Curling: an Illustrated History

For Hazel

Linlithgow curlers at play on Linlithgow Loch. A sketch from their minute book, 1854, by Andrew Philp, one of their members

Curling: an Illustrated History

SIC SCOTI: ALII NON AEQUE FELICES
Duddingston Curling Society, 1802

DAVID B. SMITH M.A. LL.B.
Sheriff of North Strathclyde at Kilmarnock

JOHN DONALD PUBLISHERS LTD
EDINBURGH

ISBN 0 85976 074 X

Printed in Scotland by Bell & Bain Ltd., Glasgow, Scotland.

Introduction

For centuries in Lowland Scotland the game of curling was played on loch, river, or artificial pond, whenever there was ice. Games were arranged on a parochial basis and the curlers of one parish vied with those of the surrounding parishes. Such was the enthusiasm of the curlers, and so fickle the Scottish climate, that as soon as the ice was bearing, all work stopped, and bonspiel followed bonspiel till the thaw.

Since the 1930s and the increase in the number of artificial ice rinks, the outdoor game has declined. Curling ponds lie overgrown with reeds, curling houses are derelict, and the stones they sheltered are scattered in the mud of many an erstwhile pond — or gracing many a doorstep.

Even in colder countries than Scotland, such as Switzerland and Canada, where the problem was rather excess of cold than lack of it, most curling is now carried on indoors.

Many, if not most, of the present generation of curlers have no experience of the original outdoor game. The passions and excitement which were crammed into the few days of a hard curling frost are now spread more thinly over a season of six or seven months.

It therefore seems an appropriate time to take stock of curling, and to remind curlers of the long and interesting history of 'Scotland's ain game.'

The best part of a century has passed since the publication of the Rev. John Kerr's monumental *History of Curling*, which is still the standard history of the game.

Kerr's researches were thorough, and the sources he used comprehensive. Unfortunately, some of the primary works he used, such as minute books, have since been lost; some minutes unknown to him have been discovered; but the broad picture he paints with love and affection remains unchanged. For fifteen years I have been immersed in the history of curling. Kerr's *History* has been my Bible. My researches have taken me to all parts of Scotland. I have been privileged to see medals, trophies, photographs, and pictures, belonging to curling clubs, and individuals, that few beyond their owners have ever seen. There is a wealth of *actual* tangible history in these objects. My purpose in writing this pictorial history of curling is to share with other devotees of the roaring game the pleasure I have had in discovering and studying them.

The majority of the illustrations depict curling of many years ago. This choice is deliberate. Not only has there never before been published a comprehensive selection of photographic illustrative material — I am confident that most readers will never have seen most of the objects and the pictures in this book — but also my purpose is to celebrate an era that is gone in the hope that through seeing what has gone before curlers of the present day will appreciate their great sport the more.

The first publication on curling, *An Account of the Game of Curling*, by a Member of the Duddingston Curling Society, Edinburgh, 1811, is very rare. Even the reprint by Captain John Macnair, which appeared in 1882 under the title of *Curling, Ye Glorious Pastime*, in a limited edition of 250 copies, is seldom encountered. The first Canadian work on curling, *The Canadian Curler's Manual*, Toronto, 1840, is even rarer. Ramsay's *Account* is important: apart from being the first description of the game and its history, it contained the first printed rules, and therefore had a great influence on the development of curling in Scotland. The *Manual* gives us an early glimpse of how the game was developing in the land in which it was destined to flourish luxuriantly.

I am grateful that my publishers have agreed to reprint both these little books as Appendices to this volume.

Acknowledgements

In writing this book I have been helped by many people.

To the staffs of the National Library of Scotland, the Scottish Record Office, the Mitchell Library, Glasgow, the National Library of Canada and the Public Archives, Canada, I give thanks. To Stuart Maxwell of the National Museum of Antiquities of Scotland, and his colleagues, I am grateful for photographing many items, and for allowing me to reproduce the photographs. Doug Maxwell and Air Canada were more than helpful, in particular with Air Canada Silver Broom material.

For kind and gracious permission to reproduce the following items I owe a debt of gratitude to:
The Duke of Atholl, Figs. 20, 102; The Marquess of Bute, p. 48; The Earl of Elgin, Fig. 13; The Earl of Mansfield, Fig. 100; The Earl of Perth, Fig. 63; Ursula, Countess of Eglinton, Figs. 66, 139, 140, 141, plate 7; Lord Kinnaird, Fig. 33, plate 13; R. Baird, Dunblane, Fig. 21; Sir John Clerk of Penicuik, Bart., plate 15; Ken Andrew, Prestwick, Figs. 41, 55; Big Four Curling Club, Calgary, Fig. 77; Brown, Son, & Ferguson Ltd., Glasgow, p. 25; John Brown, Muirkirk, Fig. 12; Mr & Mrs E. F. Cook, Glasgow, Figs. 174, 175, 176; Copp Clark Ltd., Toronto, pp. 89-91; Richard Dennis, London, Fig. 71; Betty Gibson, McGraw-Hill, Toronto; Richard Green, London, Plates 6, 8; John Haig & Co. Ltd., Markinch, Fig. 178; Commander John Hamilton, Monkwood, Fig. 34; Ruth Howe, Bemidji University, p. 89; David Letham, Edinburgh, Fig. 68; Mrs J. Love, Perth, Plate 10; Mrs Maxtone Graham, Aberlady, Fig. 80; P. D. J. C. Maxwell Stuart, Traquair, Fig. 14; Scotsman Publications Ltd., Edinburgh, Figs. 45, 46, 75; D. C. Thomson & Co., Ltd., Dundee, Figs. 76, 82, 87, 88, 97; Lt. Col. John Inglefield-Watson, The Ross, Hamilton, Figs. 112, 156, 157, 158; Aberdeen University Library, Fig. 72; Buxton Museum, Fig. 136; Cambridge University Collection (Copyright reserved), Figs. 42, 47; Carnegie Library, Ayr, Fig. 142; Edinburgh City Museums, Fig. 92; Glasgow Museums and Art Galleries, Fig. 7; Kilmarnock and Loudoun District Council, Figs. 28, 29, 37, 85, 95, plate 16; Kirkcaldy Museum and Art Gallery, Figs. 93, 94; Koninklijk Instituut voor het Kunstpatrimonium, Brussels, Fig. 5; Kunsthistorisches Museum, Vienna, Fig. 4; Largs and District Museum, pp. 119-122; Monklands District Council, Fig. 165, plate 11; National Portrait Gallery, London, plates 4, 5; Perth Museum and Art Gallery, Figs. 106, 107; Rijksmuseum, Amsterdam, Fig. 6; Smith Institute, Stirling, Figs. 16, 17; Stewartry Museum, Kirkcudbright, Fig. 73; Warwickshire County Museum, Fig. 137.

To all the curling clubs and others who have permitted me to borrow, photograph, photocopy, and quote from minute books, I give thanks.

I am also especially grateful to the Royal Caledonian Curling Club and their Secretary, Robin Welsh, not only for making all their material freely available to me, and for lending me a complete set of *Annuals* from 1839, but for permission to reproduce illustrations of many of the Club's possessions.

Contents

1

The Beginnings of Curling

When curling originated will probably never be known, although it can be stated with perfect confidence that whenever there was a sheet of ice there would be young boys throwing or sliding stones or other objects over it, and grown men playing ice games upon it.

The historian of golf and football has early evidence. These were sports which could occupy a significant part of a fighting man's time throughout the year, and keep him from his archery practice. In the fifteenth century it was rightly thought that skill in shooting, with bow and arrow, the Auld Enemy, the English, was more important than the ability to drive straight, or kick a football, and on three occasions the Scottish Parliament legislated against these games. But curling has never been the subject of legislative stricture and the curling historian has to wait until 1638 to see the words 'curling' and 'curling stones' in print for the first time. In that year was published a curious poem, *The Muses Threnodie or Mirthfull Mournings on the Death of Mr Gall,* and for long it was thought that in it were contained not only the first references to curling in the English language, but the first references to the game at all.

The poem is a sort of *In Memoriam* composed by Henry Adamson, who writes

> Of Master George Ruthven the teares and
> mournings,
> Amids the giddie course of Fortunes turnings,
> Upon his dear friend's death, Master James Gall
> . . .

and he causes Ruthven to call upon various objects from his cabinet to help him

> for to roare, And of my wofull weeping take a part,
> Help to declare the dolour of mine heart.

The poem begins with a long inventory of George Ruthven's possessions, 'which, by a Catachrestick name,

he usually calleth *Gabions.*' According to the poet, in his preface, Ruthven was almost a centenarian at the time the poem was written, which suggests that his curling days extended far back into the sixteenth century.

Amongst the very many objects mentioned in the inventory are these:

> His cougs, his dishes, and his caps,
> A Totum, and some bairnes taps;
> A gadareilie, and a whisle,
> A trumpe, an Abercorne mussell,
> His hats, his hoods, his bels, his bones,
> His allay bowles, and curling stones,
> The sacred games to celebrat,
> Which to the Gods are consecrat.

Having completed the list, Ruthven goes on and calls upon his *Gabions* to help him mourn the deceased:

> Now must I mourne for *Gall,* since he is gone,
> And yee my *Gabions* help me him to mone; . . .
> Now first my *Bowes*[1] begin this dolefull song,
> No more with clangors let your shafts be flung
> In fields abroad, but in my cabine stay,
> And help me for to mourn till dying day . . .
> And yee my *Clubs,*[2] you must no more prepare
> To make your bals flee whistling in the aire, . . .
> And yee my *Loadstones*[3] of *Lidnochian* lakes,
> Collected from the loughs, where watrie snakes
> Do much abound, take unto you a part,
> And mourn for *Gall,* who lov'd you with his heart:
> In this sad dump and melancholick mood
> The *Burdown* yee must bear, not on the flood,
> Or frosen watrie plaines, but let your tuning
> Come help me for to weep by mournfull cruning.

---

1 Bows
2 Golf clubs
3 Curling stones

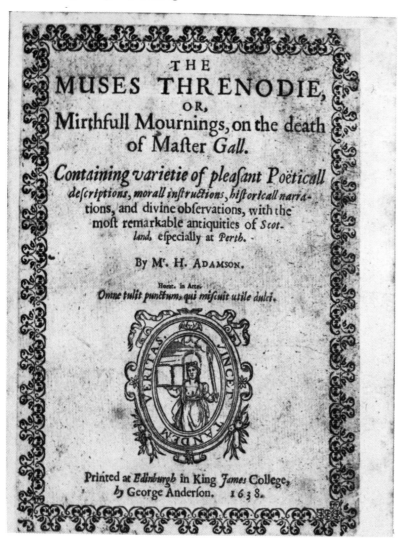

Fig. 1 The title page of *The Muses Threnodie,* 1638, the curious poem in which the first printed references to the game are to be found.

ANent the defunct, his name was *M. James Gall,* a Citizen of *Perth,* and a Gentle-man of a goodly stature, and pregnant wit, much given to pastime, as golf, archerie, curling, and Joviall companie. A man verie kinde to his friends, and a prettie poet in liberall merriments, and tart satyres; no lesse acquaint with *Philœnus,* and the *Acidalian* Dame, than with the Muses.

Fig. 2 The preface to *The Muses Threnodie.*

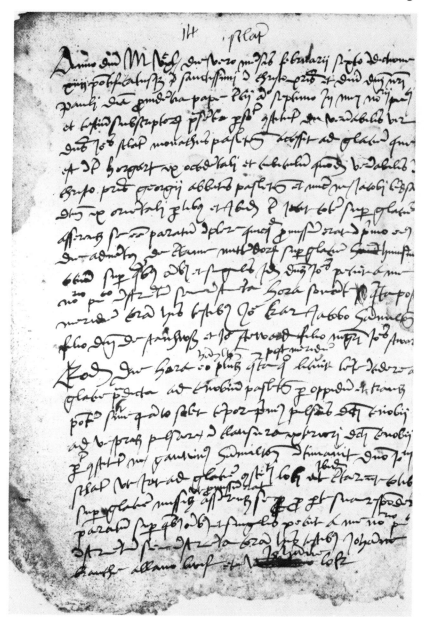

Fig. 3 Protocol book of John McQuhin, notary, Paisley. Under the date 16th February 1540/1 are two protocols which are probably the earliest references to curling so far discovered.

The significant matter for our purpose is that the three objects he selects for special mention are his bows, his golf clubs and his curling stones. It is clear that these were chosen because he and Gall both enjoyed the three sports of which they are the implements.

In fact, in the preface to the book it is said of the deceased: 'his name was M. James Gall, a Citizen of Perth, and a Gentle-man of goodly stature, and pregnant wit, much given to pastime, as golf, archerie, curling; and Joviall companie.'

What is interesting is that curling and curling stones are mentioned in such a prominent way at the outset of the poem as to indicate without a shadow of a doubt that curling was a popular pastime in the Perth of the early seventeenth century. Its very popularity rendered it possible for the poet to allude to curling stones in such flowery language as 'loadstones of Lidnochian lakes.'

In 1977 some sixteenth century notary's protocol books were deposited in the national archive of Scotland, Register House, Edinburgh. In an age when few could write, the notary performed the useful function of recording, in an offical capacity, all sorts of matters which

Fig. 4   Detail from *Hunters in the Snow*, oil painting by Pieter Breugel, 1565. This and the following illustration added fuel to the controversy as to whether the game of curling had a continental origin.

were regarded as important to the participants. He recorded in his protocol book a note — in Latin — of the transaction which he was called upon to witness, so that if need be he could draw up a formal document, an instrument, as evidence of the transaction.

John McQuhin was a notary in Paisley, a small burgh in Renfrewshire, in which lay a wealthy Cluniac abbey. His protocol book was one of those deposited in 1977, and in it the notary records a challenge between John Sclater, a monk in Paisley Abbey, and Gavin Hamilton, representative of John Hamilton the abbot.

On February 6, 1540-41, he formally records that Sclater went to the ice which was between Horgart and the late abbot's room and there threw a stone along the ice three times, asserting that he was ready to carry out what had been promised on the first day of Gavin's arrival concerning a contest of throwing this sort of stone over the ice:

> . . . venerabilis vir dominus Joannes sclater monachus pasletensis accessit ad glaciem que est inter horgart ex occidentalj et cubiculum quondam venerabilis in christo patris georgii abbatis pasletensis . . . ex orientali partibus et Ibidem ter Iecit cotem super glaciem asserens se esse paratum implere quicquid promissum erat in primo eius die adventus de certamine mittendorum super glaciem hujusmodi cotium . . .

Hamilton, a short while later, responded by intimating to Sclater that he would go to the ice in the appointed place and that they would there have a contest with stones thrown over the ice:

> . . . magister gawinus hammiltoun intimavit domino Joanni sclater vt Iet ad glaciem constituti loci et Ibidem certarent cotibus super glaciem missis vt promissum erat asserens se pro parte sua respondere paratum . . .

The result of the contest is not, unfortunately, recorded.

Was this a curling challenge? It certainly looks like it, but because the notary restricted himself to Latin it is impossible to be dogmatic. His choice of word for 'stone' may be significant, and certainly suggests to me that he was referring to curling. 'Cos-cotis' was not a common Latin word for 'stone.' It resembles in sound the word 'quoit', and 'quoit' and 'quoiting' were common terms in the West of Scotland for 'curling stone' and 'curling' in the eighteenth and nineteenth century. It is tempting to think that McQuhin chose this particular Latin word because it reproduced most nearly the sound of the word actually used in his day for curling stones.

If the Paisley protocol is evidence for curling in Lowland Scotland in the first half of the sixteenth century, it still leaves unresolved the question as to where the origins of the game are to be sought.

To say that a controversy about this matter raged in Scotland in the nineteenth century would be to overdramatise the situation. Scotland has always been a poor country on the periphery of Europe, which depended on trade with other northern European

Fig. 5 Detail from *Winter Landscape with Skaters and a Birdtrap,* oil painting by Pieter Breugel, 1565. It certainly resembles curling!

nations. Centuries of warfare with its southern neighbour, England, meant that Scotsmen looked overseas for markets, to the Low Countries, to France.

Commercial ties involved cultural ties. For example, the law of Scotland developed in parallel with the Roman-Dutch law of the Low Countries, uninfluenced by the common law of England.

There has always been an element in Scotland, who wish to ascribe to foreign influences, achievements which to others appear to have sprung from the native genius of the Scots.

One such person was the Reverend James Ramsay, minister of Gladsmuir, member of the Duddingston Curling Society, and writer of the first book, a pamphlet, on the game. In his *An Account of the Game of Curling* by a Member of the Duddingston Curling Society (Edinburgh, 1811) he raised for the first time in print the problem as to the country of its origin. 'Upon this subject,' he says, 'curlers are divided in their sentiments. Some seem to think that it was an amusement originally

Scottish: others that it was introduced into this country from the continent.'

Ramsay concedes that in his day curling was known only in Scotland, or in places like England, and Canada, to which it had recently been exported; and that there was no evidence that a similar game existed on the continent; but from the terminology of curling which, he says, is 'all Dutch or German', 'there is a very strong probability, that the game of curling was introduced into this country by the Flemings, in the fifteenth, or about the beginning of the sixteenth century.'

Eighty years later, another East Lothian minister, the Rev. John Kerr, in his *History of Curling* (Edinburgh, 1890), expatiates at some length on the problem. He concludes that there is no proof of the Flemish origins of the game:

'Wherever there was ice, there must have been, since man existed, games on ice, and the likelihood is that, long before any Fleming ever landed on our shores, our ancestors had ice-games of a kind; for John Frost is a pre-

Navita sic gelido subductâ classe Decembri **HYEMS** *Securus glaciem ferratâ compede sulcat.*

Fig. 6   Engraving by C. van Wieringen after a painting by C. van Baudous, entitled 'Hyems', or 'Winter'. The players appear to be using large discs of wood. The player to the farthest right is cleaning the bottom of this implement with a besom, and some other besoms are to be seen.

historic monarch, older than any of the mythical Kings of Scotland whose doubtful doings are recorded by our early historians. It is more difficult for us to believe that no kind of ice-game ever existed in Scotland than it is to believe that such a thing was only thought of in the sixteenth century for the first time; and, if it be said that we cannot prove this native origin, we reply that the *onus probandi* has been thrown upon those who deny it, and we leave the origin of curling where we have to leave other origins, in the midst and haze of an unknowable antiquity.'

Some curling apologists for the foreign view went so far as to suggest that curling might have had its origins in the game *knattleikr*, as it is glimpsed in the Icelandic sagas. How such a game should have been transported to Scotland, and how it should have not only survived but thrived, alone in Europe, only in precisely those parts of Scotland which were least subject to Viking influences, are questions which were of no moment to such persons, concerned, as they were, solely to find **any** origin (other than a Scottish) for the game.

For the sake of completeness, however, I consulted Magnus Magnusson, the Scots-Icelandic broadcaster, writer, and scholar, who has translated some of the sagas. His opinion is that *knattleikr* simply means: 'ball-game' from *knöttr* (which means 'ball', or 'sphere') in its genitival form, and *leikr*, meaning 'play' (you will recognise a cognate Scots form in 'laik', meaning 'toy').

'It is difficult to define the game precisely: it seems to have been a mixture of shinty, American football, and all-in wrestling! There is no single source that gives the rules: it seems to have been played between two teams of indeterminate number, involving a ball, with the players armed with bats of some kind (which they frequently applied to one another!). Body-checking seems to have been allowed. The purpose seems to have been to force the ball across a line by fair means or foul, and in the Sagas it frequently led to punch-ups, killings, and subsequent blood-feuds (that is why the games are recorded at all). How unlike curling! (Am I right??!).

'The confusion with curling may have arisen from the fact that it was sometimes played on ice: not formal rinks, but frozen waterlogged meadows, which made for a smoother surface. It seems to have been a winter game, chiefly, perhaps, because it was only in winter that the farmers and their households had the time to indulge in such sports.'

So much for knattleikr!

It has been noticed, since Kerr wrote, that the Flemish painter Pieter Bruegel (1525 — 1569) has unwittingly added fuel to the fire of controversy, because of detail in two of his pictures, now known as *Winter Landscape With Skaters and a Bird Trap,* and *The Hunters in the Snow,* both painted in 1565.

In each picture Bruegel fills the canvas with activity, in the fore — middle — and background. In the middle ground of each picture there are people engaged in all sorts of ice activities. In *The Hunters in the Snow* one can see on two rectangular frozen ponds skaters and sliders, 'ice hockey players' and sledgers, children playing with tops, and, more important for our present inquiry, five figures engaged in some activity on the ice involving five round objects with some sort of handles. It is a pity that these figures are not central to the design of the artist for they are small and the detail of the 'objects' is not clear. What can be said is that they look like discs each with a handle projecting at an angle of about 45° from the centre. They certainly resemble curling stones. It is, however, perhaps significant that there are no brooms, no besoms, no brushes, and no activity that looks like sweeping.

In the second picture the 'curlers' extend from the foreground to the middle, on a frozen river or canal. Again the 'stones' resemble curling stones, and one player is standing on the ice, bent over, obviously preparing to throw.

Very recently Dr Bob Cowan, a curling biochemist from Glasgow University, has added a further Flemish painting to the discussion. It is another winter scene, painted in 1575 by Jacob Grimmer, and it hangs in the Museum of Fine Arts at Budapest. The evidence here is even more tantalising, for the figures are even less distinct, but it could be said that they are engaged in the same pastime as Bruegel's figures.

Are these paintings evidence for curling in the Low Countries, played with handled stones, at a time when in Scotland the loofie reigned supreme?

When Sir Percy Bates of the Wengen Curling Club first brought *Hunters in the Snow* to the attention of the Royal Club, an article appeared in the *Annual* for 1932-3 which drew from the shape of the 'stones' the 'irresistible inference that on the continent of Europe the modern Scottish shape of curling stone was anticipated by centuries.'

If curling was a game practised commonly in the Low Countries of the sixteenth century one would expect some evidence of the fact, in the form of 'stones' or other implements. I therefore contacted the leading museums in Holland to see if there was any evidence as to what the game was that was being played in these three pictures, and also to see if any 'curling stones' survived.

My researches have unearthed conflicting views in the Low Countries. A.M. Meyerman, who is the author of a book called *Hollandse Winters* (1967) and director of the Historisch Museum, Rotterdam, has found an engraving of a game being played on ice with large circular discs with some sort of handle. By C. van Wieringen (1580-1635), it is reproduced as fig. 6. In this game besoms were used: in fact one player is depicted cleaning the sole of his upturned 'stone' with a besom. From the shape of the stones it appears that they were largish flat discs of wood with an upright wooden handle. In a letter to me Mr Meyerman says: 'I take it for granted that the game "curling" has been known in the 16th century in Holland . . . The fact that "curling stones" have not been kept here does not say anything as the game was probably played with wooden blocks that were lost later on.'

Mr B. Wander, of the Nederlands Openlucht Museum, Arnhem, is of opinion that the engraving by van Wieringen shows a variant of a game *krulbolspel*, played with large wooden discs, which are thrown along the ground to a mark. The course of the bowl is a curling course, hence the name. Mr Wander points out that the people of the Low Countries often availed themselves of smooth flat frozen surfaces to play games usually played on land, such as *kalving* (a club and ball game which, some say, is the origin of golf!) and whipping tops. He concludes: 'So there may be some association between 'krulbol' and curling, and the Flemish people may have played their favourite game on ice, but in spite of early vivid relations between the Flemish people and the Scots, the matter of origin and eventual adoption of curling is still obscure.' I cannot but agree with Mr Wander. Whatever the origins of curling — and a Scottish origin seems to me at least as likely as a foreign one — it was in Scotland that the game developed, and from Scotland that it has been given to the rest of the curling world; and there we have to leave the problem.

The fantastic growth in the game that occurred in nineteenth century Scotland when it was played in nearly every parish in the land, and by all classes of the population, at a time when golf was largely restricted to the coastal strip around the Forth, and football was in its infancy, entitles curling to claim to be Scotland's national game.

2
Curling in History and Literature

The literature of curling, or rather, the literature in which curling is mentioned, is not too voluminous: I feel that it is therefore worth quoting at least the earlier examples in their entirety.

The Paisley protocol and *The Muses Threnodie* have already been mentioned. The latter was published in 1638. In that year too we find the next reference to the game. Robert Baillie (1599 — 1622), Minister of Kilwinning and, later, Principal of the University of Glasgow, participated in the General Assembly of the Church of Scotland held at Glasgow in 1638. The bishops were all subjected to charges relating to their moral character at the Assembly, and Baillie in a letter written of the proceedings says: 'On Tuesday the 11th December was our eighteenth session: Orkney's process (*i.e.* the charges against the bishop of Orkney) came first before us. He was a curler on the ice on the Sabbath day; a setter of tacks to his sons and good sons, to the prejudice of the church; he oversaw adultery, slighted charming, neglected preaching, and doing any good there: held portions of ministers stipends for building his cathedral . . .' (Robert Baillie, *Letters and Journal*, 1775, p. 137).

The next reference in point of time occurs in a curious memorandum found among papers relating to the estate of Masterton in Clackmannanshire. In the memorandum, entitled 'Some Remarques upon severall things since the Happie restauratione of King Charles the Second', the writer says, '. . . There was a great frost in the end of '63, and continowed till 20 March '64, upon which day the ploughes went, and others and I curled the same day . . .' (Scottish History Society. *Miscellany*, vol. 1, 1893, p. 468)

Two other mentions of curling occur in the Account Book of Sir John Foulis of Ravelston. The editors of this book remark that Sir John was obviously keen on fishing, shooting, golf and bowls, from the frequency of his expenses on such pursuits, but, since curling was only mentioned twice, they infer that he was not a keen curler. The more's the pity, since his personal expenditure is meticulously detailed. It would have been invaluable to have a reference to the purchase of a curling stone.

1671, Jan 29
. . . spent at severall times
    W^r Lyon, baillies, drummond,
    Hay, johnston, Lawder, etc
    at curling   £06.12.0
1673 Jan. 13
    spent at curling   £03.12.0
        (Scottish History Society, 1894)

A law report provides the next reference. Under the date 30th December 1684 Sir John Lauder of Fountainhall records in his *Decision of the Lords of Council and Session:*

A party of the forces having been sent out to apprehend Sir William Scot of Harden younger, because Tarras and Philiphaugh deponed, that they communicated remotely their design to him, as a man of good fortune; and one William Scot in Langhope, getting notice of their coming, by the Cadgers or others, he went and acquainted Harden with it, as he was playing at the curling with Riddel of Haining, and others; who instantly pretending there were some friends at his house, left them, and so

Fig. 7 Pen and ink sketch by Sir George Harvey, inscribed 'First sketch for the Curlers.' The finished painting is reproduced in colour.

fled. Haining having delated thus, the said William Scot, and James Scot of Thirlstone, old Harden's brother, are brought this day to Edinburgh: Thirlstone is liberate, as finding nothing to say to him: but William is put in the irons, because he declined to tell who gave him advertisement of the party's coming.

In the same year Sir Robert Sibbald, in his work *Scotia Illustrata Sive Prodromus Historiae Naturalis,* Part II, Book IV, Cap III, p. 46, when dealing with the different kinds of stone or marble to be found in Scotland, says:

Lapis niger, quo super glaciem
luditur, nostratibus *a Curling stone.*

(Black stone, with which a game is played over the ice, (called) by our folk: a curling stone).

The very next year supplies the next reference. On 21st April 1685 General Thomas Dalyell of the Binns, in West Lothian, died. He was a soldier who had been instrumental in persecuting the Covenanters, but it is his home life that concerns us. An inventory of all the plenishings of his house was made up at the date of his death, and among the swords, whingers, pistols, bows, arrows and golf clubs listed in the 'Sadlehouse' were:

A Curling stone of stone. A curling stone of leid and iron.
A Timber Curling stone . . .

The editors of this inventory remark:

Our visitor could enjoy his game of golf in the park, or of chess by the fire of an evening. In their due season he could engage in shooting, hunting, and curling. (*Proceedings of the Society of Antiquaries of Scotland,* lviii, p. 357).

The next seventeenth century reference comes from *A Description of the Isles of Orkney, by Master James Wallace, late Minister of Kirkwall,* published in 1693. At pages 9-10 Wallace writes:

To the East of the Mainland lyes Copinsha, a little isle but very conspicuous to seamen, in which and in severall other places of this Countrey are to be found in great plentie excellent stones for the game called Curling.

For the last seventeenth century reference we are again indebted to the Church. On 28th January 1694 Gilbert Corson, Saddler, appeared before the Kirk Session of Glencairn in Dumfriesshire to answer to a charge of swearing. He 'confessed that at the Curling on the [he did] say the devill tak hime if they got that shot'. The manuscript, unfortunately, is torn at this entry and so we will never know where 'the Curling' took place. Perhaps Gilbert's candid confession did him some good, for there is no record of any punishment.

These references, and the crest of the Drummonds of Carlowrie, are the total of literary evidence, so far discovered, for curling in the seventeenth century. When taken along with finds of loofies and other dated stones, they give a picture of the game as being fairly widespread through Lowland Scotland. It is unrealistic, however, in this, as in most fields of history, to describe developments century by century, for evolution does not take account of the calendar. Indeed the next reference occurs in a poem in which the author, Dr Alexander Pennecuik of Newhall (Peeblesshire), shows that he was carrying on the same tradition as Foulis of Ravelston and Dalyell of the Binns. In his *A Geographical, Historical Description of the Shire of Tweeddale, with a Miscelany and Curious Collection of Select Scotish Poems* (Edinburgh, 1715), amongst the pleasures of winter, he writes:

> To Curle on the Ice, does greatly please,
> Being a Manly *Scotish* Exercise;
> It Clears the Brains, stirrs up the Native Heat,
> And gives a gallant Appetite for Meat.
> In Winter now and then I Plant a Tree,
> Remarking what the Annual Growth may be;
> Order my Hedges, and Repair my Ditches,
> Which gives Delight, although not sudden Riches.

Pennecuik was a neighbour and friend of Sir John Clerk of Penicuik, whose family later played such a prominent part in the history of curling.

Our next poetical reference comes from Allan Ramsay, wigmaker, poet, bookseller, entrepreneur, and another intimate of Sir John. In his *Epistle to Robert Yarde of Devonshire* he writes:

> Frae northern mountains clad with snaw,
> Where whistling winds incessant blaw,
> In time now when the curling stane
> Slides murmuring o'er the icy plain.

And in his poem on *Health,* dedicated to the Earl of Stair in 1724, curling is included among other pastimes indulged in by the vigorous healthy youth, Hilaris, who rambles, and rides, and hunts, and swims, and golfs, and plays tennis, and practises archery, and dances and

> From ice with pleasure he can brush the snow
> And run rejoicing with his curling throw.

Although in the period from 1724 to 1771 there is considerable tradition on the formation of curling societies, the written or printed page is silent. This silence is broken in 1771 by the first description of the game. James Graeme (1749 — 72), in his *Poems on Several Occasions,* published posthumously in 1773, is the first poet to devote a whole poem to curling. It was first published in the *Weekly Magazine* of 1771, and is worth printing in full, for it to a greater or lesser degree formed the pattern of most curling poems which followed: viz., a passage about the weather; the gathering of curlers for the spiel; the game; the beef and greens, and social evening which followed.

CURLING:

A POEM.

FRETTED to atoms by the poignant air,
Frigid and Hyperborean flies the snow,
In many a vortex of monades, wind-wing'd,
Hostile to naked noses, dripping oft
A crystal humour, which as oft is wip'd
From the blue lip wide-gash'd: the hanging sleeve
That covers all the wrist, uncover'd else,
The peasant's only handkerchief, I wot,
Is glaz'd with blue-brown ice. But reckless still
Of cold, or drifted snow, that might appal
The city coxcomb, arm'd with besoms, pour
The village youngsters forth, jocund and loud,
And cover all the loch: With many a tug,
The pond'rous stone, that all the Summer lay
Unoccupy'd along its oozy side,
Now to the mud fast frozen, scarcely yields
The wish'd-for vict'ry to the brawny youth,
Who, braggart of his strength, a circling crowd
Has drawn around him, to avouch the feat:
Short is his triumph, fortune so decrees;
Applause is chang'd to ridicule, at once
The loosen'd stone gives way, supine he falls,
And prints his members on the pliant snow.

THE goals are marked out; the centre each
Of a large random circle; *distance scores*
Are drawn between, the dread of weakly arms.
Firm on his *cramp-bits* stands the steady youth,
Who leads the game: Low o'er the weighty stone
He bends incumbent, and with nicest eye
Surveys the further goal, and in his mind
Measures the distance; careful to bestow
Just force enough: then, balanc'd in his hand,
He flings it on direct; it glides along
Hoarse murmuring, while, plying hard before,
Full many a besom sweeps away the snow,
Or icicle, that might obstruct its course.

BUT cease, my muse! what numbers can describe
The various game? Say, canst thou paint the blush
Impurpled deep, that veils the stripling's cheek,
When, wand'ring wide, the stone neglects the *rank*,
And stops midway? — His opponent is glad,
Yet fears a sim'lar fate, while ev'ry mouth
Cries, *off the hog,* and TINTO joins the cry.
Or couldst thou follow the experienc'd play'r
Thro' all the myst'ries of his art? or teach
The undisciplin'd how to *wick*, to *guard*,
Or *ride full out* the stone that blocks the pass?

THE *bonspeel* o'er, hungry and cold, they hie
To the next ale-house; where the game is play'd
Again, and yet again, over the jug;
Until some hoary hero, haply he
Whose sage direction won the doubtful day,
To his attentive juniors tedious talks
Of former times; — of many a *bonspeel* gain'd,
Against opposing parishes; and *shots*,
To human likelihood secure, yet storm'd:
With liquor on the table, he pourtrays
The situation of each stone. Convinc'd
Of their superior skill, all join, and hail
Their grandsires steadier, and of surer hand.

The first prose description followed close upon its heels, and not surprisingly it was the pen of a foreigner, Thomas Pennant, an Englishman, in his *A Tour in Scotland and Voyage to the Hebrides. MDCCLXXII* (Chester, 1774), that first described the game for the benefit of the world outside Scotland:

Of the sports of these parts, that of *curling* is a favorite; and one unknown in *England*: it is an amusement of the winter and played on the ice, by sliding from one mark to another, great stones of forty to seventy pounds weight, of a hemispherical form, with an iron or wooden handle at top, The object of the player is to lay his stone as near to the mark as possible, to guard that of his partner, which had been well laid before, or to strike off that of his antagonist.

Scotland, and its peculiarities, appear to have been of particular interest to foreigners in this year, for in his *New Geographical Grammar* (London, 1774), p. 139, William Guthrie also gives some attention to curling, in a passage which for its quaintness also deserves full quotation:

Dancing is a favourite amusement of this country, but little regard is paid to art or gracefulness; the whole consists in agility, and in keeping time to their own tunes, which they do with great exactness. One of the peculiar diversions practised by the gentlemen, is the Goff, which requires an equal degree of art and strength: it is played by a bat and a ball and the latter is smaller and harder than a cricket ball; the bat is of a taper construction, till it terminates in the part that strikes the ball; which is loaded with lead, and faced with horn. The diversion itself resembles that of the Mall, which was common in England ir ... middle of the last century. An expert player will send the ball an amazing distance at one stroke; and each party follows his ball upon an open heath, and he who strikes it in fewest strokes into a hole, wins the game. The diversion of Curling is likewise, I believe, peculiar to the Scots. It is performed upon ice, with large flat stones, often from 20 to 200 pounds weight each, which they hurl from a common stand, to a mark at a certain distance; and whoever is nearest the mark is the victor. These two may be called the standing summer and winter diversions of Scotland. The natives are expert at all the other diversions common in England, the cricket excepted, of which they have no notion; the gentlemen look upon it as too athletic and mechanical.

And this interest was shared in the New World, for Jedidiah Morse, in his *The Universal American Geography* (New York, 1796), plagiarised this whole passage.

It is to be regretted that Robert Burns, Scotland's greatest poet, appears not to have been a curler. What a poem could have come from the pen that wrote *The Holy Fair* and *The Jolly Beggars!* As it is, we have to be content with two tantalising mentions of the game. In *The Vision* he uses curling to set the scene for the poem:

The sun had clos'd the winter day,
The Curlers quat their roaring play,

In *Tam Samson's Elegy* the poet displays great familiarity with the game. Tam was a nurseryman and keen sportsman in Kilmarnock. Of the poem's composition Burns himself said: 'When this worthy old Sportsman went out last muir-fowl season, he supposed it was to be, in Ossian's phrase, "the last of his fields;" and expressed an ardent wish to die and be buried in the muirs. On this hint the Author composed his Elegy and Epitaph:'

When Winter muffles up his cloak,
And binds the mire like a rock;
When to the loughs the Curlers flock,
    Wi' gleesome speed,
Wha will they station at the *cock*,
    Tam Samson's dead?

He was the king of a' the Core,
To guard, or draw, or wick a bore,
Or up the rink like *Jehu* roar
    In time o' need;
But now he lags on Death's *hog-score*,
    Tam Samson's dead!

For the sake of interest, though not for their poetical merit, it may be amusing to reproduce a couple of later imitations of Burns. The first comes from *The Poetical and Prose Works* of John Gerrond (Leith, 1815). The very title, *James Gerrond's Elegy*, proclaims its paternity:

. . . When kipple¹ dirt shuts lakes and gutter,
And teals in streams kick up a splutter,
Then hardened grow the lumps o' butter,
    Can scarce be spread,
Wha now will hin' han'² clear the witter?³
    James Gerrond's dead.

Ay when the word was 'Tak ye're will o't,'
He sent it up as ony bullet,
Cries Nelson, 'L—d! he crack the skull o't,'
    Such was his dread;
But now in Death's cold arms he's lolled,
    James Gerrond's dead.

And from *On the News of Auld Jamie's Death* by Robert Hetrick, *Poems and Songs* (Ayr, 1826):

And when the North her power awakes
To whirl forth her snowy flakes,
And yatter⁴ up the lanes and lakes
    As firm's a vice,
With pure transparent limpid cakes
    O' solid ice.

When all the happy curling train,
Assembled on the glassy plain,
A parish right for to maintain,
    In curling fame;
Or bachelors and married men
    Contest the game.

Then Jamie would come stepping owre⁵
And gently rattle at the door;
'Rab there are far aboon⁶ a score,
    'Out owre the knowe,
'We'll mix amang the curling core
    'As lang's we dow.'⁷

Upon the ice he'd ne'er regard
The smile or frown of lord or laird;
Wad skite⁸ the spittle o'er his baird⁹
    And snuff his grethin;
And strike a blow or lay a guard
    Wi' ony breathing.

1 adhesive
2 playing last
3 tee
4 block
5 over
6 above, more than
7 may
8 eject forcibly
9 beard

David Davidson, the Kirkcudbright poet, in his *Thoughts on the Seasons* (London, 1789), gives not only an Augustan description of the game — who but an eighteenth century poet could describe a curling stone as 'the bracing engine of a Scottish arm'? — but a spirited description in the style of a Scots ballad of a legendary Gallovidian spiel on Carlingwark Loch, Castle Douglas. His lively piece on replaying the game 'o'er a bowl of nect'rous juice' will strike a chord in the hearts of all keen curlers!

WINTER

The sun, still urging onward in his course,
Again our region blesses.—Now, afar,
Among the snow-clad hills, the village smokes;
An' a' the jovial sons of honest mirth,
Wi' gladsome hearts, bid welcome to the day.

    Forth to the frozen lake, on frolic keen,
The youthfu' swains repair.—A medley *throng*,
On various sports intent, hither resort;
An' mixing in the band of social life,
Fondly conveen'd, upo' the river crowd.—
Old age is here an idle *looker-on*,
On revelry, in which it once did join.
E'en infants, here, mix with the multitude,
Utt'ring their puerile clamour, to the skies.
Some shoot the icy fragments.—To the goal,
Some hurl the polish'd pebble.—Some the top,
Fast whirling frae their thumbs, whip dext'rously—
An' some, bold, frae the crushed bank dart on,
String after string, the sleek well-polish'd *slide*.
Hither, the manly *youth*, in jovial bands,
Frae ev'ry hamlet swarm—Swift as the wind
Some sweep, on sounding skates, smoothly along,
In dinsome clang, circling a thousand ways,
Till the wide crystal pavement, bending, rairs,
Frae shore to shore, by th' rush o' madden'd joy.
On sledges some hurl rapidly along,
Eager, an' turning oft' to 'scape the flaws,
An' dang'rous chinks, the wind an' fun have made.
But, manliest of all! the vig'rous *youth*,
In bold contention met, the channelstane,¹
The bracing engine of a Scottish arm,
To shoot wi' might an' skill.—Now, to the lake,
At rising sun, with hopes of conquest flush'd,
The armed heroes meet.—Frae dale to doon
The salutation echoes—and, amain,
The baubee² toss'd, wha shall wi' ither fight,
The cap'ring combatants the war commence—
Hence, loud, throughout the vale, the noise is heard,
Of thumping rocks, an' loud bravadoes' roar.

1 curling stone
2 small coin

God prosper long the hearty friends
  Of honest pleasures all;
A mighty *curling* match once did
  At C*****w**k befal.

To hurl the channelstane wi' skill,
  Lanfloddan took his way;
The child that's yet unborn will sing,
  The curling of that day.

The champion of Ullisdale
  A broad rash aith[1] did make,
His pleasure, near the Cam'ron isle,
  Ae winter's day to take.

Bold Ben o' Tudor sent him word,
  He'd match him at the sport.
The Chief o' Ken, on hearing this,
  Did to the ice resort.

Wi' channelstanes, baith glib[2] an' strong,
  His army did advance—
Their *crampets* o' the trusty steel,
  Like bucklers broad did glance.

A band, wi' besoms,[3] high uprear'd,
  Weel made o' broom the best,
Before them, like a moving wood,
  Unto the combat press'd.

The gallant gamesters briskly mov'd
  To meet the daring fae[4] —
On Monday they had reach'd the lake,
  By breaking of the day.

The chieftains muster'd on the ice,
  Right eager to begin—
Their channelstanes, by special care,
  Where a' baith stout an' keen.

Their rocks they hurled up the rink—
  Ilk[5] to *bring in* his hand—
An' hill an' valley, dale an' doon,
  Rang wi' the ardent band.

Glenbuck upo' the *cockee*[1] stood—
  His merry men drew near—
Quoth he, Bentudor promised
  This morn' to meet me here.

But if I thought he would not come—
  We'd join in social play.
With that, the *leader* of the ice,
  Unto Glenbuck did say.

Lo, yonder does Bentudor come—
  His men wi' crampets bright—
Twelve channelstanes, baith hard an' smooth,
  Come rolling in our sight.

All chosen rocks of Mulloch heugh,[2]
  Fast by the tow'ring Screel —[2]
Then tye your *crampets,* Glenbuck cries—
  Prepare ye for the speal.

And now with me, choice men of Ken,
  Your curling skill display—
For never was their *curler* yet,
  Of village or of brae,

That e'er wi' channelstane did come,
  But if he would submit
To *hand to nieve*[3] I'd pledge this crag,
  I should his *winner* hit.

Bentudor, like a warrior bold,
  Came foremost o' them a'—
A besom on his shouther[4] flung;
  On's hans twa mittens bra.[5]

An' with him forth came Tullochfern;
  An' Tom o' Broomyshaw—
Stout Robert o' Heston, Ratcliff, and
  Young John o' Fotheringhaw.

An' wi' the laird o' Cairnyhowes,
  A *curler* guid an' true,
Good Ralph o' Titherbore, an' Slacks—
  Their *marrows*[6] there are few.

---

1 oath
2 keen
3 brooms
4 foe
5 each

1 tee
2 hills to the south of Carlingwark Loch
3 fist
4 shoulder
5 fine
6 equals

Of Fernybank needs must I speak,
　　As ane of aged skill.
Simon of Shots, the nephew bold
　　Of Cairny on the hill.

With brave Glenbuck came *curlers* twelve—
　　All dext'rous men of Dee.
Robin o' Mains, Clim o' the Cleugh,
　　An' fam'd Montgomery.

Gamewell the brisk, of Napplehowes,
　　A valiant blade is he.
Harry o' Thorn, Gib o' the Glen,
　　The stoutest o' the three.

An' the young heir of Birnyholm,
　　Park, Craigs, Lamb o' the lin—
Allan of Airds, a *sweeper* good;
　　An' Charley o' Lochfin.

Bentudor a Riscarrel[1] crag,
　　Twice up the ice hurl'd he,
Good sixty cloth-yards, and a span,
　　Saying, 'fo long let it be.'

It pleas'd them a'—Ilk then wi' speed,
　　Unto his weapon flew—
First, Allan o' Airds his whinstane[2] *rock*,
　　Straight up the *white ice* drew.

'A *good beginning!'* cries Glenbuck—
　　Slacks fidging at the sight,
Wi's bra *blue-cap,* lent Airds a smack;
　　Then roared out '*good night!*'

Next Robin o' Mains, a *leader* good,
　　Close to the witter[3] drew—
Ratcliff went by, an' 'cause he miss'd,
　　Pronounc'd the ice untrue.

Gib o' the Glen, a noble *herd,*
　　Behind the *winner* laid—
Then Fotheringhaw, a sidelin[4] shot,
　　Close to the *circle* play'd.

Montgom'ry, mettlefu', an' fain,
　　A rackless stroke did draw;
But miss'd his aim, an' 'gainst the *herd,*
　　Dang frae his *clint*[1] a flaw.[2]

With that stepp'd forward Tullochfern,
　　An' (saying to hit, he'd try)
A leal shot ettled[3] at the cock,
　　Which shov'd the *winner* by.

Clim o' the Cleugh, on seeing that,
　　Sten'd[4] forth, an' frae his knee,
A slow shot drew, wi' muckle care,
　　Which settled on the *tee.*

Ralph, vexed at the fruitless play,
　　The cockee butted[5] fast—
His stane being glib, to the loch-en'
　　Close by the witter past.

Stout Robert o' Heston, wi' his broom,
　　Came stepping up wi' might—
Quoth he, 'my *Abbey-burn-fit*[6]
　　Shall win the *speal* this night.

With that brisk Gamewell, up the rink,
　　His well *mill'd* rock did hurl—
Which rubbing Ratcliff on the *cheek,*
　　Around the cock did twirl.

Now stepp'd a noted gamester forth,
　　Fernybank was his name—
Wha said, he would not have it told
　　At C*****w**k, for shame;

That e'er the chief o' Ken should bear
　　The palm of victory—
Then heezing[7] his Kilmarnock hood,
　　Unto the *cock* drew he.

The *stanes* wi' muckle martial din,
　　Rebounding frae ilk shore,
Now thick, thick, thick, each other chas'd,
　　An' up the rink did roar.

---

1 hard or flinty rock
2 'a sudden dash' of fire
3 aimed
4 sprang
5 struck
6 a stone from a place of this name, on the coast south of the Abbey of Dundrennan
7 lifting up

---

1 Riscarrel, a bay on the Kirkcudbrightshire coast
2 whinstone is any black igneous rock
3 tee
4 oblique

They closed fast on every side—
    A *port* could scarce be found—
An' many a broken channelstane
    Lay scatter'd up an' down.

'Show me the winner,' crys Glenbuck;
    'An' a' behind stan' aff;'
Then rattled up the rocking crag,
    An' ran the port wi' *life*.

Bentudor flung his bonnet by,
    An' took his stane wi' speed—
Quoth he, 'my lads, the day is ours'—
    Their chance is past remead.

Syne hurlin through the crags o' Ken[1]
    Wi' *inrings*,[2] nice an' fair,
He struck the *winner* frae the cock,
    A lang claith-yard, an' mair.

The speal did last frae nine forenoon,
    Till setting o' the sun—
For when the hern[3] scraich'd[4] to her tree,
    The combat scarce was done.

Thus did Bentudor an' Glenbuck,
    Their curling contest end.
They met baith merry i' the morn'—
    At night they parted friends.

    The sportive *field* is o'er.—Now, friendly, all
Conveened o'er a bowl of nect'rous juice,
Recount the fam'd achievements o' the day—
The song goes round.—Among the jovial sons
O' health an' peace, true mirth is melody.
Regardless of, or consonance or voice, the catch, the
    glee,
The martial tale is sung—an' frae the mouths
O' the concording company, applause abounds.
The laugh, the roar, the mirthfu' story, round
The wakefu' table spread.—The banter too,
For eminence in curling pow'r an' skill,
Rings through the lighted dome.—Again, the hard,
The well-contested *speal* is called up—
The wide-spread *table* to the rink is turn'd;
An' bowls an' bottles, implements of *war*.

---

1 i.e. the opposing teams' stones
2 inwicks
3 heron
4 screeched

Here stands the *winner* by a bottle hid,
Immoveable, save by a nice *inring*—
There stands the *tee*—up through this *port* he came,
Wi' a' his might—on *this* he gently rubb'd—
On *that* he brak an *egg*—from *that* to *this*,
From *this* to *that*, thump, thump, amidst the thrang,
At length the winner struck, wi' mettled smack;
An' sent *him* birling up aboon the *fire*.

    Since jovial thus, the social sons of mirth,
The wint'ry minutes pass—be it *my* lot,
In some snug corner of my native land,
Unknowing, or *servility* or *wealth*,
Far frae the busy warld, remote to dwell;
Where, loud the sounding skate, upo' the lake,
Re-echoes frae ilk shore—where hurling sledge,
Upo' the icy pavement, boundeth far;
An' where the channelstane loud roaring, makes
The hamlet hynd depress'd wi' pensive cares,
Forget his every trouble, in his joy.
There, in some quiet retirement, would I pass
The Winter's gloomy days, wi' social friends
O' sterling wit an' jest.—With them I'd join
In a' the various scenes o' rural mirth,
An' rural joy.—With them, o' pliant soul,
I would of Nature's boundless province sing—
Admiring still the Seafon's gradual change;
An' each fair object through the varied year.

One looks almost in vain for prose references to curling in any book printed in the eighteenth century. The monumental *Statistical Account of Scotland*, published in the last decade of the century, and designed to give a comprehensive account of the whole country, parish by parish, affords glimpses of curling in only five parishes. Since each account was written by the parish minister, much depended on the interests of the incumbent: there is much geographical description, much about agriculture and manufactures, and much about insobriety and immorality, but in most instances little of the pastimes of the people. The minister of Bothwell in Lanarkshire writes jejunely: 'Curling is their chief amusement in the winter', and of Crawfordjohn in the same county it is said: 'Curling is a favourite diversion among the commonality; and even the gentlemen sometimes join in.' The two ministers from Dumfriesshire who bothered to include a piece about the game may well, from the tone of their pieces, have had an active interest in it:

Wamphray: 'We have but one general amusement, that of curling on the ice; and the parishioners of Wamphray take much credit to themselves for their superior skill in this engaging exercise. After the play is over, it is usual to make a common hearty meal upon beef and greens, in the nearest public house.'

Drysdale: 'The principal diversion or amusement is curling on the ice in the winter, when some times scores of people assemble on the waters, and in the most keen, yet friendly manner, engage against one another, and usually conclude the game and day with a good dinner, drink, and songs.'

We know from other sources that in the Ayrshire parish of Muirkirk the game had been played since at least 1750. The minister there, the Rev. John Sheppard, gives the longest and most sympathetic account:

'Their chief amusement in winter is *curling*, or playing stones upon smooth ice; they eagerly vie with one another who shall come nearest the mark, and one part of the parish against another;— one description of men against another;— one trade or occupation against another;— and often one whole parish against another,— earnestly contend for the *palm,* which is generally all the prize, except perhaps the victors claim from the vanquished, the dinner and bowl of toddy, which, to do them justice, *both* commonly take together with great cordiality, and, generally, without any grudge at the fortune of the day, or remembrance of their late combat with one another, wisely reflecting, no doubt, that *defeat* as well as *victory* is the fate of *war.* Those accustomed to this amusement, or that have acquired dexterity in the game, are extremely fond of it. The amusement itself is healthful; it is innocent; it does no body harm; let them enjoy it.'

The first decades of the nineteenth century saw the publication of several, now little-known, curling pieces. Most occurred as part of larger works devoted to a description of the seasons in general, or of winter in particular, but one, entitled *A Game at the Ice,* by George McIndoe, from his *Poems and Songs, Chiefly in the Scottish Dialect* (Edinburgh, 1805), is merely a short celebration of the game:

> WHEN on the rink we take our stand,
> Each with a broom-kowe[1] in his hand,
> We fix our cramps,[2] our stane's a—se[3] clean,
> We bend our knees, and raise our chin;
> Then frae the other end we hear
> A voice, (perhaps not very clear)
> 'Johnnie, direct yoursel' for me,—

---

1 broom
2 according to McIndoe, an iron triangle, with fangs, to keep the foot of the player from sliding
3 arse

> 'Notice my kowe, look here's the tee,
> 'Be straight how-ice,[1] and dinna[2] ride,
> 'Nor sell your stane by playing wide;—
> 'Ye're well set on man, but ye're roaran,
> 'Whatna way's that to play a forehan'?'[3]

> Another fills the cramps, and he
> Lays down his stane plump on the tee,
> 'A fair pat-lid![4] Od there's a snuff,
> 'I'm hang'd but that deserves a ruff.'

> Just break an egg on't[5]—gie him days,[6]
> Supe,[7] supe him up —another says:—

> 'Now risk a hog to guard that stane,
> 'This end, I think will be our ain,'

> When mony a straight drawn shot's been play'd,
> And mony a bonny guard's been laid,
> And mony a nice out-weik's[8] been ta'en,
> Eggs broken upon mony a stane:—

> And now the game draws near an end,
> Another shot, and 'twill be kend
> Wha pays the greens, and wha the drink,
> Wha carries laurels frae the rink.

> 'A fow hillhead,[9] the winner guarded,
> 'Is what our hin'-haun never fear'd yet;—
> 'Tak' ye the goose a gouff'e cheek,
> 'And if ye get a right in-weik,
> 'Then down the port like a kings cutter,
> 'Your stane'll slide into the whitter.'[10]

> 'He's a' the curle!'—the game is ended,
> And that is all that was intended.

The year 1809 saw the publication of *British Georgics* in which James Grahame, having sung the praises of Duddingston Loch near Edinburgh, goes on to describe a parish bonspiel:

---

1 hollow ice
2 do not
3 lead stone
4 'a stone so well play'd that it covers the tee as a pot-lid covers a pot'
5 in modern parlance, freeze
6 'use every lawful endeavour to keep the stone running'
7 sweep
8 outwicks
9 a full house
10 tee

Plate 1. Curlers at Canonmills Loch, Edinburgh, before 1796. Water colour by David Allan (1744-1796). Ramsay informs us that the town council of Edinburgh were wont to proceed ahead of the curlers to the loch with a band of music at their head. This is the earliest picture of the game. The Canonmills Curling Society also inspired the first curling publication, *Songs for the Curling Club held at Canonmills,* Edinburgh, 1792. Some stones from Canonmills are to be found in the Huntly House Museum, Edinburgh.

Plate 2. A heraldic achievement from the front board of the minute book of Muthill Curling Society. The sketch is dated 1821, and probably depicts the game about a decade before. All the stones have looped handles; one of them is not circular. The player throwing the stone is set upon two trickers.

Plate 3. Curling at Curling Hall, Largs. Oil painting by McLennen, ca. 1833. This is the famous rink constructed by John Cairnie at the end of 1827 in the grounds of his house. Cairnie, the first president of the Grand Caledonian Curling Club, and author of *Essay on Curling and Artificial Pond Making*, Glasgow, 1833, is shown delivering a stone from his famous foot-iron. Against the garden seat lie a large pair of compasses, used for measuring shots.

Plate 4. Curlers. Oil by Sir George Harvey (1806-1876). This picture has long been a favourite with curlers. It has appeared as a vignette in every edition of the *Annual* since 1843. Several versions of the picture exist, including some copies, but this is the original, which has never before been reproduced. The National Gallery of Scotland possesses a smaller version than this one, which is described as a study for this, but it may be a second version done by the artist for the engraver, as the original owner was unwilling to allow the picture from his custody. The noteworthy features of the curling are the diversity of the stones and handles, though all are circular, the crude broom cowes, and the crampits upon the feet of several of the curlers. One pair of crampits can be seen lying beside the whisky jars.

Plate 5. This attractive water colour sketch by Jemimah Wedderburn probably depicts the family of Sir George Clerk of Penicuik at play on one of the ponds at Penicuik House, Midlothian, in 1847. It is the first sketch of "mixed" curling.

Plate 6. Curling at night at Penicuik by the light of a lantern, 1847. Water colour by Jemimah Wedderburn.

Plate 7. The first Grand Match, Penicuik, 1847. Water colour by Jemimah Wedderburn.

Plate 8. The Grand Match at Linlithgow, 1848. Oil by Charles Lees. This is a composite portrait of all the curling notables of Scotland, several of whom are represented by virtue only of artistic licence, since they were absent on the great day. In the left-hand corner can be seen stones of the single-soled variety. In the background are the ruins of the royal palace.

Plate 9. Curling at Rawyards Loch, Airdrie, Lanarkshire, 1857. Oil by John Levack. This composite portrait of the notable curlers of the district is interesting for its setting in an industrial landscape: the winding gear of the Blue Doo Colliery can be seen in the background. Also noteworthy is the fact that all the stones are of the modern, double-soled variety, though the sweeping implement is still the broom cowe.

Plate 10. Medal of silver, gold and semi-precious stone, Coupar Angus and Kettins Curling Club, 1859. This is perhaps the finest medal of a small group in which there are curling stones, of silver or semi-precious stone, and implements on the surface. In this medal one pair of stones has looped handles, the other conventional screw-on handles. One pair is of bloodstone and the other is alleged to be made from stone from the walls of Sebastopol! The object between the besoms is a tee marker, or "bottle".

Plate 11. Curling at New Farm Loch, Kilmarnock, ca. 1860. Oil by McKay. This vigorous, though primitive, picture is noteworthy in several respects. It shows the Kilmarnock pattern of stone, high in relation to width, and with wooden handles; the hair brushes favoured in and around the town; and the cloth, or carpet, boots used by the Kilmarnockians in preference to the barbarous crampit. The loch, into which water was let in November and drained out at the end of March, was of several acres in extent, and provided the curlers and skaters of the town with a venue for their sport for over a century from 1845.

Plate 12. The Countess of Eglinton, her daughter, Lady Egidia Montgomerie, and lady friends at play on one of the four shallow water ponds in the policies of Eglinton Castle, February 1862. Pen, ink, and water colour by A. A. A. In the middle distance are the spires and chimneys of Irvine, and the background is the island of Arran in the Firth of Clyde. In central Ayrshire the hair brush was preferred to the broom cowe, or the besom.

Plate 13. Curling on Duddingston Loch, 1866. Oil by Charles Lees (1800-1880). In the background can be seen Duddingston Kirk, and among the trees is the manse. On the lochside is the octagonal curling house designed for the society by William Playfair in 1824.

Plate 14. The Curling Match. Oil by John Ritchie (fl. 1858 x 1875). This painting, which has never before been published, shows the game in a truly urban setting.

Plate 15. Curlers on loch near Dunkeld. Water colour by William Evans of Eton (1798-1877). This typifies the Highland scenery in which, erroneously, many people think the game began.

Plate 16. The Grand Match, Carsebreck, 1899. Oil by Charles Martin Hardie (1858-1917). This painting was commissioned to celebrate the jubilee of the Royal Club, and it illustrates the curling establishment of the day. The clerical figure on the left is the Reverend John Kerr. This picture, and Plate 8, were damaged by vandals in Perth Ice Rink in 1977, but have since been repaired and cleaned on behalf of the Royal Club.

Now rival parishes, and shrievedoms, keep,
On upland lochs, the long-expected tryst[1]
To play their yearly bonspiel.[2] Aged men,
Smit with the eagerness of youth, are there,
While love of conquest lights their beamless eyes,
New-nerves their arms, and makes them young once
more.

    The sides when ranged, the distance meted out,
And duly traced the tees,[3] some younger hand
Begins, with throbbing heart, and far o'ershoots,
Or sideward leaves, the mark: in vain he bends
His waist, and winds his hand, as if it still
Retained the power to guide the devious stone,
Which, onward hurling, makes the circling groupe
Quick start aside, to shun its reckless force.
But more and still more skilful arms succeed,
And near and nearer still around the tee,
This side, now that, approaches; till at last,
Two seeming equidistant, straws or twigs
Decide as umpires 'tween contending coits.[4]

    Keen, keener still, as life itself were staked,
Kindles the friendly strife: one points the line
To him who, poising, aims and aims again;
Another runs and sweeps where nothing lies.
Success alternately, from side to side,
Changes; and quick the hours un-noted fly,
Till light begins to fail, and deep below,
The player, as he stoops to lift his coit,
Sees, half incredulous, the rising moon.
But now the final, the decisive spell,
Begins; near and more near the sounding stones,
Some winding in, some bearing straight along,
Crowd justling all around the mark, while one,
Just slightly touching, victory depends
Upon the final aim: long swings the stone,
Then with full force, careering furious on,
Rattling it strikes aside both friend and foe,
Maintains its course, and takes the victor's place.
The social meal succeeds, and social glass;
In words the fight renewed is fought again,
While festive mirth forgets the winged hours.—
Some quit betimes the scene, and find that home
Is still the place where genuine pleasure dwells.

    The next work, which is perhaps best known for containing the earliest woodcut of the game, is James Fisher's *A Winter Season* (1810). Though a prose work,

it is written in a kind of poetic and religious ecstasy, and from the various pastimes of winter the writer draws morals, with copious citation of scripture. Nonetheless his description of a curling match, told in breathless, rhythmic prose, does convey the excitement of the occasion:

    With tramps, and brooms, and stones, a crowd now comes, with jocund glee, the long-projected speel to play, for beef and greens, in manly sport; the rink now chosen out, and distance fixed, the tees both made, and hog-scores justly drawn, the best of three, 9 or 11 shot games; agreed upon, the dinner to decide; a piece of coin is then tossed high in air, to show which side shall first begin the sport; or not so heathenish this to know, a stone is played by one on either side, and now the keen-contested curling match begins; stones roar from tee to tee the ice along; lye here; strike this; well done; guard that; well played, alternate cry those who the game direct: soon as a stone the hog-score o'er has got, and judged by those concerned to stop too short, sweep, sweep! then's all the cry; how then the brooms are plyed to sweep it on; but when the distant score one does not reach, 'tis hog it off with laughter much and loud, and still the healthful sport goes on, till three huzzas declare the victor side; now off they go with appetite to dine, and drink, and spend in social glee the evening all.*

    John Struthers, in *The Winter's Day, with other Poems* (Glasgow, 1811), displays a real appreciation of the pleasures of the game, although the descriptive verses have to be sifted from a mass of moralising about the cruelty and vanity of mankind:

The cottage smoke, upon the view,
In middle air rolls, wreathing, blue,
And scarce, so light the shifting winds,
To right or left an impulse finds;
When neighbours round, assemble gay,
In rural sport to spend the day.

---

1 Appointment
2 A match at the game of *curling* on the ice
3 The marks
4 In some parts of Scotland, the stones with which *curlers* play are called *cooting*, or *coiting stones*.
(These are Grahame's glosses.)

*For the information of those of our southern neighbours who may not be acquainted with the game of *curling*, so much practised in many parts of Scotland, it may not be amiss to observe, that the tramps are made of iron to go upon the feet, something after the form of stirrup irons, with sharp prominences at the bottom to prevent the curler from sliding while engaged in play. The curling-stones are of different forms and various weights, but always uniformly flat and smooth on the bottom, with a handle of iron or wood affixed in the top: the tee is of a circular form, with a small hole cut in the middle; the rink is the distance betwixt the two tees, and is shorter or longer according as the ice will admit; the hog-score is drawn at the distance of about four or five yards from each of the tees.

II.

The curling stones, by this, have been,
Examin'd with inspection keen,
And hands anew with care supply'd,
That chance, or time, may have destroy'd.
Provided too, the tapering broom,
Still breathing, fresh, a strong perfume,
With rags, to wrap th' unfiery foot,
Nor is the needful crisp[1] forgot,
Though these, when join'd, in trial's hour,
Are judg'd to mark a player poor.
    Thus, all accoutr'd, on the loan
    Each o'er his shoulder heaves his stone,
    And seeks the meadow's frozen bounds,
    Where high the voice of mirth resounds.

X.

Frequent, meanwhile, the curlers' roar
Rolls round the meadows icy shore,
As tee-drawn shots the smooth-lead fill,
Or ports are wick'd with hair breadth skill,
Or needful guards, are cautious, plac'd,
Or, vile, the lagging hog disgrac'd.
    Tho' boisterous is th' exulting cheer,
      Spontaneous from the heart it springs,
    More grateful to the well-tun'd ear,
      Than all the brazen pomp of Kings.

XI.

How amiable! here, to see
All ranks dissolve in social glee,
    From beardless youth to hoary age;
And from the prating village fool,
To him, with birch, made bold to rule
    The realm of learning sage.
Even titled Grandeur, flings aside
The stiffness of Baronial pride,
    And to his satisfaction finds,
Beyond the precincts of the great,
Unfetter'd with the forms of state,
    That Pleasure sometimes sports with hinds.

XII.

The Pastor, too, by all approv'd,
For pious word and deed belov'd,
    The mental feast forgoes a while,
With cheerful friends,—refreshing air,
His flagging spirits to repair,
    And brace his nerves with healthful toil.

And rashly, here, let none suppose,
That RANK its influence thus will lose,
Or, that respect will less be shown,
To PIETY for being known

XXII.

At length, dark clouds the sky deform;
And from the south the blust'ring storm,
    Sweeps o'er the darkening day,
Slow, round the hill, the cattle come,
And drench'd, the Curlers make for home,
    Cut short their roaring play:
Drawn from a tuft of wither'd grass,
    Prepar'd with previous care,
The bottle comes, in frugal glass,
    Which cordially they share.
And, Gamesters, with a merry heart,
Blythe look, and fair good-day they part.

One of the liveliest nineteenth century pieces comes from the pen of Alexander Boswell of Auchinleck, son of Dr Johnson's famous biographer, who was a member of the Duddingston Curling Society. The following duet was sung by him at a dinner in McEwen's Tavern, Edinburgh on 11th December 1816 'and received with unbounded applause, was ordered to be recorded in the Minute Book of the Society; and the thanks of the meeting were voted to Mr Boswell.' In fact the secretary of the society failed to carry out his order but the text was already preserved, for the poem had been printed in the *Ayrshire Magazine* of March 1816:

LOCHSIDE.

Let feckless[1] chields,[2] like crookit[3] weans,[4]
Gae[5] blaw[6] their thums[7] wi' pechs[8] and granes,[9]
Or thaw their fushionless[10] shank banes,[11]
    And hurkle[12] o'er the ingle:[13]

---

1 crampit

1 feckless: spiritless
2 chields: fellows
3 crookit: decrepit
4 weans: children
5 gae: go
6 blaw: blow
7 thums: thumbs
8 pechs: gasps
9 granes: groans
10 fushionless: without strength
11 shank banes: legs
12 hurkle: huddle
13 ingle: fire

But lads o' smeddum,[1] crouse[2] and bauld,[3]
Whase[4] bluid[5] can thole[6] a nip o' cauld,
Your ice-stanes[7] in your grey plaids fauld,
    And try on lochs a pingle.[8]

Chorus.
When snaw[9] lies white on ilka[10] knowe,[11]
The ice-stane and the gude broom kowe,[12]
Can warm us like a bleezing lowe:[13]
    Fair fa'[14] the ice and curling!

Soop[15] the rink, lads, wide enough;
The hog-score mak', and mak' ilk brough;[16]
And though the game be close and tough,
    We aiblins[17] yet may bang them:
Stan' on, Tam Scott; ye've a gude e'e;[18]
Come creeping up the ice to me,
Lie here,—my besom's on the tee,
    Let's hae a stane amang them.
        When snaw lies white, &c.

DAMBACK.

Johnny Gray, mak' this your rest,
A gude calm shot is aye[19] the best;
He's fled it raging like a pest:
    O! what's come ower ye, Johnny?

LOCHSIDE.

Stand on, Pate Boag, and gie's a guard
I ken ye can play; cautious, laird,
Just lie ahint[20] our stane a yard:
    I like ye weel, that's bonnie.
        When snaw lies white, &c.

DAMBACK.

Now, Rob Roy, mind the ice is gleg,[1]
Aim for the guard, and break an egg;[2]
But O! be cautious, man, I beg;—
    He's roaring in the corner!
Soop, gi'e him heels, he's aff the ice;
The chiel is fou,[3] or else no wise!
For gudesake! will ye tak' advice,
    And play in your auld ord'nar.
        When snaw lies white, &c.

LOCHSIDE.

Now, Geordie Goudie, here's a port,
Be canny, and we'll soop ye for't,
I carena though ye're twa ells short:
    Han's up,—there's walth o' powther.[4]

DAMBACK.

Now, Willie, here's a fine inring,[5]
Play straught,[6] and rub him like a king:
He's slipt his foot, and, wi' a fling,
The stane's out ower his shouther.[7]
    When snaw lies white, &c.

Sin'[8] I was born, and now I'm gray,
I ne'er saw siccan[9] wretched play;
Our fallows are clean wud[10] the day,[11]
    Their stanes like gowks[12] are hurling:
But bring the whisky and the baiks,[13]
Though Fortune has played us the glaiks,[14]
A bumper to the 'Land o' Cakes,
    And her ain game o' curling.'
        When snaw lies white, &c.

---

1 smeddum: character
2 crouse: happy
3 bauld: bold
4 whase: whose
5 bluid: blood
6 thole: endure
7 ice-stanes: curling stones
8 pingle: battle, contest
9 snaw: snow
10 ilka: every
11 knowe: hill
12 kowe: broom
13 lowe: flame
14 fair fa': good luck to
15 soop: sweep
16 brough: circle
17 aiblins: perhaps
18 e'e: eye
19 aye: always
20 ahint: behind

---

1 gleg: keen
2 break an egg: freeze on the stone
3 fou: drunk
4 walth o' powther: wealth of powder, i.e. lots of weight
5 inring: inwick
6 straught: straight
7 shouther: shoulder
8 sin': since
9 siccan: such
10 wud: mad
11 the day: today
12 gowks: fools
13 baiks: biscuits
14 played us the glaiks: cheated us

The *Annuals* of the Royal Club record year by year throughout the nineteenth century the efforts of curling poets and songsters, though many of their efforts suffer from being composed for particular clubs on particular occasions. From these one song stands out. 'Cauld, cauld frosty weather', written by the Rev. James Muir of Beith, was sung by him at an anniversary meeting of the Duddingston Curling Society, and was reproduced from time to time because of its general sentiments as well as its skilful use of Scots dialect: since curling was the national sport it was natural that it should be celebrated in the Scots language:

Whan chittering[1] birds, on flicht'ring[2] wing,
  About the barn doors mingle,
And biting frost, and cranreuch[3] cauld,
  Drive coofs[4] around the ingle;[5]
Then to the loch the curlers hie,
  Their hearts as light's a feather,
And mark the tee wi' mirth and glee,
  In cauld, cauld, frosty weather.

Our buirdly[6] leaders down white ice
  Their whinstanes[7] doure[8] send snooving,[9]
And birks[10] and brooms ply hard before,
  Whan owre the hogscore moving;
Till, cheek by jowl within the brough,[11]
  They're laid 'side ane anither;
Then round the tee we flock wi' glee,
  In cauld, &c.

Wi' canny hand the neist[12] play down
  Their stanes of glibber[13] metal,
Yet bunkers[14] aften send aglee,[15]
  Although they weel did ettle:[16]

---

1 chittering: shivering
2 flicht'ring: fluttering
3 cranreuch: hoar frost
4 coofs: fools
5 ingle: fire
6 buirdly: large, well made
7 whinstanes: hard black stones
8 doure: hard
9 snooving: moving smoothly
10 birks: birch (brooms)
11 brough: ring
12 neist: next
13 glibber: keener
14 bunkers: bumps on the ice
15 aglee: awry
16 ettle: aim

'Now strike!' — 'No! draw:' — 'Come, fill the port,'
  They roar, and cry, and blether;[1]
As round the tee we flock wi' glee,
  In cauld, &c.

A stalwart chiel, to redd the ice,[2]
  Drives roaring down like thunder,
Wi' awfu' crash the double guards
  At ance are burst asunder;
Rip-raping on frae randum wicks,
  The winner gets a yether;[3]
Then round the tee we flock wi' glee,
  In cauld, &c.

Our chief, wha's skill and steady arm
  Gain mony a bonspel dinner,
Cries, — 'Open wide, stand off behind,
  'Fy, John, fy, show the winner:'
He goes — he moves — he rides him out,
  The length of ony tether;
Huzzas wi' glee rise round the tee,
  In cauld, &c.

But now the moon glints thro' the mist,
  The wind blaws snell and freezing,
Whan straight we bicker[4] aff in haste
  To whare the ingle's bleezing;
In Curler Ha', sae bein[5] and snug,
  About the board we gather,
Wi' mirth and glee, sirloin the tee,
  In cauld, &c.

In canty[6] cracks,[7] and sangs, and jokes,
  The night drives on wi' daffing,[8]
And mony a kittle[9] shot is ta'en
  While we're the toddy quaffing:
Wi' heavy heart, we're laith[10] to part,
  But promise to forgather,
Around the tee, next morn wi' glee,
  If cauld, &c.

---

1 blether: chatter
2 redd the ice: clear the stones out of the ice
3 yether: severe blow
4 bicker: move speedily
5 bein: comfortable
6 canty: cheerful
7 cracks: chats
8 daffing: gaiety
9 kittle: tricky
10 laith: loath

A nice example of another genre, the paeanistic account of a parish's victory in a particular bonspiel, is to be found in *Poems and Songs*, by James Kennedy, Sanquhar (Dumfries, 1823):

AN EPISTLE TO MR. M'———,
Relating a Curling Match betwixt the parish of Crawfordjohn and the parish of Sanquhar.

Dear friend, a wee bit tale I'll gi' ye,
In hame-spun verse or poetry,
But that it's dull and scant o' glee
    I'm really fear't,
However, ye the judge shall be
    When ance ye hear't.

Folk lo'e the place from whence they sprang,
And a' their friends they've liv'd amang,
And wish nae body them to wrang,
    Or do them harm;
So Sanquhar ye will lo'e as lang
    As ye are warm.

And now, my Cronie, to reveal't
Bleak Boreas had the *Ward** congeal'd,
And on the glitt'ring icy field,
    As you may think,
Our Curlers keen their bodies wield
    For pies and drink.

John Crawford to regain his glore,
That he had lost in days o' yore,
Us summon'd wi' a double score
    O' men weel picket,
To field o' weir,[1] and solemn swore
    We should be licket.

Tho' bauld the brag and bauld the threat,
We neither trembl'd nor look'd blate,
But trusted still that smiling fate
    Would lead us on
To vict'ry, as of ancient date
    'Gainst Crawfordjohn.

A council's called speedily,
In which our curlers a' agree
To fight it out right manfully
    While they were livin',
Aiblens John might fa' or flee
    For a' his deavin'.

Th' accepted challenge to convey
An answer's fram'd without delay,
And by the bearer sent away
    That vera e'en;
While every bosom for the fray
    Was beating keen.

John kept the tryste[1] ye needna fear,
A Parson, front, and Elder, rear,
Their uniform like men o' weir,
    Was rigg and furr[2]
White stockings, and their living gear
    A dawtit cur.

A gillock[3] scarce their heart had warm'd
Till a' our lads were fully arm'd,
Then to the Loch, and Ward, they swarm'd
    To try their maught,[4]
Frae far and near folk cam alarm'd,
    To see the faught.[5]

Had that auld singer 'mang the Greeks,
But heard their Crawford moorland speaks,
Their outer, and their inner wicks,*
    And witter shot,†
He'd kittle been to p——[6] his breeks
    Upon the spot.

O musie be na shy nor thrawn,
To sing how Johnny Crawford's fa'n
Upo' the field, and a' his blawin'
    Is fairly settl'd;
'Gainst Sanquhar he could never stan'
    Tho' weel he ettl'd.

No truly generous mind you know
Exulteth o'er a fallen foe,
Tho' foolish pride hath laid him low;
    Yet all agree,
Others may learn by his o'erthrow
    Humility.

* A loch in the neighbourhood of Sanquhar
1 war

1 engagement
2 ridge and furrow, i.e. ribbed
3 gill of whisky
4 might
5 fight
6 pish
* The out-ring and in-ring of a stone.
† When the stone rests on the tee.

Auld Sanquhar, lang and lang hast thou
Wore twisted round thy bonnie brow
The laurel'd wreath sae fair to view,
    The victor's pride,
Nae rival curler could it pow,
    Tho' often try'd.

Lang has the frozen north confess'd
The Sanquhar curlers for the best;
And mony ane they've soundly dress'd
    And fairly dung,
As Wilson, that fine poet has't
    Sae fitly sung. *

While circling seasons onward roll,
And boisterous billows barks control;
While loadstone points unto the pole
    Or norland star,
May Sanquhar's sons attain the goal
    At icy war.

As the foregoing examples show, most curling poems stress the keen, but sportsmanlike, competition; and the goodwill which follows the game. It obviously was not always like that, as the following poem shows: it is cast in a different mould: it comes from John Mactaggart's *Gallovidian Encyclopedia* (1824), and is intended to satirise the attitude of upstart lairds to their curling. The very names the poet chose for the protagonists, Nurgle and Nabble, are satirical; Mactaggart defines the words 'nabble' and 'nurgle' as 'a narrow minded, greedy person,' and 'a short, squat, savage little man,' respectively.

'The highest game at curling — the chief *spiel*', is the bonspiel, writes Mactaggart: 'When one parish, for instance, challenges another to play it, at the famous Scottish game of curling or *channlestane*, that bout on the ice is called a *bonspiel*. The best players on these occasions are selected to play, and when not only their own honour, but that of the parish is at stake, they do, or at least strive to do, their very best; though often good players are put in such a flutter at these times, that they lose the *steadiness of their han'*, and play badly: those who keep unmoved amid the crowd, and pay no attention to either damns or huzzas, play always best . . .

* Alluding to a poetical description of a former curling match betwixt the same parties, in which Sanquhar was victorious.

Sometimes *cock-lairds*[1] challenge each other to fight a *bonspiel*, and often these concerns turns out to be wars indeed. The following poem depicts a *broolzie*[2] of this nature: —'

THE BONSPIEL

In Auld Scotlan' whan winter snell[3]
    Bin's up the fosey yirth,[4]
Than jolly curlers hae a spell,
    O' manly fun and mirth:
Whanere the ice can har'ly bear
    Ahame lie hurkling[5] nane,
Wha liketh independant cheer,
    And can a channel-stane
        Owrhog[6] that day.

But whiles[7] our grand peculiar game,
    Which ithers a' surpasses;
Is hurt by Gomfs,[8] weel worth the name,
    Vain bullieing senseless asses:
Akin tae them brave Hallions[9] twa,
    Laird Nurgle and Laird Nabble,
'Bout wham I mean tae croon awa,
    Or like a wilesteg[10] gabble
        A while this day.

Their habits, tempers, a' are bad,
    They're saucy, glunchy,[11] greedy;
Lan' they alike ay nearly had,
    And tenants starving needy:
For far abroad they baith were bred,
    Sae are o' kindness scarce ay,
A savage life they lang had led,
    And lash'd puir Massa's arsie
        On mony a day.

1 Cocklairds: small proprietors who cultivated their own land
2 broolzie: a fight
3 snell: keen, sharp
4 fosey yirth: wet earth
5 hurkling: drawing the body together (for warmth)
6 owrhog: overhog, i.e. throw the stone beyond the hogscore
7 whiles: sometimes
8 Gomfs: fools
9 Hallions: clowns
10 wilesteg: ? term of abuse
11 glunchy: disdainful

To curling they did baith pretend,
    Sae challeng'd ane anither;
Their farming slaves a han' maun[1] lend,
    And neither whinge nor swither;[2]
Twall[3] on a side, the place Loch Lum,
    The rink just forty ell;[4]
The bet a puncheon o' gude rum,
    Upon the ice itsell,
                        Fu' fu' that day.

And 'ere they did the play begin,
    Ilk stamock gat a cauker,[5]
For nane did think it was a sin
    Most bonnily to tak her.
Ahin the quickly toomed[6] glass,
    How the wee finger twirled,
Than up in air a bawbee[7] was,
    For heads or tails hie birled[8]
                        To lead that day.

Laird Nurgle had that triffling luck,
    Sae his first player led;
The stane to his direction stuck,
    But by the cock[9] it fled;
At which began to fidge[10] the laird,
    And muttering to blame him;
Laird Nabble's man na better fared,
    For Nabble loud did damn him,
                        At first that day.

'Lay your stone right upon the tee,
    'My sickar[11] handed fellow;
'My broom, if you're not blind, ye see,'
    Fat Nurgle now did yello'.[12]
The trimling[13] player stells[14] his tramps[15]

Wi' mony a stamping stog;[1]
Af gangs his stane, and ay it clamps,[2]
    But hoh portule,[3] a hog —
                        It grunts that day.

What language now frae Nurgle fell,
    His phiz had on a horrid thraw;[4]
What oaths he let, ne'er heard in Hell,
    Warm frae the Gulph o' Florida.
Lean Nabble than gaed out the word —
    'Be white ice to the witter,[5]
'You're, ye are not worth a t——d,
    'Ye seem tae hae the sk——r,[6]
                        'Or bloit[7] this day.'

O! was na that a darling game,
    And worthy imitation;
Ye wha do understand the same,
    Ye standards o' our nation —
Had they been on Loch Duddingston,
    And no Loch Lum, we're thinking,
Few ends indeed they wad hae thrown,
    But aff been hissed linking,[8]
                        Fu' fast that day.

Whanere a Scotchman turns a slave
    He is na worth a boddle;[9]
Before the brave — below a knave
    Will cringe, they'll want the noddle.[10]
Though there are some, we're wae to tell,
    Feet soles are fond o' licking,
Will stick to tyrants, even to Hell,
    And bear their sneers and kicking
                        Frae day to day.

But still the bonspiel drives awa,
    The ice was weak and slagie;[11]
The stanes wad scarce gang up ava,[12]
    They grew sae unco clagie.[13]

1 maun: must
2 swither: hesitate
3 twall: twelve
4 ell: yard
5 Ilk stamak got a cauker: each stomach got a drink
6 toomed: emptied
7 bawbee: small coin, penny or halfpenny
8 birled: twirled
9 by the cock: past the tee
10 fidge: get restless
11 sickar: sure
12 yello': scream
13 trimling: trembling
14 stells: places
15 tramps: crampits

1 stog: a sturdy footstep
2 clamps: goes noisily
3 portule: a loud cry
4 thraw: anger, ill-humour
5 witter: the tee
6 skitter: diarrhoea
7 bloit: diarrhoea
8 linking: walking smartly
9 boddle: a small coin of very little worth
10 noddle: head
11 slagie: soft, in a thawed state
12 gang up ava: go up at all
13 clagie: sticky

Ill nature pued[1] down every brow,
  The lairds they swore and choked;
There common sense did loit[2] and spue,
  And wisdom aften boked[3]
              Wi' a brash[4] that day.

Thus frothing on, ilk noble side
  Wi' blustering wan a game;
A' corked were alike wi' pride,
  A Gomeril's[5] near the same.
This minute was a bullierag,[6]
  And that a blue erruction;[7]
At length did burst the meikle[8] bag
  Which caused the destruction
              O' the spiel that day.

As Nurgle raved about the cock,
  A stane came up the rink,
And hit his heel a canny shock,
  On that wi' joy we think —
For down he whurled upon Loch Lum,
  Some crawing cockaleerie;[9]
And span awhile upon his bum
  Like Toutom[10] or queer peerie,[11]
              About that day.

But sprachling[12] up a madman now,
  See how he lays about him;
Laird Nabble cudna see his crew
  Abused — never doubt him.
A battle general began,
  Wi brooms and neives[13] they linged,[14]
And mony a wee bit foolish man
  Was getting himsell swinged[15]
              In stile that day.

---

1 pued: pulled
2 loit: spew out
3 boked: vomited
4 brash: a transient bout of sickness
5 gomeril: fool
6 bullierag: hectoring abuse
7 erruction: spewing forth
8 meikle: big
9 cockaleerie: the sound made by a cock crowing
10 toutum: a kind of spinning top
11 peerie: a kind of spinning top
12 sprachling: sprawling
13 nieves: fists
14 linged: flogged, beat
15 swinged: beaten

Till hah! the lochen gaed a rair,[1]
  And af in blawds[2] divided:
Down sank the gows[3] amang the glaur,[4]
  Or else the water lided.[5]
Yet han' in han' they reached dry lan',
  Up to the chin weel cooled;
Then hame puir draggled cuifs[6] they ran,
  Magnificently fooled
              And dub'd[7] that day.

Dear social honest countrymen,
  Let despots never dinnle[8]
Your manly bosoms — for will then
  Nae pleasure through them trinnle.[9]
Detest those sooking turkey-cocks,
  For ever jibing, jeering,
And heed as little's yon grey rocks,
  Their guldering[10] domineering
              On ony day.

Since curling was an integral part of Scottish life, it received mention in prose as well. Even J.M. Barrie, the Scottish novelist and playwright, perhaps best known for his children's play, *Peter Pan,* thought it necessary to include a humorous curling chapter in his first novel, *The Little Minister* (1891), and vigorous descriptions of bonspiels can be read in H. Johnstone's *Kilmallie* (1891), A. N. Simpson's *Bobbie Guthrie* (1905), and Neil Munro's novel, *Fancy Farm* (1910). The first is notable for a toast proposed at the 'beef and greens' after the match: 'May the hinges of friendship never rust.'

In the twentieth century the flow of curling literature has all but ceased. It seems that writers required to draw their inspiration from frozen loch and roaring stone: as the game has retired indoors, so the Muse has departed.

Of the poets writing in Scots, W. D. Cocker is the last successfully to have sung the praises of curling:

---

1 lochen gaed a rair: lochan, or small loch, gave a roar
2 blawds: big pieces
3 gows: fools
4 glaur: mud
5 lided: made mellow
6 cuifs: fools
7 dub'd: soaked in a dub, or pool, of water
8 dinnle: cause pain to
9 trinnle: roll
10 guldering: roughly threatening

The Roarin' Game

A cauldrife[1] sun keeks[2] ower the hill,
Shines on the snaw it canna thowe,[3]
An' sparkles on the scruntit[4] birks[5]
That gaird[6] the lochan[7] in the howe.[8]
There curlers to the ice hae ta'en,[9]
While winter hauds[10] the land in grip,
An' clear upon the frosty air
I hear the voice o' Jock, their skip —
The weel kent[11] voice that aft[12] I hear
Shout to his collie on the hill.
I pause an' listen to his cries,
His exhortations lood an' shrill.

Hey Tammas, can ye see this stane?
Weel, dunt[13] it oot noo; here's the port.
I like ye, aye, I like ye fine.
Soop, soop 'er up! eh, man, ye're short!
Weel, try again then, elbow oot.[14]
Can ye get roon'? That's no' sae bad.
Ye're comin', dod! ye'll get 'm — dune!
You for the curler, Tammas lad.

He wrings puir[15] Tammas by the haun'.[16]
His nieve[17] can gi'e a frichtsom[18] grip.
Oh! wae betide the denty loof[19]
That gets a shake frae Jock the skip.

He gies nae praise that's no' weel-earned,
An' whiles he proves an unco rager;
He'd flyte[1] upon the laird himsel'
Gin[2] he was no' weel up, I'se wager.

Noo, Doctor, juist a canny[3] shot.
Ye see this stane? — weel, chap an' lie.[4]
Soop, soop, like bleezes, fine, Sir, fine! —
Man, but this roarin' mak's me dry'.
It's aye a 'roarin' game' wi' Jock,
His voice could droon a clap o' thun'er.
A guid shot gars[5] him loup[6] for joy,
A bad ane gars him grue[7] wi' scunner.[8]

Can ye get through atween[9] thae[10] twa?
Aye, pit your specs[11] on, Doctor Chisholm.
Gey weel laid doon![12] she'll come hersel'.
Haud aff there, canny wi' the besom'.
But noo the mirk is fa'in'[13] fast,
The lichts[14] are gleamin' in the clachan;[15]
The inn-door, sweein'[16] wide agee,[17]
Lets oot a burst o' merry lauchin'.

Aye, this maun he oor hinmaist[18] en'.[19]
We've bate[20] ye fair an' square, I'se war'n:
An', gin it doesna thowe ower nicht,
Ye'll get your licks[21] again the morn.[22]

---

1 cauldrife: cold
2 keeks: peeps
3 thowe: thaw
4 scruntit: stunted
5 birks: birch trees
6 gaird: guard
7 lochan: small loch, or lake
8 howe: hollow
9 ta'en: taken
10 hauds: holds
11 weel kent: well known
12 aft: often
13 dunt: knock
14 elbow oot: elbow out, i.e. an out turn
15 puir: poor
16 haun': hand
17 nieve: fist
18 frichtsom: frightsome
19 loof: palm

1 flyte: scold
2 gin: if
3 canny: careful
4 chap and lie: strike and stay in the house
5 gars: makes
6 loup: jump
7 grue: shudder
8 scunner: disgust
9 atween: between
10 thae: those
11 specs: spectacles
12 gey weel laid doon: very well laid down
13 mirk is fa'in': darkness is falling
14 lichts: lights
15 clachan: village
16 sweein': swinging
17 agee: open
18 hinmaist: hindmost, last
19 en': end
20 bate: beaten
21 ye'll get your licks: you'll get beaten
22 the morn: tomorrow

3

Some Early Curling Clubs

One matter must be affirmed at the outset of this chapter: an early reference to curling in a parish does not mean that there was a curling club constituted in the parish at that date. It is therefore wrong for clubs such as the present Duddingston Curling Club in Edinburgh to claim a genealogy dated back to 1761, for the historical record is clear, that the famous Duddingston Society was constituted on 24 January 1795. Any reference to curling in Duddingston at an earlier date is merely evidence that the game was played then in the parish. Moreover, the historical record is also clear that the Duddingston Society petered out about 1854-5, when the active members formed the new Coates Club, with a pond nearer the capital city, and retaining custody of the Duddingston Society's Minutes and Gold Medal. The present Duddingston Club is a new formation dating from 1894. The club itself acknowledged this *fact* until 1904 when for the first time it claimed 1795 as its date of institution in substitution for 1894 which had appeared in every *Annual* since 1895, and it was not long before the new club took its origin back to 1761.

Likewise the present Kinross Club celebrated its tercentenary in 1968 in defiance of the evidence contained in its own minute books, which clearly show that the club was a new formation in 1818.

The situation in these parishes was no doubt much the same as existed in Kirkpatrick Durham in Dumfriesshire, where the situation prevailing before the formation of the club is pithily described in the preamble to a small manuscript volume, entitled 'Curliana of Kirkpatrick Durham': 'The Curlers of Kirkpatrick Durham enjoying like other Parishes the healthy and invigorating game of curling for a period almost unparalleled in modern times in the winter of 1838; and finding from experience the want of order and arrangement in the mode of rinking, there was a general desire to follow a more systematic course of procedure than had been generally observed.

Hitherto in this Parish curling was entirely left to casualty in all its details and exercises without rule or regulation, without plan or purpose, and without authority or precept to guide and stimulate the players in the science and spirit of the game. As there was no system to regulate and no authority to decide every person played with stones of whatever shape, size, weight or material he happened to be possessed of or which accident threw in his way; and the leaders and rules of game had always to be chosen and determined on the ice if not previously arranged by the parties who were principals in the spiel. To obviate these inconveniences, and to practise more scientifically the manly art of curling it was generally conceded that method and order ought in future to be adopted.' And so they *formed* a club.

That there was curling in the parish of Kirkpatrick

Fig. 8   Silver badge of the Duddingston Curling Society, 1802, struck to 'distinguish the members from any other gentleman.' The curlers are at play on Duddingston Loch, with circular stones. This is the first club badge and one of the earliest depictions of the game.

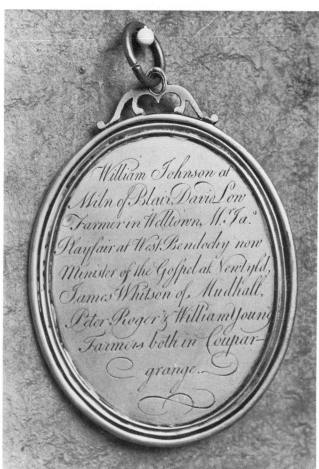

Fig. 9A Silver medal of Coupar Angus and Kettins Curling Club, 1772. This and fig. 10 are the two earliest surviving medals. Obverse.

Fig. 9B Reverse of fig. 9A.

Durham before 1838 no one doubts: that there was no curling club before then is also without doubt.

Similarly, no one doubts that there was curling in Duddingston parish before the society was formed, and in Kinross, although what the alleged evidence for the date 1668 in the latter instance is I have been unable to discover.

While the desire to claim an ancient lineage is understandable, the Royal Caledonian Curling Club has done the history of the game a disservice in acknowledging spurious claims to antiquity based on legend and in the face of historical evidence.

The clubs which can legitimately claim an unbroken history going back to the eighteenth century are very few in number. Kerr notes that in his day there were 42 clubs which claimed eighteenth century origins. Although he does not say so in terms, it is clear that he feels he cannot affirm these claims in any but 10 cases because of the

want of written records. Nonetheless the other 32 clubs do provide some evidence that the game was played in their areas.

Of Kerr's 10 clubs, one, Canonmills, was evidenced only by the publication in 1792 of *Songs for the Curling Club held at Canon-mills*. Neither Dunfermline nor Duddingston had any right to be in Kerr's list, for the former, as he points out, was formed in 1827 under the title of the New Dunfermline Curling Club (i.e. it was regarded by its founders as a new foundation), and the latter, as has already been shown, ceased to be a club 35 years before Kerr wrote. There is now no Muirkirk Curling Society.

That leaves in order of antiquity, Muthill, Coupar Angus and Kettins, Sanquhar, Hamilton (now Hamilton and Thorniehill), Blairgowrie, and Douglas.

Of these clubs Muthill has records which, from internal evidence, were written about 1823 but clearly contain

Fig. 10A   Silver medal of Coupar Angus and Kettins Curling Club, 1772 and 1774. Obverse.

Fig. 10B   Reverse of fig. 10A.

information from other documents then in existence, which showed a historical continuity. The records of Hamilton have been lost since Kerr wrote, as have the records of the older Dunfermline Club.

To Kerr's list has to be added Sorn in Ayrshire, which came into existence in 1795, and which thrives today.

Two additional sets of eighteenth century minutes, those of the Wanlockhead Curling Society formed in 1777 and Leadhills Curling Society in 1784, which appear to have been unknown to Kerr, have been discovered by my researches.

It is not altogether clear why groups of curlers in the last two decades of the eighteenth century and first two of the nineteenth century thought it necessary to form themselves into organised groups with constitutions and rules, although some of the possible reasons can be seen in the Kirkpatrick Durham 'preamble.'

Very few of the older constitutions are specific about

this: the curlers of Sorn in 1795 being 'sensible that it will not only be proper for themselves but for the Benefit of the whole Curlers and Community at large; They are resolved to erect themselves into a Society by the Name of the Sorn Curlers . . .'

In Kilmarnock in 1810 'a number of persons residing in the townend of Kilmarnock met in the house of Robert Carswell when they resolved to form themselves into a Club for their improvement in Curling . . .'

At the inaugural meeting of the Meikleour curlers in 1814 it was resolved 'That this meeting aware of the many advantages resulting from Societies in general do most heartily and cordially approve that they themselves may be formed into such . . .'

In Penicuik in 1815 at a meeting of curlers 'it was observed that in order to produce that improvement in Curling which when put in competition with our neighbours was so much wanted the Curlers in the Parish

Fig. 11A   Silver medal of Tarbolton Curling Society, Ayrshire, 1814. One of the first acts of the club at its inaugural meeting in 1814 was to commission this medal. It is the oldest medal in the world which is still regularly played for. Obverse.

Fig. 11B   Reverse of fig. 11A.

should constitute themselves into a Society to be intitled the Penicuik Curling Club, and by confering some honourary distinction upon merit it would naturally create an emulation which would terminate in improvement . . .'

The curlers of Peebles in 1821 were likewise 'satisfied that it would be of much advantage to the Curlers of Peebles in general to constitute themselves into a Curling Club.' It is fortunate for posterity that they did, for on Christmas Eve 1821 they adopted a set of regulations which is unique for the polished urbanity and deep emotion of its language.

'None of the Pastimes in which Scotsmen indulge have given occasion to such a diversity of opinion as our National Manly Game of Curling. By some it has been reprobated in the severest terms, and represented as an encouragement to idleness a temptation to profane swearing an incitement to quarrelling and an inducement to dissipation: By others it has been extolled in the language of unqualified paneygric and declared to be friendly to innocence conducive to health favorable to temperance and contributive to social intercourse.

'For our part without minutely discussing its merits or demerits but weighing them in a strict balance we can state from experience that curling so far from promoting idleness is an active and laborious recreation, an enemy to every spirit of sensual indulgence debarring those who engage in it for the time being from tippling in Taverns, lounging laziely & effeminately at a fire side or devoting themselves to worse imployments; peculiarly adopted also to the preservation of a sound constitution by favoring its Votaries with these two grand preventatives of disease and restoratives of health "Air and Exercise."

'At a season of the year when the Plough is arrested in the furrow, when Masonic & many other handicraft impliments are laid aside, and when the Mill wheel refuses to revolve on its axis, what can be more harmless, what more salubrious, what more social, than for those who are in possession of health, indowed with muscular strength blessed with a keen eye and a steady hand to repair to the still river Cuddies pool or the flooded Gytes, the waters whereof are bound in icy fetters and the surface smooth as the polished Mirror and transparent as the crystalion Cup and there give a display of strength dexterity and skill, united in a Game the darling of our forefathers.'

Compared with these sentiments the motives of the founders of the Linlithgow Town and Parish Curling Club appear selfish and parochial: 'considering that much misunderstanding and want of cooperation has of late taken place by reason of Individuals taking on Bonespeals with Curlers of other Parishes, without the

Fig. 12A   Silver medal of Muirkirk Curling Society, Ayrshire, 1823. The couplet is adapted from a popular curling poem by Sir Alexander Boswell of Auchinleck, son of the celebrated James Boswell, biographer of Dr Samuel Johnson. The medal is obviously, from its lack of sophistication, a local product. Obverse.

Fig. 12B   Reverse of fig. 12A.

knowledge of many of the Principal Players, whereby the reputation of the Curlers of the Town and Parish at large was in danger of being compromised Resolves to form a Society or Club . . .'

Another factor which motivated some groups of curlers was the undoubted and almost masonic feeling of brotherhood that existed amongst curlers. Having played a game, the unmarried men against the married, on Sanquhar Loch on 21st January 1774, the curlers dined in the Duke of Queensberry's Arms and agreed to form the Sanquhar Society of Curlers. A Committee was then chosen 'of the best qualifyed to examine and try all the rest concerning the Curler word and grip. Those who pretended to have them and were found defective were fined and those who were ignorant and made no pretensions were instructed.'

The same mystical motivation appears to have underlain the foundation in 1792 of Douglas St Brides Curling Club, for two years after the formation it was agreed 'that a distinguishing word should be adopted and given gratis to the present members.' And the appropriate 'word' in the form of question and answer is duly thereafter recorded. It is of interest to note that part, at least, of the Douglas 'word' was adopted at the very first meeting of the Montreal Club. Was one of the first members a man from Douglasdale?

The regulations adopted by the Sorn Curling Society involved the 'examination' of each old curler at his admission, and the transfer from members to the directors of the power 'to make a Brother or Brothers.' What this 'brotherhood' could mean in real terms is graphically illustrated by the terms of Regulation 5th. Regulation 4th had provided means for resolving 'all differences among the Brethren as to curling.' Regulation 5th was astoundingly comprehensive in its application:

'5th. That this Institution may be the more useful to all its members and to prevent them from throwing away their money in Courts of Law. They become bound to submit all Disputes in civil matters in the same Terms as the last regulation only in place of expulsion in Case of refusing to abide by the Decision of the Society he or they may do so on paying ten Shillings. In which Case the Society adopt the cause of the Person or Persons, in whose favour the Decision was given, and will support the same in any Inferior Court so far as their Funds will allow.' And by Regulation 8th it was in the power of the Directors 'to assist misfortunate Members or Brethren so far as the funds will allow.'

So the curler in Sorn not only became a member of a curling club, but of an arbitration club, and a legal aid society! and a friendly society! A veritable welfare state!

As far as concerned regulating the game by rules, most of the early constitutions are tantalisingly silent. What is usually expressed is the organisational structure of the club in terms of office bearers, annual meetings, and dinners.

One area that concerned many an old club was behaviour of its members both on and off the ice.

Muthill, Coupar Angus and Kettins, Sanquhar, Blairgowrie, Duddingston, all in their own way prohibited swearing and attempted to limit gambling on the results of games.

The earliest prohibition, that of Muthill in 1739, should perhaps be quoted in full: 'Fourthly. That there shall be no wagers Cursing or swearing or any Disrespectfull Language used during the time of Game Under the Penalty of Two pence Sterling for each oath or disrespectful Term, The fines and bywagers to be at the Discretion of the Precess and other members present and the Wagers of themselves Void & null.'

That fines were actually exacted by clubs is shown in the account of the treasurer of Coupar Angus and Kettins Club in 1795. Five shillings of 'cash for oaths' was collected on four dates in 1795. At 2d per oath that sum represents thirty infractions of the rule!

By the 1830s the practice of fining delinquent members had become, in clubs such as Abdie, a humorous and convenient way of augmenting the club funds and adding merriment to the annual dinner. (See p. 195.)

Since the influence of the Duddingston Curling Society was so great in the early years of the nineteenth century before the institution of the Grand Club, it may be appropriate to give a brief sketch of its history. That curling had existed in the parish of Duddingston in some form before 1795 is clear from the first minutes of the Society, but it was on 24th January of that year that a proper club was constituted with rules and regulations in terms of the following resolutions:

'1st Resolved, That the Sole Object of this institution is

Fig. 13   Gold medal, presented to Drum Curling Club, near Edinburgh, in 1820.

the enjoyment of the Game of Curling; which while it adds Vigour to the body contributes to vivacity of Mind, and the promotion of the Social & Generous feelings.

'2nd Resolved, That peace and Unanimity the great Ornaments of Society shall reign among them, and that virtue without which no Accomplishment is truly valuable and no enjoyment really satisfactory, shall be the Aim of all their Actions.

'3rdly Resolved, That to be Virtuous is to Reverence our God, Religion, Laws & King; And they Hereby do declare their reverence for and Attachment to the Same.'

Most of the first members were local people but because the village was situated near the large and convenient loch of Duddingston, and 'near to the Metropiles' (in the words of the secretary), it soon began to attract curlers from the city. In 1800 was admitted an advocate, James Millar, who was not only the first of a veritable deluge of legal talent to join the club, but was one of the committee which devised and promulgated the club's rules of curling and was responsible for the pithy Latin motto adopted by the society, and reproduced on their badge: *Sic Scoti: alii non aeque felices* (loosely translated: This is the way the Scots play:

the rest of the world isn't half so lucky.) Concerning him, Richard Broun, in manuscript notes he compiled for a second edition of *Memorabilia,* includes the following: 'The attitudes of the late James Millar Esquire Advocate will long be remembered upon the Duddinston ice as unique in their kind. His practice was invariably to squat on his belly after throwing his stone. His humour too was rich and racy — it was He, we believe, who upon one occasion gave his directions as follows — 'Dight youre doup my bonny Principal, & come your ways up, & break an egg upon Davie's backside'! — We would translate the same for the uninitiated — did not our reverence for the club . . .' The note remains incomplete, no doubt because of Broun's indecision as to whether to include a pun of such coarseness.

By 1801 the society had designated three members respectively as masters of brooms, stones and rinks, and Hugh Bairnsfather was elected surgeon to the society.

The next ten years were perhaps the most fruitful in the society's history. In 1802 came a proposal that 'a medal with proper insignia' should be struck 'as a badge to distinguish the Members from any other gentleman,' and by the next anniversary meeting the medals had already been distributed, at a cost of 10/6d each. The medal, no doubt designed by John McGeorge, subsequently the first medallist of the Grand/Royal Club, depicts curlers at play on Duddingston Loch, with the parish kirk in its background. In this respect the Duddingston curlers were far in advance of any other curling club, for it is many years before we hear of another club badge, though in 1834 Abdie decided upon a club uniform and had special buttons struck. In 1803 the Society again showed its foresight by setting up a committee to devise a code of curling laws. In its report the committee stated they had prepared the rules with the greatest care, 'most of which are strictly observed in those Counties in which the Game of Curling prevails,' and the new Code was duly approved on 6th January 1804. In this respect, too, the Duddingston curlers appear to have been first in the field, and by having the laws printed they made them accessible to other curlers and thus exerted considerable influence throughout Scotland. For example, in 1829 the Lochmaben Curling Society resolved to incorporate the Duddingston rules with their own, and the first rules of the Grand Caledonian Curling Club were substantially the Lochmaben/Duddingston rules.

In 1806 the society was joined by the Very Reverend George Baird, Principal of the University of Edinburgh, and in 1808 the Reverend John Ramsay was admitted. The admission of these two men had the immediate result of a request that members communicate to the secretary 'any curious Information with regard to the Art of Curling which they may be able to obtain, as, when and where it was invented, in what part of the Country it was first generally practised, the meaning of its technical terms etc. It was further resolved to receive thankfully any antient Curling stones or any other piece of antiquity relative to Curling, In fine whatever might tend to throw a light upon the Nature and history of the Game.'

This scholarly interest in the game bore fruit in the first publication about curling, *An Account of the Game of Curling by a Member of the Duddingston Curling Society,* published in 1811 (see Appendix A). Ramsay was the author but he had the support of the society in the form of a distinguished committee 'to take all necessary steps towards the publication of Mr Ramsay's Essay upon Curling.' In 1813 Principal Baird gave intimation that an article on curling would appear in the next edition of *Encyclopedia Britannica.* The Principal's scholarly interest in the game is further shown by his donation to the Society in 1822 of five loofies; but he was no mere scholar: he remained a president of the Society until his death in 1841, and in 1830 Broun records that he had in active contemplation a wooden rink, which would be cheaper than Cairnie's or Sommerville's.

Meantime further innovation was going on apace, for at the Society's summer meeting in July 1809 unanimous approval was given to James Millar's proposal that a Prize Medal should be instituted, 'as no sport was more deserving of encouragement, and as none seemed to offer a juster, or more interesting competition than curling.' By November 1809 rules had been drawn up for the world's first points competition, which was to consist of five ends at each of drawing, striking, and inwicking, in a house of five feet in diameter.

The simple elegant gold medal, which was the only trophy played for throughout the Society's history, was lost from about 1911 until 1977, when merest chance saved it from the jeweller's melting pot. It was purchased by the present Duddingston Curling Club, and is one of their most prized possessions.

By 1811 the Society numbered among its 52 members two baronets, a marquis, the Principal of Edinburgh University and the Professor of Greek there. This was obviously no ordinary curling club. In 1812 Alexander Boswell of Auchinleck, son of the famous biographer of Dr Samuel Johnson, and a writer of curling poetry (pp. 18-19), became a member, and in 1814 both Sir George Clerk of Penicuik, on whose pond the first Grand Match took place in 1847, and also James Hogg, the Ettrick Shepherd.

In 1821 the Rev. Mr Sommerville, minister of Currie, and Cairnie's rival in inventing artificial curling ponds, joined the society.

Fig. 14   Curling scene, oil, early eighteenth century. This primitive, but accurately observed, painting is the earliest picture of the game in Scotland. The landscape looks Scottish enough although the bridge does not. The picture hangs in Traquair House in Peeblesshire, which is advertised as being the oldest inhabited house in Scotland.

By 1823 it had become apparent that the old curling house built in 1796 at a cost of £2.16.0 was woefully inadequate to house the stones of a rapidly expanding club. The result was a decision to build a new house on the minister's glebe, and the committee charged with the task of planning and building it might well have felt thoroughly satisfied not only at obtaining the services of Mr Wm Playfair, one of Edinburgh's outstanding architects of the time, but at obtaining his services free!

The new curling house, built by the lochside, and shown in Lees's painting, still stands, though roofless. A plan for its restoration is being actively supported by the present Duddingston Curling Club.

The elegant octagonal building was designed to have two floors. The top floor, which entered from the manse garden, was designed as a studio for the minister, the Rev. John Thomson, Scotland's first landscape painter; and the bottom storey was designed to accommodate the curlers. It is a pity that John Thomson, who was a member of the Society from 1807, appears never to have painted the sport!

At the meeting in 1823 which approved Playfair's plans, there were admitted no fewer than 70 new members, amongst whom the most notable was Henry Cockburn, who was immediately elected one of the four presidents, a post he retained while Solicitor General for Scotland from 1830-34. As Lord Cockburn, judge in the Court of Session, he wrote so interestingly of life in the Scotland of his day that it is again a matter of regret that nothing about curling has survived from his pen!

By this time the creative period in the club's life was over, though it continued to attract curlers: in 1845 there were 210 members; but no more advances were made.

The formation of the Grand Caledonian Club in 1838 came and went, without even a mention in the Minutes. In fact the Society never became a member club.

The demise of the Duddingston Society is rather curious. The last minute in the minute book is dated 2nd March 1853 and several new members were admitted, but by 1854 it appears that the majority of members wished to curl nearer their homes in the New Town of Edinburgh and to that end they formed a new club, Coates Curling Club. The very last minute of the Duddingston Society is the first in the Coates minute book.

Despite John Kerr's remark that the old Duddingston records were in the safe custody of the Coates Club, when the present writer tried to inspect them, no one knew where they were. A chance remark in a conversation with one of the Keepers of the Records of

Scotland, that he thought an old curling minute book had recently been deposited among legal papers in H.M. Register House, sent me to the Register House, and the Duddingston records were rediscovered. They had lain, for years unnoticed, among legal papers in the safe of the legal firm of a deceased secretary of the Coates Club and had been deposited with other legal relics in the national archives of Scotland.

4

Stones

We are able to infer from poetical and prose references to the game in the eighteenth century how it was played then.

What curling was like in earlier times has to be guessed from the shape of the few stones which survive, and my purpose in this chapter is to describe the evolution of the curling stone and with it the evolution of the game. It appears that the earliest form of stone was the 'loofie', so called from its small size, which meant that it was held in the 'loof', or palm, of the hand.

A small number of such stones has been found in various localities. They are normally small — 15lb. to 25lb. in weight — flat in shape, and without handles. There is incised in the bottom surface a groove to accommodate the fingers, and in the top a hole for the thumb. A typical example is the famous Stirling stone. Although it bears the date 1511, experts in inscriptions assign the date and the rest of the inscription to a considerably later period. There are no verbal descriptions of stones or curling from the sixteenth century or seventeenth century. The only depiction occurs in the crest of the family of Drummond of Carlourie.

When the coat of arms of this family was first matriculated between 1672 and 1677, the crest was described in words as 'a hand dexter, holding a curling stone.' At that date it was, unfortunately, not the practice to include in the register of arms a sketch of the armorial achievement. However, Alexander Nisbet (1657-1725), a lifelong student of heraldry, prepared a series of armorial plates for a work on heraldry. The book, *System of Heraldry,* was published in 1722 and 1742 and a second edition in 1816. For some reason some of Nisbet's plates did not find their way into either edition. When they were discovered in 1890 it was decided to publish them as a supplementary volume. Amongst these plates were the arms of Drummond of Carlowrie. The editors of the supplementary volume are of opinion that the plates were engraved for Nisbet about 1695. The 'hand dexter' which appears in the crest of the Drummond arms is holding a roughly circular disc; the thumb against one side of it, and the fingers obviously

Fig. 15   The armorial 'achievement' of the family of Drummond of Carlowrie, which is close to Edinburgh airport. It comes from a copperplate engraving made for Alexander Nisbet's *System of Heraldry* at the end of the seventeenth century. The crest is matriculated in the Register of All Arms and Bearings in Scotland as 'a hand dexter holding a curling stone.'

Fig. 16 Loofie, Stirlingshire, seventeenth century. The groove was for the fingers; a depression on the other side accommodated the thumb.

Fig. 17 The Stirling Stone. Loofie, bearing the inscription: 'St Js B STIRLING 1511' and on the top side 'A GIFT'. The inscription must have been added long after 1511, but the stone is undoubtedly ancient. Length: 9 in., width: $7\frac{1}{2}$ in., height: $4\frac{3}{4}$ in., weight: 26 lb.

against the other. This is the earliest picture of a curling stone, and it displays what Alexander Nisbet, at any rate, thought a curling stone should look like. By the late seventeenth century heraldry performed little useful purpose and was, in fact, an archaic survival from earlier days. It may be therefore that the Nisbet plate deliberately displays an old-fashioned stone.

Be that as it may, the plate is the only contemporary evidence for what a seventeenth century stone looked like and how such a stone was held in the hand. It is interesting to note that the artist who prepared the plates for a later armorial, *The Royal Book of Crests of Great Britain and Ireland* (1883), draws a hand holding a conventional nineteenth century curling stone.

From the shape of loofies it is reasonable to assume that they were thrown along the ice to a mark, in the manner of quoits.

Early references to quoiting show that that game was originally played with stones. Indeed a fifteenth century Anglo-Latin dictionary gives *petreludus*, or stone-player, as the Latin equivalent of 'quoiter.' There seems to be no Scottish evidence for quoiting, but what more natural than that a game involving throwing of stones in fields during summer should be adapted to the ice during winter? That that was the evolution may be inferred from the terminology used for curling in some parts of Scotland, at least until the mid-nineteenth century. In Ayrshire, Lanarkshire and Renfrewshire 'quoit', 'quoiter' and 'quoiting' were the terms used for 'curling stone', 'curler' and 'curling.'

James Grahame, in his *British Georgics* (Edinburgh 1809), writes:

> But more and still more skilful arms succeed,
> And near and nearer still around the *tee*,
> This side, now that, approaches; till at last,
> Two seeming equidistant, straws or twigs
> Decide as umpires 'tween contending coits.

And he glosses the last word thus in a footnote: 'In some parts of Scotland, the stones with which curlers play are called *cooting*, or *coiting* stones.'

Moreover, John Cairnie in his *Essay* (p. 93) quotes a contemporary letter from Andrew Crawford of Lochwinnoch, about a game 'against the Brig-o'-Weir quoiters, with 14 a side.'

Some of the loofies described by Kerr have vanished since he wrote; a few more have been discovered, the latest being found by Willie Jamieson on the farm of Gateside of Fulwoodhead at Beith in Ayrshire; no doubt many more are lying about still awaiting discovery, but it is significant that the counties in which they have been found, Stirling, Perth, Fife, Ayr, West Lothian, Mid Lothian and Kirkcudbright, comprehend most of the areas in which curling later prospered.

Kerr proposes as the age of the loofie the period 1500 to 1650, and with the proviso that there was no sudden change from one form of stone to the next, there seems to be little reason to dispute that conclusion.

The next stage in the development of the stone was the handle. With a handle it was possible to lift a much greater weight than before, and very quickly such

Fig. 18   This display of stones belonging to the Royal Caledonian Curling Club shows samples of all the old types of stone. There are three loofies at the bottom left. The three rough boulders with iron handles, channel stones, include the famous 'Jubilee Stone' presented to the Royal Club in 1888, the year of its jubilee. Of the three circular stones, one has a double iron handle; one, The Earl of Buchan, is bored to take a central bolt to hold the handle; and the third has a permanently fixed iron handle. In the centre is the hammer-dressed boulder thought to have belonged to the Rev. William Hally of Muthill in 1700. Its three-legged iron handle is unique. The triangular giant at the top of the picture is one of the 'Grannies' from Meigle.

Fig. 19   Another view of four of the stones shown in fig. 18.

Fig. 20   Channel stane, eighteenth century, Blair Atholl, Perthshire. The immense size of this stone can be gauged by the twelve-inch ruler lying on its top. Weight: 183 lb.

Fig. 21   Single-soled, roughly circular stone from south-west Perthshire, late 18th or early 19th century. The iron handle is fixed at both ends with lead. Height: 7½ in., circumference: 31 in., sole: 7½ in., weight: 52 lb.

channel stones — so called from their being picked from the channels, or beds, of burns and rivers — developed into enormous size.

If the game was ever played with a mixture of loofies and channel stones, the puny loofies cannot have long sustained the unequal competition. The earliest dated channel stone is one found at Roslin in 1826, and it bears the date 1613. The illustration of it in the *Annual* for 1843 shows it to be a roughly triangular stone, resembling the tailor's 'goose', or flat iron. 'It served both as a "leader" and a "wheeler"; in the first capacity it was a most dangerous shot when well played, leading many a stone directed against it "a wild goose chase" by fairly turning round like a "Jim Crow", as it never moved from the spot except when hit exactly in the centre. As a "wheeler" it was banished from the rink, and has lost the confidence of all parties. The broken nose of the Roslin stone bears strong marks of its "striking qualities" and hard encounters. It was found in the bottom of a pond deeply immured in mud, and was about to be consigned to the walls of the New Chapel of Roslin, when the mason, by the merest accident, discovered, upon removing the mud, the date of "the channel stane".' Most channel stones are, however, undated and undatable. There are, nonetheless, some examples of dated stones, later than 1613. In Dunfermline Museum resides a large oval stone of 66lb. weight with the date 1696 and the initials D M incised on its top.

Two other examples from the eighteenth century complete the list of dated channel stones. The first is an oval stone of 45lb. with the inscription MWH 1799 JA. This is thought to refer to Mr William Hally of Muthill who became minister there in 1690 and was a founder member of Muthill Curling Club in 1739. It was found when a pond on the estate of Mr Drummond Murray of Ardoch was being drained. Fortunately, it has been preserved by being donated to the Royal Club. Its interest lies not only in the early date, but in the well-preserved three-legged handle. The last is a smaller triangular boulder with a swan-necked iron handle, inscribed W Mc G 1720. It weighs 22lb. and is preserved in the Stewartry Museum, Kirkcudbright.

It is unfortunate for the curling historian, but scarcely surprising, that most channel stones bear neither distinguishing dates nor owner's initials. Such marks of ownership became necessary only when something like uniformity in the shape of stones came in at the end of the eighteenth century. The individuality of most channel stones was a sufficient badge of ownership. Unmarked they may be, but identity they did have, for many of them bore names with which all the curlers of the club would be familiar, and which no doubt recorded long since forgotten incidents and people. Thus there was a stone at Hawick known as the Town Clerk, while Coupar Angus had its 84lb. Suwaroff,* its Black Meg of 66lb., and its Saut Backet of 116lb.

---

* No doubt an allusion to Marshall Suvorov (1730-1800), the brilliant Russian soldier.

Fig. 22 One of a pair of single-soled stones, Duddingston, first quarter of the 19th century. The iron 'L'-shaped handle is run into the stone with lead. This shape of handle was by far the commonest of the iron handles. The initials 'J R' carved on the top may indicate that the stones belonged to the Rev. John Ramsay, author of *An Account of the Game of Curling*, 1811. Height: 5 in., circumference: 29 in., sole: 7 in., weight 31 lb.

Fig. 24 One of a pair of single-soled stones from (?) Fintry, Stirlingshire, first half of 19th century. The flat top with its sharp edge is typical of the earlier round stones. The handles are cast of solid brass, and are permanently fixed with lead into holes bored into the top of the stone. Height: $5\frac{5}{8}$ in., circumference: 30 in., sole: 6 in., weight: 39 lb.

Fig. 23 Another view of fig. 22.

Fig. 25 Another view of fig. 24.

Perhaps Blairgowrie had more named stones than most clubs. At any rate their names were woven nearly a century ago into an amusing Centenary Ode by John Bridie:

> In early years the implements were coarse,
> Rude, heavy boulders did the duty then,
> And each one had its title, as 'The Horse';
> One was 'The Cockit-hat', and one 'The Hen';
> 'The Kirk', 'The Saddle', 'President' and 'Soo',
> 'The Bannock', 'Baron', 'Fluke' and 'Robbie Dow'.

Kerr tells us that Robbie Dow was called after one of the baron bailies of Blairgowrie, son of the parish minister of the time, and President of the club when almost all its energies were channelled into the provision of curling stones.

Such channel stones were in use throughout the eighteenth century. Some, like the Jubilee Stone, reached the enormous weight of 119lb., and there is an even greater stone outside Blair Castle, the residence of the Duke of Atholl, which weighs, incredibly, 183lb. The immense weight of this stone has suggested to some

Fig. 26 One of a pair of single-soled stones, mid-19th century. The engraved pattern on the top side of the stone shows how some curlers paid regard to the appearance of their stones. The handles, of cast brass with wooden grips, fit onto a permanently fixed metal peg on the top of the stone. They are held in place by a metal screw. Height: 5 in., circumference: 32 in., sole: 5 in., weight: 38 lb.

Fig. 27 Another view of fig. 26.

people that it was not a curling stone, but a means of proving manhood, the idea being to carry it for long distances. The fact remains, however, that it is exhibited in company with a large collection of undoubted and early curling stones, and the shape of the iron handle, and the fact that its sole is completely flat lead the writer to conclude that it is indeed a curling stone.

It must not be supposed that *every* curler used gigantic stones: they would be beyond the power of most men then, as they would today, and in fact the majority of the surviving channel stones are from 35lb. to 45lb. in weight.

An exciting glimpse of the manner of channel stone play can be got from David Davidson's *Thoughts on the Seasons*, 1789:

The *stanes*, wi' muckle martial din,
Rebounding frae ilk shore,
Now thick, thick, thick, each other chas'd
An' up the rink did roar.

They closed fast on *every* side —
A *port* could scarce be found —
An' many a broken channel stane
Lay scatter'd up an' down.

'Shew me the winner', cries Glenbuck;
'An' a' behind stan' aff';
Then rattled up the rocking crag
An' ran the port wi' *life*.

Bentudor flung his bonnet by,
An' took his stane wi' speed —
Quoth he 'My lads, the day is ours' —
Their chance is past remead.

Syne hurlin' through the crags o'Ken,
Wi' *inrings*, nice and fair,
He struck the *winner* frae the cock
A lang claith-yard an' mair.

Brute force must have characterised channel stone play in its heyday. The irregularity of the stones, and the inequality of their weight, must have meant that luck played too great a part in the game. If a stone like the massive triangular Grannie from Meigle (115lb.) could be got safely to the tee it could be allowed to lie unguarded, for even direct hits can scarcely have done more than make it 'birl', and anyone who has played a game involving stones of greatly disparate weight will know that a hard strike with a puny stone against one twice its size will cause the small stone to rebound rather than propel the giant forward.

The use of heavy natural boulders was, however, part of the strategy of the game. The following minute by the exultant Secretary of Meikleour Curling Club, dated 19th January 1820, recording Blairgowrie's first defeat for 55 years, explains how these stones were utilised: 'The Stones which the party choose for this Match were of a mixed sort, Very heavy Natural Stones was played by the three first leading men and so on lessening in weight towards the end, They were principally hammer dressed polished stones.' The reference to three first leading men becomes intelligible when one realises that each rink was composed of *eight* men plus a director, each playing *one* stone.

Such clubs as Blairgowrie and Meikleour persisted in the use of channel stones at least into the 1820s. In fact as late as January 1819 the Meikleour club appointed

Fig. 28 One of a pair of single-soled stones, from Kilmarnock, ca. 1842. The painted decoration includes the name of the owner and his club. The handles are cut from a single piece of wood, and are inserted into a circular hole in the top of the stone, and held in place by wet cloth wrapped round the dowel. The owner, Charles Aird, used them from his joining the Townend Club in 1842 until 1892. Height: 6½ in., circumference: 29 in., sole: 7 in. but convex, weight: 42 lb.

Fig. 29 Another view of fig. 28.

two of their members 'to go to the water in the course of the summer to search for Stones at the expense of the Society,' and when they reported their failure to find suitable stones at the 1820 Annual General Meeting they were ordered to go and look again. Moreover Kerr informs us that the Ardoch club curled with natural boulders until 1828.

By the middle of the eighteenth century a feeling was growing in some parts that the game should be more

Fig. 30 Pair of curling stones presented to the Prince of Wales by the Royal Caledonian Curling Club in 1863. They have only just come to light at Sandringham. No doubt, in view of the rank of their recipient they were not only the finest that could be obtained, but also of the most up-to-date design. The double-soled stones were of green serpentine from Crieff; the grips of the handles were made of oak from the old royal palace of Linlithgow, richly mounted in silver. Note too the box for the stones. *Illustrated London News*, 8 April, 1863.

scientific, and the manner in which this was achieved was the introduction of the circular stone. The reasons for its introduction are so obvious that one must wonder why this shape was not thought of sooner. (Yet many civilisations have managed without the equally obvious advantage of the wheel!)

It is obvious that in some parts of the country the circular stone was in universal use from the second half of the eighteenth century. Pennant's description of 'great stones of forty to seventy pounds weight, of hemispherical form' shows that this was so, at least in Dumfriesshire.

Broun, in *Memorabilia*, page 42, writes: 'Old Bonaparte who flourished cir. 1750 and downwards was the first who had a regular formed polished Curlingstone upon our ice' — 'our ice' being one of the many lochs about Lochmaben.

In 1803 the Duddingston Curling Society set up a committee to prepare a code of curling laws 'in order to prevent disputes and ensure concord and harmony amongst the Members when upon the Ice.' They reported that 'the rules had been prepared with the greatest care, most of which are strictly observed in those counties in which the game of curling prevails': Regulation V states *inter alia*: 'All curling stones to be of

Fig. 31   One of a pair of single-soled, machine-made stones, 1853. The handles of cast brass with wooden grips fit onto two metal pins permanently fixed into the top of the stone. Height: 5⅛ in., circumference: 32½ in., sole: 7¾ in., weight: 42 lb.

Fig. 32   Another view of fig. 31.

Fig. 33   A very handsome pair of green serpentine stones presented by Rossie Priory Curling Club to Lord Kinnaird in 1867. The handles, of solid silver, are fixed to the stone by means of an iron screw which secures them to triangular iron pins leaded into the stone. On the top of the stones is a low relief silver casting of the coat of arms of Lord Kinnaird.

circular shape.' The influence of the Duddingston Society was considerable. It numbered among its members many notable Scots from different parts of the country. For instance, John Cairnie, of Curling Hall, Largs, Ayrshire, who was to become the first President of the Grand Caledonian Curling Club, was admitted to the Duddingston Society on 6th January 1804, the very day on which the Duddingston rules were approved. He was not the only Ayrshire member. Both the curling poets, the Rev. James Muir of Beith and Sir Alexander Boswell of Auchinleck, were members, and it is not fanciful to suppose that they took modern curling ideas back with them from the capital city to their respective parishes.

The family of Muir Mackenzie of Delvine Curling Club in Perthshire was also represented on the roll of members of the Duddingston Society and thus, no doubt, the society's influence spread to Perthshire also.

There are very few old minute books which actually set out the rules by which the club played the game; but one of the few is that of Fenwick, near Kilmarnock. In 1814 it was enacted by Regulation 1st, which was obviously not directly based on the Duddingston Rules: 'Every member of this Society when appearing on the Ice to Play must have two stones of equal weight and direct *round* (my italics), a Besom and one cloth shoe.' Whether the words 'direct round' were merely an unsophisticated translation of the Duddingston term 'a circular shape' or whether they represent a conscious change from former barbarity is not clear, but the author has found no old stones of anything but 'direct roundness' in the parish of Fenwick.

At this juncture it may be appropriate to pause and consider what steps were necessary for the provision of suitable stones for curling. The first surviving minute book of Blairgowrie Curling Society, which covers the years 1796 to 1811, displays an obsession with the provision of curling stones. Regulations approved on 20th December 1796 provide that each person admitted to the society 'shall be bound within three months from the date of his admission to provide himself with two Curling stones, which must be approved of by the society Or in case he fail to do this within the above period he forfeits five shillings that the society may therewith provide stones for him and he shall not be at liberty to carry them away as they are understood to belong to the society.'

As one can see from a later minute, the cost of a curling stone was about 2/9d, so the fine of 5/- was intended to be a compulsitor towards activity.

Fig. 34 One of a pair of double-soled, machine-made and polished stones presented to Commander Alexander Hamilton of Rozelle, Ayr, by Ayr Agricultural Curling Club in 1875. Though double-soled, both soles are of equal polish, but one is 7 in. broad and completely flat, and the other is 4 in. and slightly hollow. Height: 4 in., circumference: 36½ in., Weight: 41 lb.

Fig. 36 One of a pair of double-soled, machine-made and polished stones, 20th century. The stone is Red Hone from Ailsa Craig. The handles are of cast brass, silver-plated, in the form of oak leaves and branches. Both soles are only slightly hollow. The author's own outdoor stones. Height: 4 in., circumference: 34 in., sole: 5½ in. on the less polished side, 4 in. on the more polished, weight: 36 lb.

Fig. 35 One of a pair of double-soled, machine-made and polished stones, late 19th or early 20th century. The stone is Crawfordjohn, which was popular at that time, because it took a very high polish. The large black crystals of augite in a lighter matrix produced a handsome pattern, though the stone was brittle. The handle is an example of the most sophisticated stage in the development of the double handle. Such handles were in vogue in the 1890s. Height: 5 in., circumference: 32 in., sole: 6 in. and slightly hollow on the less polished side, 3½ in. on the more polished side, weight: 38 lb.

Regulation 9th provided for 'a proper number of stones not less than three dozen to be kept in proper repair at the expence of the society'; and the duty of inspecting the stones annually was laid upon the president.

On 4th January 1797 the Society decided to go further: 'having taken into their consideration that there is not a sufficient varaity of stones, they . . . agreed . . . that the following members be appointed as a Committee to furnish two dozen of stones at the general expence of the society . . .'

Thus began the saga of the provision of curling stones. At the annual meeting of 1798 no stones were available. At the meeting of 1799 the committee failed to report. However, the summer of 1799 saw some activity. The convener of the committee wrote to the members 'requiring and directing' them to turn out on 15th July 'should the river Ericht not be more swollen that day'.

Three members and the convener attended, according to their report, 'And proceeded up the water of Ericht and they have to report that they found and laid aside a considerable number of stones out of which Eighteen or twenty very Excellent Curling stones may be picked and the Committee request as they have been at considerable pains in searching out the stones that another committee should be named to bring them home . . .'

The choice of the word 'picked' in the preceding paragraph, and the fact that a later minute recording the expenses involved in turning the natural stones into curling stones makes no mention of anything other than boring holes for handles, the cost of iron handles, and lead, suggests strongly that the sort of stones that were in contemplation were natural channel stones from the River Ericht.

Fig. 37   This photograph, of New Farm Loch, Kilmarnock, ca. 1895, shows wooden-handled, single-soled stones still in use.

On 1st January 1800 the society changed its tack and proceeded to enforce regulation 3rd: 'The young members who have not yet provided stones in terms of the regulations to have their stones in readiness within one month.' In 1801 none of the young members had complied and ten of them, then present, including the Rev. James Johnston, had the fine of 5/- imposed, with power to the Clerk to prosecute all the other delinquents in the club's name for this fine. Three members subsequently got a refund by speedily producing their stones.

In 1804 a committee for providing curling stones to the number of two dozen was again appointed. In 1805 it was appointed yet again and the Clerk was appointed 'to see and recover as many of the old stones as can be found and any expence to be incurred to be paid out of the funds in his hands — any of the members that may bring such stones as may be approved to be handled out of the funds.'

The accounts relative to these matters are interesting:

1805		£.	s.	d.
July	To paid Carriage of a quantity stones	2	-	
	To paid Sundrie expenses at collecting stones		13	4
Dec 18	To paid at Committee for settling handling and boring stones		2	10

1806		£.	s.	d.
Jan 1	To boring 24 stones		9	
	To handling — d, — with Iron & L[ead]	1	14	
	To lead		2	6
	To sorting the Jumpers for boring		2	
	To 3 lb lead left with Baillie Brown for handling the rest of the stones		1	6

On 1st January 1806 the saga was brought to a close by a minute noting the happiness of the meeting that 'The Preses Clerk and Committee appointed at the last meeting for providing Curling Stones have amply discharged their duty in that respect by having provided and handled two dozen of Stones, besides a great number of others ready for handling', for which they were thanked.

By 1820 most curling clubs had adopted the new shape, though some lagged far behind the times. John Cairnie inveighed against the curlers of the small island of Cumbrae in the minutes of his Noddle Curling Society, of which he was then Secretary (20th January 1820): 'This day the following party went to Cumbraes to play the players in that quarter . . . An equal number opposed them with stones quite unfit to appear on any rink of curlers, some were oval, some triangural and only one of them fit for Muster.'

Fig. 38 A pair of stones displaying an unusual design of handle. 20th century. The stones are common Ailsa.

The earliest dated circular stone is to be found in the Museum at Hawick. It is a single-soled stone with a fixed iron handle. Not only does it bear the date 1772, but it has the name of the owner, or owners, inscribed upon it: 'Geo. War Henderson'. There are at least two other dated eighteenth century stones: one, dated 1781, comes from the Henderson Bishop collection of *curliana* recently rediscovered in the Highland Folk Museum at Kingussie; the other in the Gladstone Court Museum, Biggar, is a pinkish stone with an iron pin for a detachable handle and has the initials GL and the date 1794 carved upon its top.

Circularity did not, however, cure all the problems. Since curling was organised on a parochial basis, each parish tended to have a preference for a particular size and form of stone. Some parishes tended to prefer the large, flat, and heavy; some preferred height in relation to breadth; and others, such as Tarbolton, favoured small stones. The advantage of a small stone was that it could pass through a narrower port than a large stone, but there were occasions when this advantage was overcome by climatic conditions:

6 February 1830
This day a Curling Match took place betwixt the players of Loudon and Torbolton 12 Rinks on each side which terminated in favor of Loudon players by above 100 shots. The great loss sustained by Torbolton players was caused by the wind blowing their small stones completely off the ice — whereas the Loudon people having larger stones and weigher (*sic*) they were not so easily blown away — in fact the ice was so keen and the storm so great, that it was scarcely possible to remain on the ice, that day therefore has ever since been called stormy Saturday.

As we have already seen, the provision of stones for play was a matter not only for individuals but also for clubs. Many clubs provided in their rules for the proof of ownership of a stone, or stones, as a condition of membership, with elaborate rules for payment, or fines, in default. Some clubs had provisions for quality control, only approved stones being permitted. Other clubs used subtler means. Thus at Sorn Curling Society (Ayrshire) on 14th January 1805, 'The meeting considering that there may be an improvement made in the forming of Ice stones, resolve to give the following premiums for the four best and most useful fore-hand stones, to be produced at next Annnal meeting by any of their members and to be determined by the Directors, viz. 4/- for the first, 3/- for the second, 2/- for the third and 1/- for the fourth. The stones to be produced on the ice any day the Directors shall appoint before said meeting . . .'

Fig. 39   Silver inkstand given by Penicuik Curling Club to James Jackson in 1838 for his services as secretary for 24 years. The stone is a good example of the shape of a stone of that date, with a handle that becomes thicker at its open end.

Fig. 40   An early and ornate example of the so called 'goose neck' variety of handle, which in its modern form is the only type. The handle is handforged from iron. The grip consists of wood, embellished with white metal. First half of the 19th century.

Whether the prizes produced results we do not know, for nothing further about the matter is recorded.

Writing in 1831, the secretary of Penicuik Curling Club attributes their having 'arrived at a high pitch of perfection' not only to enthusiasm, discipline and practice, but to the club's having an 'excellent collection of Stones for any sort of weather', that is, keen-soled stones for drug ice, and less polished soles for keen ice.

Stones would be made, usually locally, by stonemasons and the handles fashioned by the local blacksmith, or out of wood by the curler himself. The whole process, from the finding of a suitable stone in the burn by Rab, to his shaping it by chipping and clouring, his polishing it to 'a lustre rare', and his making and fitting a fine handle, is celebrated in a poem of extraordinary feeling by the Rev. George Murray, minister of Balmaclellan.

My Channelstane

ALTHOUGH my muse on rustic wing
  Ne'er saw Parnassus' witching spring,
  She yet together lines can string
      In humble strain,
  And all thy praises loud to sing,
      My channelstane!

Where lone Penkiln, 'mid foam and spray,
O'er many a linn leaps on his way,
A thousand years and mair ye lay
    Far out of sight;
My blessings on the blythesome day
    Brought thee to light.

Though ye were slippery as an eel,
Rab fished ye frae the salmon wiel,
And on his back the brawny chiel
    Has ta'en ye hame,
Destined to figure at the spiel
    And roaring game.

Wi' mony a crack he cloured[1] your crown,
Wi' mony a chap[2] he chipped ye down,
Fu' aft he turned ye roun' and roun',
    An aye he sang,
A' ither stanes ye'll be aboon,
    And that ere lang.

Guided by many a mould and line,
He laboured next, with polish fine,
To make your mirrored surface shine
    With lustre rare —
Like lake, reflect the forms divine
    Of nature fair.

A handle next did Rab prepare,
And fixed it with consummate care —
The wood of ebony so rare,
    The screw of steel —
Ye were a channelstane right fair,
    Fit for a spiel.

___

1 a hard knock
2 knock

Fig. 41 Sunset at Turnberry with Ailsa Craig in the background. The Craig provided stones for one of Scotland's national games; Turnberry's championship golf course, venue of the British Open Golf Championship in 1977, provides the opportunity for the other.

Ye had nae name for icy war —
Nae strange device, nor crest, nor star —
Only a thread of silver spar
    Ran through your blue;
Ilk[1] curler kenned[2] your flinty scar,
    And running true.

When first Loch Ken ye glided o'er,
I stood upon its eastern shore;
Your onward course ye truly bore,
    Then struck the land,
Old Lowran echoed back your roar,
    With welcome grand.

Oh, 'twas a glorious sight to view
Ken's frozen waters, firm and true,
Each object clad in silv'ry hue,
    Or grey with time;

The heavens above, so calm, so blue —
    The hills sublime!
'Twere long to tell where ye have been,
How many gallant games ye've seen;
How oft the brooms of curlers keen
    Waved o'er your head,
Whene'er ye took the winner clean,
    In time of need.

Nae doubt misfortunes we have met wi',
Right ugly customers been set wi' —
Some honest chiels we are in debt wi'
    To try't again;
Such *accidents* maun never fret ye,
    My bonnie stane.

But truth to tell — for truth should still
Be freely told, whether the rill
Speeds on its way or waxeth chill
    At winter's blast —
Though vanquished, we with hearty will
    Fought to the last.

1 every
2 knew

A time will come when I no more
May fling thee free from shore to shore;
With saddened heart I'll hand thee o'er
  To some brave chiel,
That future times may hear thy roar
  At ilka spiel.

Sev'n heartsome lads — weel may they be —
Run blythe about their father's knee;
To them I'll give right cannily
  This sage advice:
'Auld Scotland love, and love like me
  Her game of ice.

'Let spiel be lost, or bravely won,
Enjoy like men the glorious fun;
From morning's rise till set of sun
  Be frank and free;
And still let manly deeds be done
  Around the tee.'

It was always necessary for the early curlers to bestow a lot of care and attention on the soles of their stones. No matter how rough and coarse the body of a stone, the sole was honed — often with Water of Ayr stone (which still plays an important part in their manufacture) — to a considerable polish, as the following anecdote, composed by Richard Broun for a quite different purpose, clearly illustrates. It comes from his hitherto unpublished notes for a second edition of *Memorabilia*: 'Upon the morning of our memorable bonspiel with Dumfries 1829-30, their President a great amateur and determined to secure victory "by all appliances and means to boot" had all the sixteen stones of his Rink brought to his house — and as the day promised to be soft from a fall of snow, he had a man at work water-of-ayring them from an early hour. By ten, the ennamel was complete that the polish was exquisite — We met at eleven, & tho the snow lay four or five inches deep — the ice when unrobed was splendid, & exceedingly keen. The consequence was, from the high polish of his stones, they were all regularly played out at the tee head. He was highly provoked, & tried to roughen them by rubbing with freestone, but without effect, & he lost the game having only 6 shots. After dinner — whilst discussing to some friends with no little acrimony the mischance of his polishing — the door opened and the servant interrupted his narrative with a question which set the table in a roar — "John is here Sir, just come from the loch, & he wants to ken whether ye'll hae your stanes rubbed the night or no?"'

Though the rules of curling have always made provision for the breaking of a stone — the largest fragment counts! — the occurrence nowadays is almost

unheard of. When stones were home-made it must have been a good deal more frequent. James Kennedy, in his *Poems on Scottish and American Subjects*, (2nd. edition, New York, 1883), describes the feelings of a Scoto-American curler when faced with the demise of the stone his own hands had created:

THE CURLER

Saw ye e'er a vet'ran curler
  Mourning owre a broken stane,
When the game is at the thrangest[1]
  Ere the hin'most[2] shot is ta'en?

How the past comes up before him,
  Like a gleam o' gowden[3] light!
How the present gathers o'er him,
  Like a stormy winter's night!

Doun he sits upon his hunkers[4] —
  Lifts the pieces ane by ane;
Mourns the day he cam to Yonkers —
  Vows he's lost a faithfu' frien'!

Doun the rink comes Davie Wallace,
  Tears o' pity in his e'e,
Vex'd an' sad his very saul is,
  Sic a waesome sight to see.

Weel he kens that throb o' anguish
  Wring the vet'ran's heart in twa;
Davie's feelings never languish —
  Davie kens we're brithers a'.

An' he speaks him kindly — 'Saunders,
  Weel I wat you've fash[5] aneuch:[6]
But let grieving gae to Flanders —
  Keep ye aye a calmer sough.[7]

Stanes will gang to crokonition,
  Hearts should never gang agee;
Plenty mair in fine condition —
  Come an' send them to the tee.'

'Wheesht!'[8] says Saunders, 'dinna mock me —
  Cauld's the comfort that ye gie;
Mem'ries gather like to choke me
  When ye speak about the tee.

---

1 busiest
2 last
3 golden
4 haunches
5 trouble
6 enough
7 always keep calm
8 be quiet

Fig. 42 Aerial view of the island of Ailsa Craig from the north-west. The quarries from which the metal for curling stones was won can be discerned in the left of the picture.

Whaur's the stane I could depend on?
   Vow my loss is hard to bear!
Stanes an' besoms I'll abandon —
   Quat[1] the curling evermair.

Weel I mind the day I dress'd it,
   Five-an'-thirty years sin' syne,[2]
Whaur on Ailsa Craig it rested—
   Proud was I to ca' it mine.

Owre the sea, stow'd i' the bunkers,
   Carefu' aye I strave[3] to fend,
Little thinking here at Yonkers
   I would mourn its hinder end.

Saw ye aft how ilk beginner,
   Watch'd it aye wi' envious eye.
Canny aye it chipp'd the winner —
   Never fail'd to chap an' lie.

Ne'er ahint the hog-score droopin' —
   Ne'er gaed[1] skitin[2] past the tee;
Skips ne'er fash'd[3] themsel's wi' soopin[4]
   When they saw my stane an' me.'

Round the ither curlers gather,
   Some lament wi' serious face;
Some insist it's but a blether —
   Aft they've seen a harder case.

Davie lifts the waefu' bodie,[5]
   Leads him aff wi' canny care,
Brews a bowl o' reekin[6] toddy,
   Bids him drown his sorrows there.

---

1 leave
2 ago
3 strove

1 went
2 sliding
3 bothered
4 sweeping
5 sorrowful person
6 steaming

Fig. 43 At one period the blocks were cut by a diamond saw on Ailsa Craig before being shipped to the mainland. These blocks are ready for shipment.

But his heart is like to brak aye,
   An' he granes the tither grane,[1]
Gies his head the tither shake aye,
   Croons a cronach[2] to his stane.
Sune the toddy starts him hoisin,
   Sune he grows anither chiel —
Glorious hameward reels rejoicin'
   Wi' his senses in a creel!

It was not until the second half of the nineteenth century that curling stone manufacture became mechanised. Until then there can have been no masons who were exclusively curling-stone makers, but there were masons who specialised in making curling stones, as the following passage from a correspondent of Cairnie shows: 'The first improvement in stone-making at

1 groans another groan
2 lament

Lochwinnoch, was immediately after the Duke's visit in 1784, *in imitation of the Hamilton fashion,* for the Lanarkshire stones were bored through the centre admitting a screw. Hence these stones were called at this village *Duke-hand* for many years afterwards. They began to make them neater. John Cochrane took up the trade of polishing them. He continues the same ingenious craft to this day. He puts in an iron handle, and hews the stone to a perfect circle. William Sutherland was the second maker. He made the Castle Semple stones and many others, after the Duke's fashion, or *Duke-hand.* Garthland's stone, made by Sutherland, passed into the hands of Mr Orr, Merchant. It was quite flat and very broad. It was broken a few years ago.' An example of Sutherland's work, 'The Earl of Buchan', which now belongs to the Royal Club, can be seen in fig. 18.

As late as 1845 the curlers of the newly formed St Mirren Curling Club in Paisley resorted to a mason in Auchinleck, thirty-five miles away, to make stones for

Fig. 44 Loading the blocks onto the *Ailsa Lady* at the Craig.

them of 30 to 34lb. at the rate of one pair per week for five weeks at a cost of 4 pence per pound. The metal for stones was, at first, found locally: there is no part of Scotland where suitable stone cannot be found. Common sources of stones were the beds of the rivers and the sea shore, but as early as the 1830s it is clear that stone from particular localities was beginning to be sought by curlers from further afield. For example, the frontispiece to John Cairnie's *Essay on Curling and Artificial Pond Making* (Glasgow, 1833) depicts Cairnie's sailing cutter arriving off the shore opposite his house at Largs 'with', as he says, 'a few selected pieces of granite for Curling Sport, taken from the shore of Ailsa Craig,' and Broun (page 44) informs us that, in 1829, 200 pairs of Ailsa Craig stones were shipped for Canada.

Ailsa Craig is a small volcanic islet in the Firth of Clyde about thirty-five miles from Largs as the crow flies. In the later nineteenth century and well into the twentieth it provided the metal for by far the majority of curling stones in the world — but of that more later.

Dr Renton, member of Penicuik Club in 1824, seriously suggested that any of the Iceland traders in Leith might bring some 'Basaltic Blocks in Ballast at less expence than good Blocks could be brought from Lanarkshire, and no stones in earth could equal them, in hardness, or keenness.'

Nowadays the manufacture of curling stones in matched sets for ice rinks and clubs has removed any element of personal taste from their design. Splendid uniformity is the result.

Before the introduction of machine-made stones the diversity, even within the confines of circularity, was considerable. The first circular stones were single-soled; that is, the handle was permanently fixed to the top surface of the stone. It was usually of iron or wood, but sometimes of brass. Naturally many more handles of iron have survived than those of wood, although most old stones that one comes across today lack even their iron handles, and such as do survive are often rusty and bent. The common pattern was L-shaped, with the short limb

Fig. 45   Ailsa Craig, 1961. Rough-hewing a block of Blue Hone at the quarry face with a blocking hammer.

of the 'L' leaded into a hole cut eccentrically, about two-thirds across the diameter of the stone. The actual shape of the handle depended on the views of the curler. In some localities the grip ran parallel to the top surface of the stone; in others the open end of the handle projected slightly upwards. Some handles are constructed entirely of iron; others have, or had, grips of wood or bone.

A permanently fixed handle was liable to be damaged by rough treatment when the stone was in store during the long non-curling months. Not only that: during the winter the stone with a fixed handle was available for use by anyone when the owner was not present on the ice. Kerr (page 40) records that the Alyth stones were kept in the open: 'Instead of a house, the curlers had only a small piece of ground fenced in with a rough paling in the form of a circle, and in the centre the stones were all tumbled together in a heap.' To overcome these difficulties a removeable handle was devised. At first made of iron and latterly usually of cast brass, these handles fitted onto a triangular or square pin permanently set into the top of the stone and they were held in place by a screw. See fig. 26. Another form of detachable handle was developed in central Ayrshire. In this form the handle was screwed on to a thick threaded bolt permanently fixed in the centre of the stone.

The last form of detachable handle was the so-called goose-neck variety, now practically the only shape. This form became universal with the advent of machine-made double-soled stones, with a keen and a dull surface. The possibility of having a stone with running surfaces suitable for different ice conditions made necessary a handle which could be fixed at will to both sides of the stone, and the modern form which screws on to a bolt running right through the stone was the result. The earliest form of this type of handle was an angular affair, forged from iron. See fig. 40.

An appreciable number of old circular stones had looped, or closed handles, that is, handles both ends of which were fixed to the stone. The heavier the stone, the more natural such a handle, but this form was not restricted to very heavy stones. Looped handles were never common, and the surviving examples are usually early.

In some areas the looped handle was the norm. Muthill Curling Society in Perthshire was founded in 1739. Rules from that date exist but the surviving minute book containing them has evidently been written about 1823. The book does, however, incorporate the 1739 rules in their original form, and the front end-paper is embellished with a most interesting 'coat of arms', supported by thistles, and topped by a 'crest' of a whisky bottle and two glasses. The top half of the shield is a heraldically arranged pattern of three trickers, three besoms, and three stones. All of the stones are of the closed handled variety, two of them circular, and the third roughly rectangular. The bottom half of the shield contains a drawing of four curlers at play. They are dressed in the mode of 1810 and one curler is playing a circular closed-handle stone. The picture is initialled and dated 1821, and in the opinion of Mr Stuart Maxwell of the National Museum of Antiquities in Edinburgh it is an attempt to portray curling as it was practised in Muthill at that time, or maybe ten years before. See Plate 1.

There are, however, some comparatively sophisticated examples of handles cast in brass from the 1840s and 1850s. The author has in his collection one pair of stones with permanently fixed solid brass handles, and another dated 1853 with a double closed handle screwed on to pins fixed in the top surface of the stone. See figs. 24 and 31.

The commonest form of decoration on circular stones was the incised initials of the owner. In other cases the stones were embellished by incised stars and other emblems, and one in the author's collection has the masonic insignia of crossed square and dividers. Two early circular stones at Penicuik House have a star and a horn respectively sculpted on the upper surface.

Fig. 46 Ailsa Craig, 1961. Imparting a more accurate shape with hammer and punch. In this state the blocks were shipped to the mainland.

Another form of decoration was painting. This was by no means common, but it can be seen to advantage in a handsome pair of stones in the Dick Institute, Kilmarnock. They are of the Kilmarnock pattern, high in relation to width, with varnished wooden handles. The top surface is decorated with gold lines running round the circumference. The name of the owner, Charles Aird, and his club, the Townend, are likewise neatly painted on the top in gold letters, and the numbers of the stones are painted in red and blue. Charles Aird used the stones for at least fifty years from 1842 until 1892. Another reference to painting stones comes also from Kilmarnock. In 1827 it was agreed by the Townend Club 'that the Stones be all painted in one manner black with the Initials of the owner and the letter T for Townend below the handle.' This suggests that other patterns of painting had hitherto existed. Another fine pair is preserved in Blair Castle. Below the handle is painted the crest of the Duke of Atholl.

Sir Richard Broun, in his *Memorabilia Curliana Mabenensia* (Dumfries, 1830), and John Cairnie, in his *Essay*, had gathered and published information as to shapes, sizes and materials of stones from various parts of the country. Their researches disclosed an unacceptably high variation in size and weight. One of the first tasks undertaken by the newly formed Grand Caledonian Curling Club in their first *Annual* for 1839 was to make recommendations as to stones. The following appeared at page 22: 'The Committee consider an equalization in the weights and sizes of Curling Stones to be of such paramount importance, as to justify them in submitting the following scale as the most preferable.

When the weight is under

35 lb. imp.	the height not to be less than $4\frac{1}{4}$ in.
38 lb. imp.	the height not to be less than $4\frac{1}{2}$ in.
41 lb. imp.	the height not to be less than $4\frac{3}{4}$ in.
44 lb. imp.	the height not to be less than 5 in.
47 lb. imp.	the height not to be less than $5\frac{1}{4}$ in.
50 lb. imp.	the height not to be less than $5\frac{1}{2}$ in.

Whatever be the diameter or weight, the height ought never to exceed 6 or at most $6\frac{1}{8}$ inches, nor be less than $4\frac{1}{4}$ inches.

Fig. 47 Aerial view of the quarries at Trefor, North Wales.
The stone comes from the top terrace.

'Too broad stones are bad; they cannot pass through a narrow port, as has often to be done towards the conclusion of an end. None ought to be allowed in a set game of greater diameter than 12 inches, nor of a greater weight than 50 lb imperial.'

One area in which personal preference had full rein was in the choice of sole. Argument about the relative merits of flat, concave and convex soles continued throughout the nineteenth century.

The earliest area of controversy concerned the width of the sole, or running surface, of the stone. Some clubs swore by broad flat soles of five, or six, or seven inches; others extolled the virtues of narrow soles. From Cairnie's *Essay* it is clear that considerable experimentation had been going on in the early years of the nineteenth century, for he illustrates not only broad and narrow soles, but the precursors of all modern curling stones, running on a ring; and a very curious stone which ran on three separate prominences extending slightly out from the sole.

A stone which ran well on a broad sole on keen ice might be impossible to get up when the ice was soft; and although a narrow sole could cope with drug ice, it was difficult to control for direction, because the small area of the running surface made it pick up the slightest bias, of which there is an abundance on natural ice.

The modern shape of sole was developed in Canada by J.S. Russell of the Toronto Club. A native of Lanarkshire in Scotland, Russell worked ceaselessly in the promotion of curling in the land of his adoption. He is probably best known in Canada as one of the fathers of the Ontario Curling Association, of which he was secretary from 1882 until 1902, and as a member of the all-conquering 'Red Jacket' rink of the Toronto Curling Club. Russell's other great contribution to curling, the improvement of the curling stone, is nowadays overlooked, for most curlers take the stone for granted. In an article printed in the second *Annual* of the Northwestern Curling Association of America (1893-94) Russell thus describes the situation he found about 1870 in Canada and the U.S.: 'Most of them (*scil.* curling stones) had the convex for the 'keen' bottom, and the 'dull' bottoms were about equally divided between the 'flat' of various widths, and the 'concave', with a bearing about one inch or more in breadth, around a slightly depressed hollow of about 4 inches in diameter.'

He went on: 'The keen bottom was used only when the ice was soft: and could be played "up" even in slush, but did not obey the turn or twisting motion given to stones in the act of being delivered from the hand to guide their course on the ice, and was used only as a last recourse when to play with the other bottom down was impracticable. The other bottom suited fairly well when the ice was rough or damp, but when the ice was smooth and hard it could not easily be controlled, running "over all ice" with the application of a very gentle force; and with the introduction of covered rinks, and the skilfully prepared ice which followed, they were found to be unsuitable, and a change became necessary to meet the altered condition of the ice; and for this the curling community are indebted to Mr J.S. Russell of Toronto. This change was found by making the bottom concave, and having it "curl" on a narrow "aridge" or "arras" surrounding the concave. Many diameters of the concave were tried and various depths, and different forms of "arras" were experimented with until, in 1879, Mr Russell having become satisfied that he had succeeded in perfecting a form of bottoms that gave satisfactory results on all kinds of ice, introduced his new style of Curling Stones under the name of "Russell's Improved," and they were found to be immensely superior to those previously in use, and are now accepted everywhere as the standard Curling Stone, and the only model which gives satisfaction to the expert player. The "keen" bottom is made slightly concave and the surrounding "arras" is oval and about $\frac{3}{8}$ to $\frac{1}{2}$ inch in breadth, and the "dull" bottom is also concave to a depth of about $\frac{1}{4}$ of an inch, and is bounded by an "arras" well elevated, and of very

Fig. 48   Thomas Thorburn's curling stone factory, Beith, Ayrshire, ca. 1895. This posed photograph was obviously designed to show as many of the manufacturing processes as could be demonstrated outdoors. The lady on the left is dealing with a pair of finished stones. Beside her a man is checking with calipers the diameter of a partly turned stone. The chucks for holding the stone in the turning machine are still in position. The third man from the left, with the rough block in front of him, has in his right hand a knapping hammer, used for trimming the block to the approximate size required for turning. The two seated boys are finishing off the striking bands. The boy with upraised right hand is boring the hole for the bolt to hold the handle in a roughly shaped block. The boy at the extreme right is holding a knapping hammer. In the foreground are what appear to be used stones in for treatment.

narrow width, and not flat but rounded or oval. The diameter of the concave varies from 5 to 5½ inches, the wider diameter giving the stone increased resistance, and greater "borrowing" power, and the breadth of the "arras" mainly determines the resistance of the stone. The wider the face of the "arras," the stone is more easily played, and vice versa. The diameter of the concave on the keen side is proportioned to that on the dull side, so as to give the stone the same "borrow" when played with the keen bottom down, on wet or soft ice, as it takes when played with the dull bottom on hard, dry ice. Many other considerations have influenced the changes introduced in "Russell's Improved," and which are still being modified as increased knowledge, and better mechanical appliances warrant.

'While the credit of devising the improvements belongs to Mr Russell, the merit of working them out belongs to the late Mr Andrew Kay of Haugh, Mauchline, in

Scotland. Mr Kay accepted Mr Russell's ideas with enthusiasm, and invented his curling stone grinding machine to produce the pattern with perfect exactness. Mr Kay's is the only patented grinding machine for curling stones in existence, and without it, it is impossible to produce a curling stone approaching in perfectness of model, and in excellence of playing Russell's Improved.'

At this stage it is appropriate to mention the manufacture of stones by machine. Reference has been made in the above article to Andrew Kay of Mauchline (Ayrshire), whose patent machine is illustrated. See fig. 49. The firm of T & A Kay, of which he was a partner, was one of the two earliest firms producing curling stones in numbers by machine. The other early manufacturer was Thomas Thorburn of Beith, whose advertising proclaims him to have been the earliest, biggest and cheapest manufacturer of stones. His factory was also situated in Ayrshire within easy reach of Ailsa Craig,

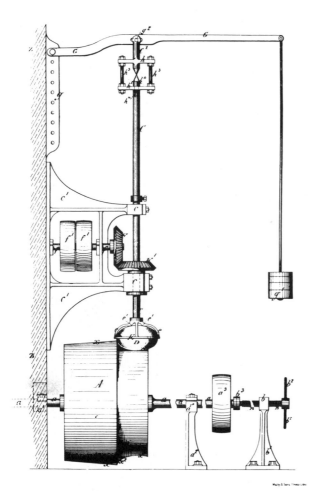

A.D 1881. Oct 13. Nº 4459.
KAY'S SPECIFICATION

Fig. 49 The drawing which accompanied the patent specification of Andrew Kay's curling stone grinding machine. 'A' was the large revolving grindstone. The curling stone 'D' was kept in contact with it by gears and weights and was revolved by 'E'. 1881.

Fig. 50 The block undergoing initial cutting in the lathe at the factory of Andrew Kay & Co. (Curling Stones) Ltd. in Mauchline.

Crawfordjohn, Burnock Water, and the other favoured sources of the raw material. These companies were in operation in the late 1870s.

T & A Kay were established in 1876 at Haugh near Mauchline, in a building which still stands. On the death of Andrew Kay in 1888 his widow procured the lease of the factory and, having evicted her brother-in-law, set up in competition with him. For twenty-five years the two Kay companies operated in close proximity in Mauchline with, one assumes, more than usual rivalry. The original firm came to an end in 1915 but its offshoot, now known as Andrew Kay & Co. (Curling Stones) Ltd., has continued to the present day and is in fact one of the only two manufacturers of curling stones in the world.

Thomas Thorburn, who is shown on his business card as a tall man with a broad, spade-shaped beard, delivering one of his own stones, gave up production in 1914 and his business was taken over by John Keanie in the neighbouring village of Lochwinnoch. Keanie had begun manufacture about 1890, and in various forms the firm was continued by his descendants until about 1939.

D. R. Gordon, curling stone manufacturer and wholesale ironmonger, produced stones in Bathgate, West Lothian from 1881 until 1892; David Beveridge in Perth from 1891 until 1907; and W. & J. Muir in Beith for five years from 1900. In 1904 Beveridge was advertising the virtues of his 'Steam Polishing Works.' The only other maker to have advertised in Royal Club *Annuals*, in which it is reasonable to assume that all manufacturers would have offered their wares, was Donald & McPherson, Glasgow, from 1890 to 1915. Interestingly, their works were situated at Stair, also in Ayrshire.

If one measures commercial success in terms of longevity, only those firms working in the West of Scotland were successful. Even in the heyday of curling stone manufacture, at the beginning of this century, the market was sufficient to employ only seven companies.

Fig. 51 The first cut.

When Donald & McPherson and Beveridge gave up making stones they retained a curling connection, for they sold other people's stones for many years.

Despite the present boom in curling the demand for stones is small. In the 1960s a rival company to the old-established Andrew Kay was formed in Glasgow, but after some years, and after an unsuccessful move to Inverness, it has ceased to trade. An associated company, the Bonspiel Curling Stone Company Ltd., has since 1978 been producing, for the Canadian market, a small number of stones at The Quay, Deganwy, North Wales. The reason for the small demand is simple: curlers curl in ice rinks whose matched sets of stones do service for thousands of players. Hardly a curler now owns a pair of stones, and individuals who purchase a new pair are rare indeed.

Although the older price lists, and books, abound with picturesque names of stones such as Crawfordjohns, Burnock Waters, Carsphairn Reds, Tinkernhills, Douglas Waters and Blantyre Blacks, it was from Ailsa Craig that the majority of blocks for curling stones came.

Ailsa Craig is a rocky islet in the Firth of Clyde, about ten miles out from the small harbour of Girvan. In height about 1100 feet, in length about 1300 yards and in breadth 870 yards, the Craig is what geologists know as a volcanic plug, the solidified lava in the vent of a volcano, the remainder of which has long since been eroded away. Though light in relation to their bulk, the various types of Ailsa Craig stone have been found since the early nineteenth century to produce excellent metal for curling stones. Three main types of stone were quarried: Red Hone, Blue Hone and Common Ailsa.

Fig. 52   Checking the weight of roughed-out stones.

On the Craig quarrymen resided throughout the summer, producing rough blocks of 80 to 100 lb. in weight. These were transported by boat to Girvan, and thence by rail to one or other of the curling stone factories. There the blocks were reduced in size by hand before being subjected to Kay's patent, or other similar, grinding machines. Nowadays, the cost of maintaining even a small workforce on an island otherwise uninhabited, apart from the crew of a lighthouse, has become prohibitive. Moreover, the quarries from which the superior stone, namely Blue and Red Hone, was won, had become progressively more difficult and dangerous to work: fewer and fewer top quality blocks were costing more and more effort to obtain. In 1973 the quarries were abandoned, and another source of stone had to be found for the curlers of the world. The quarry of Trefor, twelve miles west of Caernarvon in North Wales, provided the answer, and now all the raw rock for curling stones is produced by a small band of about half a dozen Welsh-speaking quarrymen, the tiny remnant of what had once been a large workforce operating one of the largest quarries in Britain. The quarry plunges in terrace after terrace down a mountainside into the sea, but the blocks for curling stones are obtained from a small area near the top of the mountain.

The present steps in production are as follows: First, a large mass of rock weighing many tons is blasted from the quarry face. It is then split by hand, using plugs and wedges, into roughly rectangular blocks, which are further refined by hand-held hammers into coarsely circular cylinders, like large cheeses, each weighing about 100 lb. In this state they are transported to Mauchline.

Kay's patent machine, which consisted of a large revolving sandstone grinding wheel, exists no more. The rough blocks are now first attached to large chucks and about 50 per cent of their weight is cut off by tough steel blades. After this process, it is possible to discern flaws in the stone which would cause it to break on impact, and an appreciable percentage are discarded. The second process involves more turning and there emerges the

Fig. 53 Fine adjustment to the running surface of the stone.

characteristic flattened spherical shape of the modern curling stone. Thereafter a hole is drilled through the centre, which will ultimately house the bolt which holds the handle. The stone is then spun for several hours on different polishing machines which, by use of successively finer abrasives, produce a dully polished surface at top and bottom. In the final process a high polish is imparted to the stone by revolving it at high speed in contact with putty powder.

The finishing touches, countersinking the bolt hole on each side, and tidying up the striking band, are soon carried out, and the stone is ready for dispatch.

When one considers that rough blocks from the quarry cost about £18 per pair, that about 10% are discarded at various stages of manufacture, and that about twenty man-hours are spent on each pair of stones, it is little wonder that a new pair costs as much as £220 in Scotland in 1980.

It may be thought that the characteristic feature of curling is the use of stones. However, in the area around Montreal the earliest form of 'stone' was made of iron. The Canadian iron was generally heavier than a stone, weights of 50 to 60 lb. being common. Whatever the reason for their adoption, the Montreal curlers clung to the iron game until 1947, and it was only with difficulty that they were in that year persuaded to conform with the rest of the curling world.

Wooden blocks were used as ersatz stones in various places in Canada and the U.S. in the early days of curling in an area, but never out of preference, and always only until real stones could be procured. The only place in which wooden 'stones' were used in Scotland appears to have been the leadmining village of Wanlockhead, where until about 1939 schoolboys played with light wooden 'stones' until they became strong enough to handle real stones.

Fig. 54　Finishing off the bolt hole.

Hollow iron 'stones', similar in shape to conventional stones, and quite unlike Canadian irons, were produced in Scotland, but no doubt because of the abundance of suitable stone they never took on and are consequently very rare. Such 'stones' were played by the Glasgow North Woodside Club in the early 1830s, probably because their secretary, Mr Edington, was involved in the Phoenix Iron Works. Writing to John Cairnie, Edington says, 'the improved castings for curling . . . answer very well, and play uncommonly straight; they are cast hollow, 10 inches by 5 inches, weigh 36 lb. and have one case hardened bottom or sole'.

When it appeared that the veins of easily won red and blue hone were running out, an experiment was tried by the Scottish Curling Stone Company which consisted of inserting a Blue Hone sole into a stone of baser material. The 'Ailsert' sole was held tight in place by the bolt and handle. Another experiment consisted of inserting an Ailsa Craig sole into a 'stone' cast of aluminium, but the

resilient quality of the metal was so different from that of stone that this project was soon abandoned. One aluminium stone striking another on the nose did not stop dead, but was pulled forward for several inches by the other; and if a wick was attempted the played stone slithered round the struck stone before flying off at unexpected angles, as happens when the striking bands of stone stones are coated with ice.

The reverse process, that of attaching a metal sole to a stone stone, was tried in the early years of the nineteenth century in Beith and Dalry, which were in close proximity to iron works. On drug ice the stones with polished iron soles gave the curlers who owned them such an advantage over conventional curlers that they were shamed off the ice.

Because of the rising cost of the raw material there have been a number of attempts to find a substitute for stone, such as synthetic stone, but the results have never been satisfactory. One manufacturer in Glasgow tried

Fig. 55   Before and after. The block from which a curling
stone is made and the finished article.

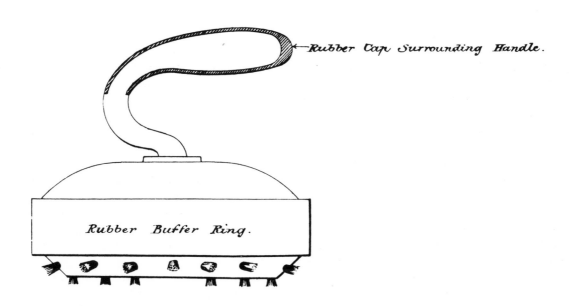

Fig. 56   A patented curling stone substitute of 1877. It was designed to be thrown along a smooth prepared surface indoors.

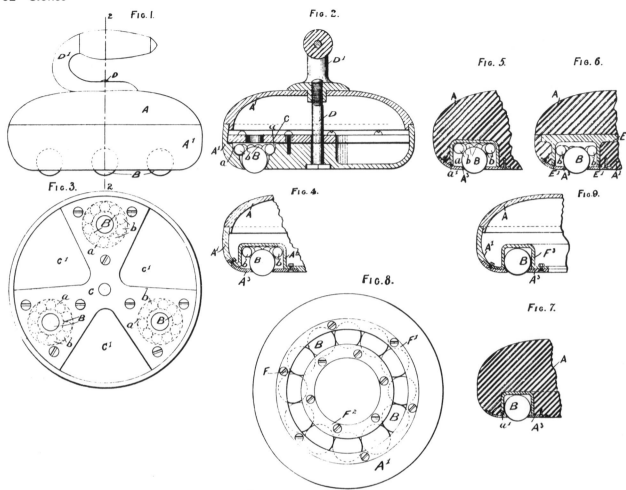

Fig. 57 Another patented curling stone substitute of 1902. It ran on ballbearings, or glass beads.

stones of vulcanised rubber, with such conspicuous lack of success that the writer knows of only one surviving pair, in the museum of the Dick Institute, Kilmarnock.

The curling season in Scotland was so short that fertile minds were constantly at work to devise methods of extending it. The lead given by the Earl of Mansfield in displaying the game to Queen Victoria on a polished wooden floor was not taken up for many years, but in the closing years of the nineteenth century various inventors obtained patents for substitutes for curling stones. The invention which obviously drew most inspiration from the Earl of Mansfield's example was patented in 1877 and consisted of a wooden 'stone', weighted with lead. The running surface, designed to be used on a polished wooden floor, was covered with tufts of bristles, something like an artificial ski-slope in reverse. Other patents for metal stones, running on ball-bearings, or castors, were granted in 1887, 1902 and 1908.

The patent specification for the first of these inventions, No. 1443 of 1877, is worth quoting in full:

SPECIFICATION in pursuance of the conditions of the Letters Patent filed by the said Robert Foulis in the Great Seal Patent Office on the 12th October 1877.

ROBERT FOULIS, of Cairnie Lodge, Fifeshire, Scotland. 'IMPROVEMENTS IN APPARATUS TO BE USED IN PLAYING GAMES SIMILAR TO THE GAME NOW KNOWN AS "CURLING".'

This invention has for its object improvements in apparatus to be used in playing games similar to the game now known as 'curling.'

The game of curling is at present played on a surface of natural ice with weights, or as they are called 'stones,' which are slidden along the ice towards a point marked upon the surface. In this form the game can only be played when a frozen surface is obtainable.

In order to admit of a similar game being played in a room or other place having a smooth floor, I

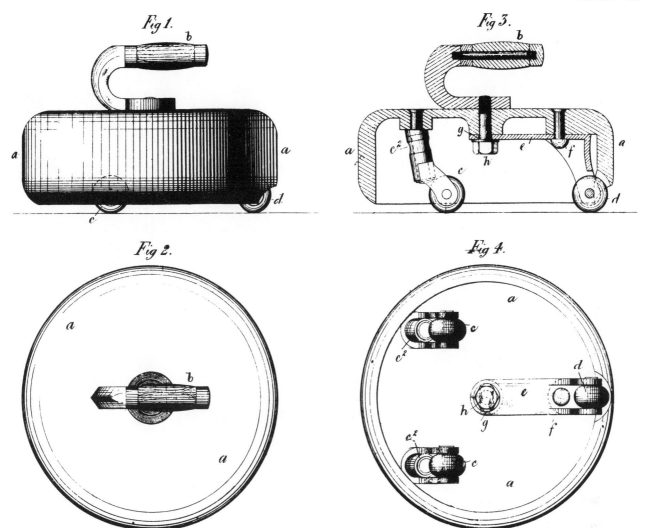

Fig. 58   This substitute, patented in 1887, ran on castors.

spread upon the floor a fabric similar to oilcloth, but somewhat lighter, and having a smooth face.

The fabric known as 'marble baize' is that which I employ, but it requires preparation to render it suitable for use, and this preparation consists in rubbing the surface with a composition of wax and turpentine.

Marble baize is especially convenient for use in rooms, but for larger sizes of the game, other smooth surfaces as wood and metal may be employed, but whatever material is employed, the surface is prepared with beeswax dissolved or rendered semi-solid by admixture with turpentine.

On this prepared surface the peculiar 'stones' which I employ slide much as do the ordinary curling stones on a surface of ice.

A special peculiarity of my curling stones, one of which is represented in the Drawing annexed, is that the bottom or frictional face of the stone is composed of short bristles set as in a brush, so that the stone stands upon the ends of the bristles.

I form the body of the stone of wood in two parts, an upper and a lower. These parts shut together boxwise, and between them I arrange a metal disc of a size to give the requisite weight to the stone.

The stone is provided with a metal handle covered so that it may not injure the surface, if from unskilful use the stone should be overturned.

The stone is also provided with a buffer ring of india-rubber all around it, so that when in the course of play one stone comes into contact with another, the elasticity of the india-rubber may prevent shock and facilitate the transfer of motion from stone to stone.

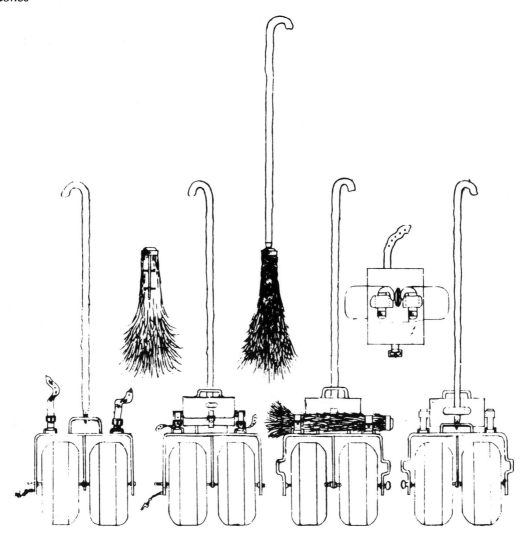

Fig. 59 'Contrivance (invented by James Weir of the Waverley Club, Edinburgh) for lightening labour in conveying curling stones to and from the ice, by rolling them instead of carrying them, the full benefit of which will be felt in attending the grand matches, or bonspiels, where the regular conveyance cannot approach within a short distance of the ice. Another advantage . . . is the keeping of the stones together, at the same time preserving the soles from damage, and running less risk in losing them altogether, which at the last great meeting at Carsebreck, there is reason to fear was the case.' *Annual*, 1854.

The surface is marked with concentric circles as when the game is played upon ice.

But curling is a game that is played on ice, and such perversions of the game were consigned, where they belong, to the show cases of museums; or became conversation pieces in a few private houses.

A Note on the Petrology of Curling Stones

Despite Kerr's troubling to obtain from the most eminent Scottish geologist of the day, Professor Foster Heddle, the opinion that *granite* was useless as a rock for making curling stones, the misconception has persisted that all curling stones that have ever been made have been fashioned from granite.

Neither the blocks from Ailsa Craig which were in use from the beginning of the nineteenth century until well into the twentieth, nor the present blocks from Trefor in North Wales, are what the petrologist would call granite. Heddle called the former granophyre; the petrological designation of the latter is a granite porphyry; made up of a fine grained ground mass, in which the large felspars lie, consisting of orthoclase and plagioclase felspar, often intergrown with clear quartz.

Both of these are igneous rocks, formed by the cooling

of the magma of which the mantle of the Earth is composed, and most curling stones will be found to have been made from igneous rocks.

The virtue of an igneous rock is that it is composed of a mass of interlocking crystals of the different minerals in its mixture. Since the crystals have formed in all directions as the molten liquid solidified, most igneous rocks have a remarkable ability to withstand hard impacts without fracture, obviously an indispensable quality in a curling stone. The trouble with granite, according to Professor Heddle, is that its main constituent, the mineral orthoclase felspar, splits most easily in two directions at right angles; and since the crystals of orthoclase in most granites lie in a polar arrangement, there is a marked propensity for the stone to split or crack. The only true granite stones that I have ever seen, a beautiful pair of red Peterhead granite, were proof of Heddle's opinion, for they had both split into two pieces along the line of the striking band.

Another disadvantage of granites is their lack of uniform elasticity, which again arises from the polar arrangement of the orthoclase, which possesses a greater elasticity in one direction than all others; the result, according to Heddle, is 'that curling-stones made of granite, while they would only travel 6 feet after an inwick on one side, would travel 8 feet if hit upon another; while if *both* stones were of granite the 8 might become 10. Uncertainty is introduced all round; and it is just in delicate play that the differences would make all the difference.'

In the earliest days stones were fashioned from whatever metal was to hand, and a not inconsiderable number are found to be made of sedimentary rocks, like greywacke and sandstone, but the preponderance of stones is of igneous origin, the commonest types of rock being diorite, and dolerite. Diorite is a plutonic rock consisting essentially of plagioclase andesine or labradorite felspars, together with augite, hornblende, or biotite. Dolerite contains augite in addition to plagioclase felspar, and iron ores.

5

Ice

The Duddingston curlers curled upon Duddingston Loch; the Lochmaben curlers played upon one of the seven lochs that surrounded their village. All of these were natural stretches of water of greater or lesser but always substantial depth. It was no doubt on such lochs as these that the game was first played. The advantage of such lochs was their size, their responsiveness to the roar of the stone, their picturesque beauty.

The disadvantage of deep water is the length of time it takes to freeze. Casual observation must have shown that nine inches or a foot of water will turn into bearing ice much sooner than water ten feet deep. Moreover, one's chances of drowning in a foot of water are markedly less, and drowning was a danger of which early curlers were well aware. Broun (page 27), having listed the numerous parishes vanquished by Lochmaben, goes on: 'and perhaps Kirkmichael might have been added to the list, but for the occurrence of a most disastrous accident by which six individuals were drowned, and a termination the most melancholy put to the bonspiel.'

The conditions in which nineteenth century curling matches were often played were atrocious. Water lying on the surface was common. Play continued in snow, and even in rain. Throughout the nineteenth century the Dundonald secretary records the state of the ice for nearly every game. The ice was often 'daughy', or damp. On 3rd February 1848 he writes, 'A few of our curlers met today on Merkland in the midst of rain and played three hours for Beef and Greens . . .' and on 25th February 1853: 'Eight players enjoyed five hours sport today on Auchans pond, tho' the water coming through the ice was rather troublesome.'

One minute in the Kilmarnock Townend minute book prosaically yet graphically describes such conditions. February 2nd, 1839: '. . . They then Met the Fenwick Curlers according to appointment for to Play the Madel Game 60 Players a side. The day was very unfavorable for Good Play. it was Proposed about 1 O Clock to Prospond (*scil.* postpone) the game to an other day but as Both Parties Could not agree it was Playd out by the Time the game was finished the water was at some of the rack heads Covering the whole of the stones . . .'

From at least the beginning of the nineteenth century curlers in Scotland therefore constructed artificial shallow ponds, which varied in size from being large enough for only two or three games to fairly large ponds covering several acres.

The mode of construction was generally much the same. An area was levelled out, embankments to contain water were piled up, and sluices were built at two ends of the pond to allow the water in and out of the pond. These ponds were not designed as permanent water surfaces: the idea was to close the appropriate sluice in November, open the other sluice and allow the burn to fill the pond to its required level, and hope that it froze. The water was then released in March when all hope of frost was gone, and the pond returned to its other function as pasturage for beasts.

The minutes of early clubs are full of material about the construction and, more commonly, the repair of such ponds. Not only did mechanical devices like sluices break down, but voles and rats could render the embankments leaky by their burrowing, and a constant expense was incurred in mowing the grass every autumn.

This type of pond was an improvement on the deep water pond, and in the early nineteenth century was the favourite sort. In 1850 the Royal Club published a curling map of Scotland on which was shown the location of each club's pond. (Extensive researches have failed to discover even a single copy of this map.)

The amount of curling afforded on shallow water ponds was greater, but not markedly greater, than on deep water, even when play was extended by artificial light. As early as 1853 Major Henderson of Park of

Fig. 60   Silver medal of New Abbey Curling Club, Kirkcudbrightshire, 1830. A fine engraving on the reverse of this medal, which is still played for annually, depicts the curlers of the parish at play on Loch Kindar.

Westerton, Bridge of Allan, introduced gas lighting to his new pond by means of gutta percha piping from the village gas supply. Some means had to be found to prolong the curling season, and the credit for finding it must go to John Cairnie, of Curling Hall, Largs.

He had the idea, about 1810, as he informs us, of making an artificial rink by creating a shallow level surface which would hold water, but he did not act upon the idea until returning home from a Duddingston Curling Society dinner on 20th December 1827. The principle upon which Cairnie's pond was built was to create and compact a level surface freed from grass and weeds. An impervious layer of clay was laid on this, and when frost seemed likely a thin skin of ice was built up from watering cans.

This invention increased beyond comprehension the number of days on which curling was possible. J. Gordon Grant, in *The Complete Curler* (1914), records a comparison made at Moffat between deep water and tarmac ponds over a period of seven years between 1906 and 1913. In that period there were 40 days of play on the deep water pond but on the tarmac pond the total was 240!

A rival claim to his invention by Dr Sommerville of Currie caused Cairnie to publish in 1833 his *Essay on Curling and Artificial Pond Making*, a fortunate occurrence, because the book is by no means restricted to the making of artificial rinks, but is a storehouse of information on the game as it was then played in many parts of Scotland. Until shortly before his death in 1842 we find Cairnie extolling the virtues of his artificial rink and encouraging clubs to form them.

Cairnie's basic idea, namely of forming a thin skin of ice on a level impermeable surface, was of course capable

Fig. 61   Though apparently a natural loch, the sluice in the foreground shows that Invernytie Loch has been adapted for curling. *Illustrated London News*, 7th January 1854.

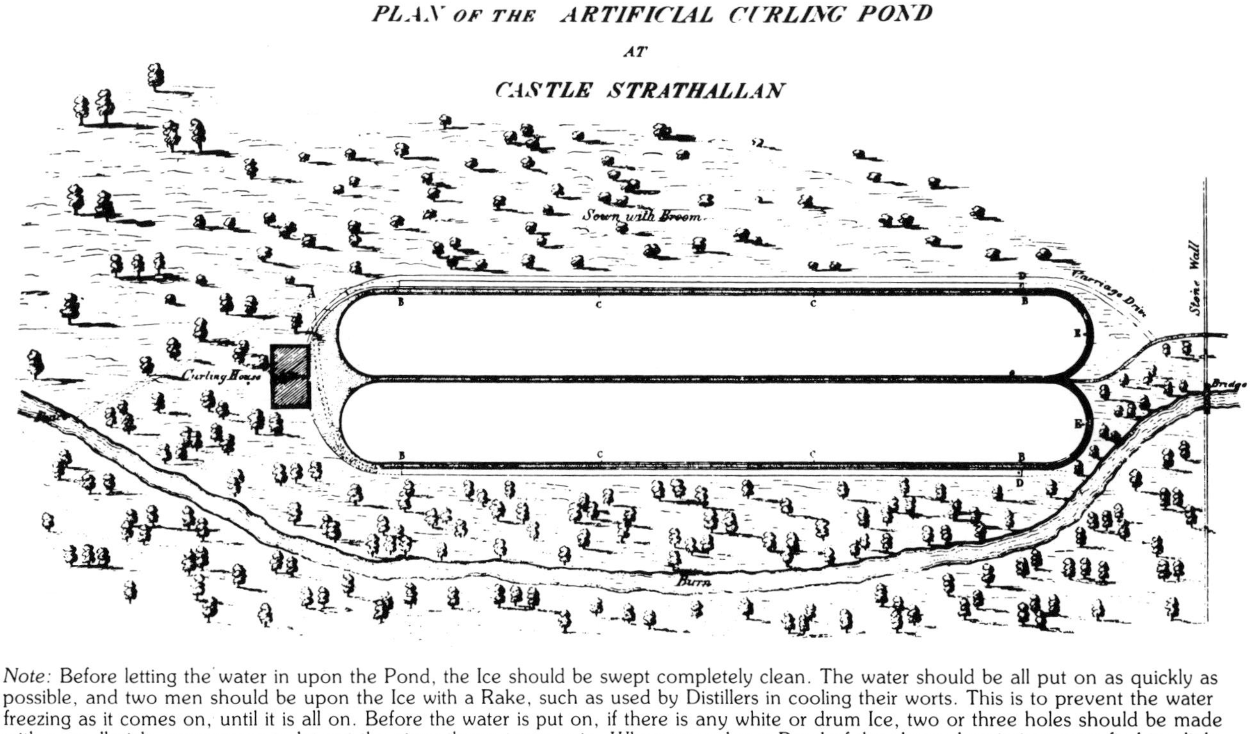

Note: Before letting the water in upon the Pond, the Ice should be swept completely clean. The water should be all put on as quickly as possible, and two men should be upon the Ice with a Rake, such as used by Distillers in cooling their worts. This is to prevent the water freezing as it comes on, until it is all on. Before the water is put on, if there is any white or drum Ice, two or three holes should be made with a small pick, on purpose to let out the air as the water goes in. Whoever makes a Pond of the above description, may find it a little difficult, until they get into the way of regulating, etc.

Fig. 62   Plan of the artificial ponds at Strathallan. The same ponds are shown in fig. 63. *Annual*, 1846.

Fig. 63 Photograph of the artificial ponds at Strathallan Castle, Perthshire, ca. 1862. The construction of the ponds was described in the *Annual* for 1846. (See fig. 62.) Note the tee marker, the single-soled stones, and the pair with looped handles. The curlers are using broom cowes.

of elaboration and improvement. Worms and weeds were his greatest nuisance. An asphalt surface was tried in some parts as a cure for these difficulties, but much more elaborate and ingenious improvements were also tried.

Thus we find Lord Kinnaird at Rossie Priory in 1852 building a complex of four artificial rinks, two lined with clay and two floored with wood; and at Coodham in Ayrshire and at Culhorn near Stranraer not only was the rink entirely constructed of wood but it was so designed as to allow a special watering machine, as wide as the pond itself, to be pulled back and forth over the pond: 'thus the watering operation is performed in the most efficient manner in less than a minute after the machine has been filled.'

What was perhaps the ultimate refinement of Cairnie's invention was also constructed in Ayrshire. The proprietor of Dalgarven pond near Kilwinning, 'considering that various materials have been tried for making the floors of artificial curling ponds, but whatever the successes of these there have always been some decided disadvantages, such as leakage or the melting of asphalte, and casting or shrinking of wood in summer,

which the projectors have been unable to overcome', decided in 1857 to adopt the suggestion of a friend and construct an *iron* pond. The 'pond' was constructed of flanged cast iron plates, 5 feet 1¼ inches square by ½ inch thick, bolted together and supported on brick piers. The *Annual* for 1859 records the success of the pond, on which it was possible to curl as late as 13th April 1858 for 4½ hours, and to resume as early as 30th October following.

Maybe the cost of an iron pond was prohibitive, for we read of no other. In fact tarmac and concrete were the floors that survived into the twentieth century, and although most tarmac ponds are now abandoned, there are still a few where play takes place every winter.

In North America the problem was not lack of frost. The early clubs played on natural ice, of which there was plenty, though often it was rough: we read of the Montreal Fire Brigade assisting the curlers in the preparation of smoother ice on the St Lawrence River by flooding the surface with their hoses. There was, however, a superabundance of snow; and biting frost and wind could render curling impossible. The solution was natural ice within a building which protected curlers from

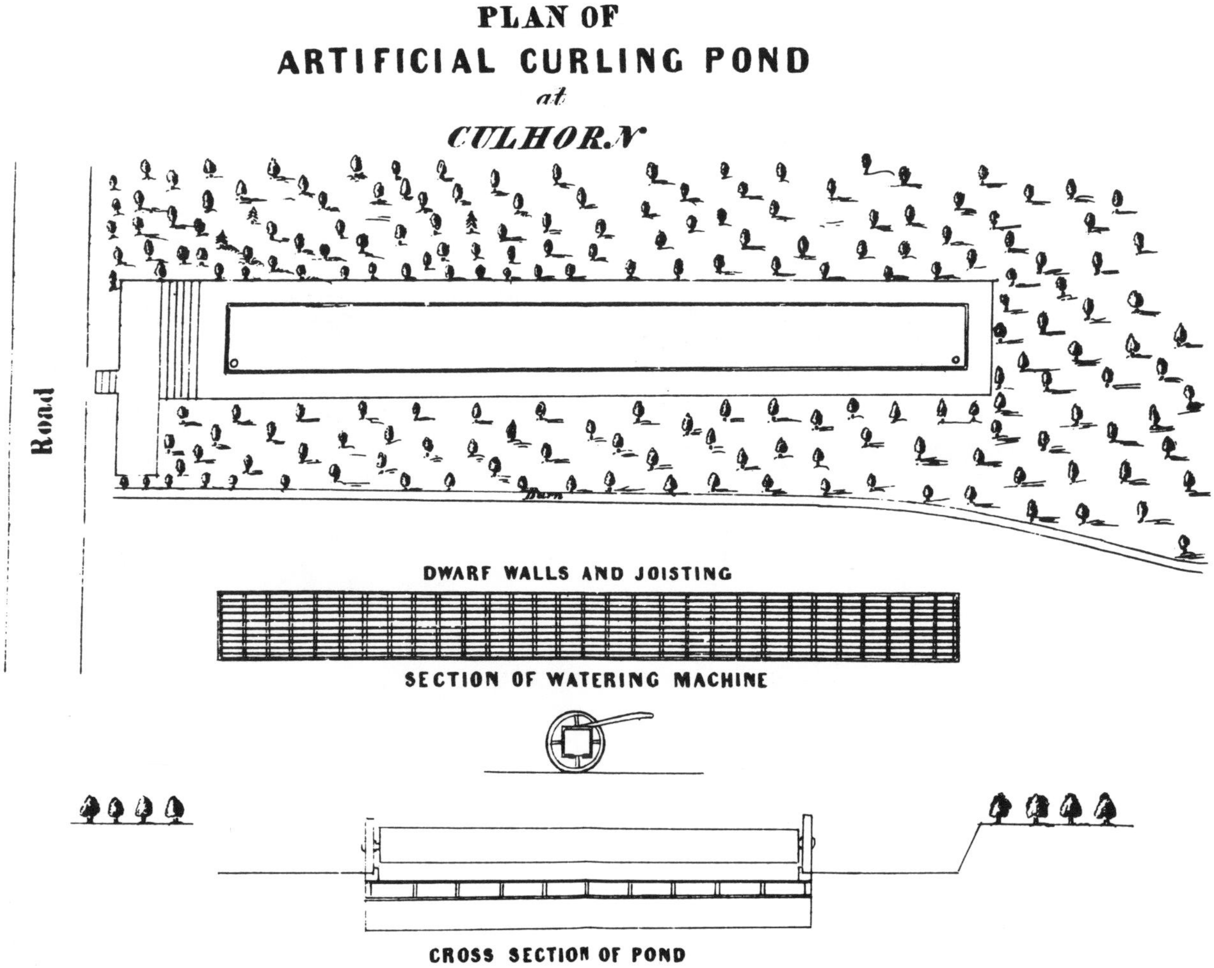

PLAN OF
ARTIFICIAL CURLING POND
at
CULHORN

DWARF WALLS AND JOISTING

SECTION OF WATERING MACHINE

CROSS SECTION OF POND

Fig. 64 *Annual, 1853.*

the weather but permitted the frost to get on with the work of providing ice. The first such rink appears to have been constructed in 1837 by the Montreal Club in St Ann suburb near the Lachine Canal. In the 1840s there are several reports of sheds for curling. For instance, in 1844 Montreal Thistle Club obtained a site in Craig Street, though it is doubtful if it was erected since in 1847 the Thistle club played their Silver Medal in the Montreal club's covered rink. The Toronto club moved indoors in 1859, the Hamilton club had covered rinks in the early '60s, and on 1st January 1868 the Ottawa club opened their covered rink, constructed at a cost of $1000.

By the time of the first tour to Canada by the Scots curlers in 1902-3, most Canadian curling was conducted indoors in specially constructed rinks. Kerr noted: 'Many of them, in the smaller towns, are built of wood; but in the larger towns and cities they are mostly of brick, and have an ice space sufficient to lay out from four to six sheets of ice for curling, 142 feet in length, with a width of 15 or 16 feet.'

Kerr's experiences in Canada drew from him the following wry reflections:

Happy Canadian Curlers

It is not simply in the quantity of frost they have that our Canadian children are so happy. Their advantage as compared with ours is that they can attend to business all day, and adjourn to the rink in the evening. The palatial nature of the majority of these rinks has been made apparent by our illustrations, which give only a faint idea of what they really are. In the majority of cases they can have every kind of comfort in their retiring-rooms, and can either play or do the plate-glass-skip business, i.e. criticise those who are playing. Then in these they have more space on which to display the trophies

CURLING PONDS
AT
ROSSIE PRIORY.

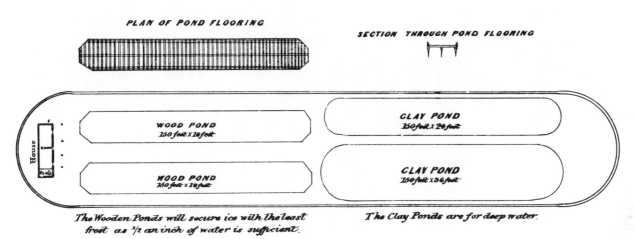

PLAN OF POND FLOORING   SECTION THROUGH POND FLOORING

WOOD POND
150 feet X 18 feet

WOOD POND
150 feet X 18 feet

CLAY POND
150 feet X 24 feet

CLAY POND
150 feet X 36 feet

House

The Wooden Ponds will secure ice with the least frost as ½ an inch of water is sufficient.   *The Clay Ponds are for deep water.*

Fig. 65   *Annual, 1853.*

won by their representatives in great bonspiels, the names being immortalised, so as to give incitement to others to emulate them. It was quite remarkable to find what valuable collections of cups and trophies of all kinds were in the keeping of nearly every club we had the pleasure of visiting. As these go on increasing they will make the curling clubs the wealthiest institutions in the Dominion.

Such ice palaces contributed in no small measure to the transformation of the game in Canada from a boisterous haphazard sport, to one in which skill and technique could be developed.

Kerr's detailed account of the preparation of rinks for curling in Canada deserves quotation in its entirety. 'Throughout the Dominion,' he writes, 'all curling is now done under cover, in large sheds called rinks, for want of a better and more distinctive name.

'In preparing the ice-bed for a curling rink the first thing demanding attention is the thorough drainage of the sub-soil, for if even a small quantity of water lodges in it, within the scope of frost, it will freeze in severe weather, and thaw out in mild weather, thereby affecting the ice sheet, making it uneven and unfit for curling.

'In the best-constructed rinks, the soil is taken out to a depth of about 2 feet, and the bed thus formed is levelled accurately; then cedar sleepers, about 6 inches in thickness, are laid on it, and on them are placed 10-inch

joists, the spaces between which are filled, up to the level, with ashes, well rammed, which makes a solid foundation for the flooring, and lessens the roaring sound of the curling-stones as they move along the ice. The flooring is from $1\frac{1}{4}$ to $1\frac{1}{2}$ inch in thickness, is tongued and grooved, and laid in white lead, to prevent leakage; and as a further precaution against this serious evil, a good coating of oil is given to the floor, in rinks, at the beginning of each curling season.

'In most of the rinks there is a platform for spectators at either end, about 8 or 10 inches above level of the ice floor, and fitted with boxes or shelves for putting away the curling-stones when not in use; and in some, this platform extends all around the interior of the rink; while others have, in addition, a gallery at an elevation of 10 or 12 feet above the platform, and extending around the inner walls of the building, from which an excellent view of the game may be had. Provision should be made by ventilators to admit cold air, as near the surface of the ice floor as possible and to allow the escape of the heated air at a higher altitude; and some means should also be provided, to quickly run off surface water from melting of ice in mild weather.

Ice-making

'As soon as a term of settled frost seems assured, a thin coating of water is sprayed over the wooden floor, and is followed by others, as soon as each successive coating

Fig. 66 The Countess of Eglinton and her ladies on a Cairnie-type artificial rink at Eglinton, February 1860.

becomes frozen, until the sheet of ice thus formed is thought to be water-tight, when sufficient water may be put on to cover freely the entire ice surface, so that the water may come to its natural level before freezing; it is safer to do this by two or even three successive floodings of moderate depth, than by one of greater depth, so as to avoid the danger of the water finding "a way of escape" through the thin sheet of ice already formed, before it is solidified by the frost.

'Now, supposing that all this has been successfully completed, we will have a level sheet of ice, about 1 inch in thickness, covering the whole of the floor, but the surface of it will not be quite uniform in appearance, some parts of it being smooth as glass, and other parts (where currents of air played upon the surface of the water while freezing) more or less rough. And as ice in this condition is not good for curling on, another process has to be used to make the surface of the ice-sheet uniform all over, which is called "pebbling," and is the finishing touch for making ice for curling. Strange as it may seem to the uninitiated, in this final process hot

water is used; and when the mercury indicates a near approach to zero the water may be almost at boiling point, the objective being that the heated water may melt a seat for itself in the ice-sheet before freezing, and so not scale off under the action of a moving curling stone; and in all the best rinks it is now applied by means of a "sprinkler", which is a watering-pot with a rose about 3 feet or so in length, pierced from end to end with a single row of very minute holes, about 1 inch apart; when in use the pot, being first supplied with water, is tilted over so that the rose comes very near the surface of the ice, and the ice-maker walks backwards, drawing the pot after, so as to deposit a thin line of water, from each hole in the rose, on the ice; which quickly becomes frozen — this is sometimes put on in straight lines from end to end of the rink, but more commonly either at right angles, forming squares, or diagonally, forming diamonds, as if the surface of the ice was covered with cobwebs in mathematical forms. The result is that the ice gives a grip to the curling-stone, and that grip uniform, over the whole rink. Some hair-splitting curlers debate, with many

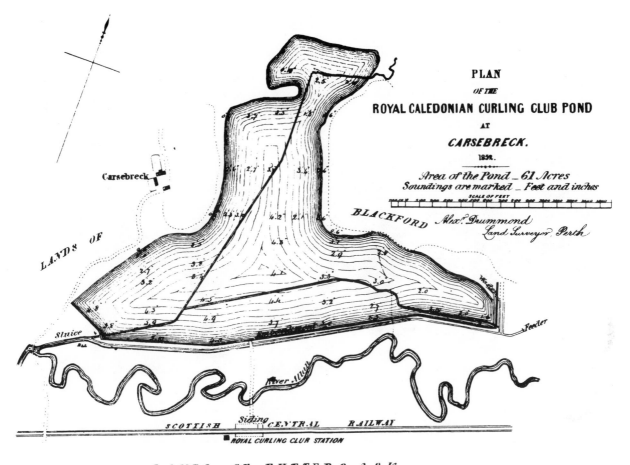

PLAN
OF THE
ROYAL CALEDONIAN CURLING CLUB POND
AT
CARSEBRECK.
1852.

Area of the Pond – 61 Acres
Soundings are marked – Feet and inches

SCALE OF FEET

BLACKFORD Alexr. Drummond
Land Surveyor, Perth

Carsebreck

LANDS OF

Sluice

Feeder

River Allan

SCOTTISH Siding CENTRAL RAILWAY
ROYAL CURLING CLUB STATION

LANDS OF BUTTERGASK

Fig. 67   The artificial curling pond *par excellence!* This plan of the Royal Club's pond at Carsebreck, Perthshire, was designed to illustrate the depth of water and allay the fears of curlers who were afraid of drowning. *Annual, 1853.*

words on either side, whether the square or the diamond formation is the better for curling, but it is not a practical question. Some excellent rinks have their ice-beds of ordinary soil well drained, and covered with a layer of sand about 6 inches in depth; this is easily levelled on the approach of winter, and under frequent rolling becomes well compacted. Ice is formed on it in the same manner as on wooden floors, and although it is not built up quite so quickly as on the wooden floor, it is not so speedily affected by mild weather, and often affords good dry ice when ice on wooden floors is covered with water. On ice built up on such floors no sound arises from the movement of curling-stones, no curring of the running stone is heard, and no groaning or moaning of the ice.'

In the outdoor curling rinks of Switzerland where, as A. Noel Mobbs in his *Curling in Switzerland* (1929) remarks, ice is 'not only a hoped-for contingency but a definite certainty', a slow and laborious method of preparation was used: 'A sunk tennis court provides an excellent and level foundation, and on the first fall of snow men set to

work. If there is not already sufficient snow on the court, more is brought on to it and spread as evenly as possible. This is then trodden down into a hard, comparatively level mass. If necessary more snow is added, and the same process repeated until a really solid foundation is obtained. Then the rink is flooded and re-flooded until the snow has ceased to absorb water and a thin level stretch of ice is formed above it.

'From now onwards the utmost care is observed, and the further construction of the rink is a matter of many days or even weeks. Flooding during the days levels off the stretch, and at night the hosepipes are set going, pointed up in the air so that the water falls in a spray so fine as to be almost a mist. Each day and each night sees another stratum added to the ice, and at last a rink is produced that is not only dead level, but has a peculiar indescribable feeling of resiliency to the feet, and, what is most important of all, can stand a long day of the fierce sunshine which Switzerland's winter is capable of producing.'

F

Fig. 68   An early curling photograph, ca. 1860. Smeaton Loch, East Lothian. Some of the stones are double-soled. The stone in the bottom left corner appears to have an iron handle of the type illustrated in fig. 40.

Fig. 69   A curling match on St Margaret's Loch in the Queen's Park, Edinburgh. *The Graphic*, 25 December 1867.

Perhaps one of the most curious places where the Swiss mode of rink construction was used was the moat of a Bavarian castle, employed during the last War as a prison camp for British officers. Offlag 1X/AH held many Scots officers of the 51st Division who were captured in June 1940 in St Valéry. The Scots, seeing the possibilities for curling in the cold Bavarian winters, got word to the Royal Club, and through the good offices of St Moritz Curling Club and the International Red Cross, several pairs of stones were delivered to the prison camp. After the War, Lt. Colonel Ian Barclay was able personally to thank the Royal Club at the Annual General Meeting of 1945 and give this description of their curling: 'Two years ago we were able to make a start with the curling stones. Our curling, of course, was carried out in a very restricted area in the moat of this old castle in which we lived. You will wonder how we managed that. There was no water in the moat and we had to beat down the snow to make a surface and water it every day and every evening until finally we got a skin of ice on it, and that was where we curled. Unfortunately, one end of the rink was about 2 feet lower than the other end, so that you had to keep your hand in when curling down the hill.

Fig. 70   A curling match at Rusholme Ice Rink, Manchester, England, 1877. This was the first curling ever played on artificial, machine-made ice. *The Graphic*, 24th March 1877.

However, that worked quite well and we had some very good sport indeed. We used to be curling from half-past eight in the morning — that was when we were allowed out of our rooms — and it just went on all day, with a few battles with the people who wanted to skate, until nightfall. The next year, that is last winter, we had this great joy again, and we offered General Fortune to take the stones to another camp, but movement of anything on the German railways was quite impossible during last winter, so our camp was fortunate again in having another very fine winter's curling. I don't suppose there were five officers in the camp who didn't play. You can imagine the number of games that we got in, starting in the morning at half-past eight with sessions of an hour each, orderlies and everybody playing, and I expect there are many officers now home who will not rest until Curling Clubs are started in England, now that they have been taught to play the game as it should be played.'

The last development, the one which has finally released the curler from bondage to the weather and allowed curling to make a tentative advance even into such places as equatorial Africa, is the artificial ice rink.

The mechanical freezing of water on a scale large enough to allow sports to be played on it was first successfully achieved by Professor Gamgee in a small tent in the Chelsea Clock House, in London, on 7th January 1876. Two other London ventures drew plaudits from the world's press, but these experiments were small, the first Chelsea rink being only 43 square yards in extent. In 1877 there was opened an ice rink in Manchester in which the ice had been created by machinery according to Professor Gamgee's patent. The area, 570 square yards, was sufficient for a curling match, and the *Graphic* of 24th March 1877 contains a sketch of a curling match taking place there, probably the first curling match ever played on artificial ice.

It was not at Manchester, however, but at nearby Southport that curling on artificial ice really developed.

Fig. 71   Curling on the River Tay at Dull, Perthshire, ca. 1890.

Fig. 72   The curling pond at Kinross, ca. 1895. A shallow water pond like this one obviously gave much more sport than the nearby Lochleven.

Fig. 73 Curling, Mossroddoch, Kirkcudbrightshire, ca. 1900. Though the stones are modern, the broom cowe is still in use.

Between 1877 and 1889 regular curling competitions took place in the glaciarium there, for a silver shield, which is now the property of the Royal Club and used as its Rink Championship trophy.

More than twenty years elapsed from the collapse of the Southport venture before the first artificial ice rink was built in Scotland, at Glasgow in 1907, and it afforded facilities for curling until 1917. After a gap of eleven years the present curling rink at Glasgow, with the possibility of seventeen sheets for curling, was opened.

The capital city was the next place in which artificial ice was established. In 1912 two separate rinks, one at Lochrin, and one at Haymarket, were opened in quick succession. The former soon languished but the latter survived until 1977. Between 1917 and 1928 it was the only ice rink in Scotland. Aberdeen also had its ice rink between 1912 and 1917.

The temporary popularity of ice hockey in Scotland resulted in the building of ice rinks at Perth, Kirkcaldy, Dundee, Falkirk, Dunfermline, Paisley, Murrayfield, Perth and Ayr all in the late 1930s. The hockey boom soon declined after the War and curling took over the

facilities. No more ice rinks were built thereafter until 1963, when a rink was constructed at Kelso. The Kelso example fired curlers, and in fairly quick succession rinks were built at Aviemore, Lockerbie, Hamilton, Inverness and Stranraer.

At this point it may be appropriate to note how curling is organised in Scotland. Curling clubs hitherto in Scotland have consisted of groups of curlers, none of which own their own artificial rinks. The rinks are run by commercial companies, albeit companies whose shareholders consist largely of curlers, and the ice provided is hired by the clubs, or individuals, according to their needs, or rather, since the ice capacity is constantly over-booked, according to their allocation. Each curler pays a fee for each game to the company, as well as a subscription fee to his individual club. In each ice rink there is also an all-embracing club, membership of which is necessary to permit use of bar, dining and changing facilities.

Stranraer Ice Rink represented an addition to this concept. The rink is privately owned and forms an adjunct of the North West Castle Hotel. As well as

Fig. 74   Duddingston Loch, 1906. The curlers are on a shallow water pond constructed beside the Loch, which can be seen beyond the fence. On the far bank is the curling house of 1824.

providing the normal Scottish facilities, Hammy MacMillan organises weekend competitions throughout the season and provides curling, and bed and board, for an inclusive, and very reasonable, fee. The Stranraer competitions are extremely popular, attracting curlers from all over Scotland. The winners of each weekend are invited to participate, *gratis,* in a closing bonspiel held on the first weekend of May; the prize, a Mediterranean cruise for four, is about the most handsome in Scotland.

In 1977 a second rink, run on the MacMillan principles, was built at Kinross, as an adjunct to the Green Hotel there.

In Canada and the U.S.A. the growth of curling has been on quite different lines. From an early period clubs acquired covered rinks for their natural ice. The addition of viewing and entertainment facilities was a natural development, and by the beginning of the twentieth century, as has already been remarked, the curling rinks of the New World were in many cases so palatial as to make the Scots tourists green with envy. The result is that the expression 'curling club' in Canada and the U.S.A.

means primarily the club's rink and buildings, whereas in Scotland 'curling club' means a body of curlers.

In Canada and the U.S.A. artificial ice has gradually replaced natural indoor ice since about 1912. The first club to install artificial ice plant solely for curling was the Brookline County Club, Massachusetts, in 1920. But even yet, the natural indoor ice survives in some localities.

The most exciting event in curling in recent years in Scotland has been the establishment of a curling club in Edinburgh on Canadian lines. Ken Gumley, an Edinburgh estate agent and keen curler, has established a four-sheet rink on the outskirts of Edinburgh at Gogar Park. An entry fee and annual subscription entitle the members to free curling throughout the season.

It is in this direction that the future of curling in Scotland surely lies. The country is full of golf clubs; it would be feasible to build a four-sheet rink on to the clubhouse of many of these, so that at times of the year, and even of the day, when the club facilities are under-

Fig. 75 Cairnie's ponds have survived well into the twentieth century. The artificial rink at Dun Alain Hotel, Aberfeldy, Perthshire, December, 1967.

used by golfers they could be utilised by curling members. A substantial proportion of the cost of establishing a rink, namely the provision of the social facilities, would be avoided in this way; and the golf club's social facilities, being better utilised throughout the year, could be run much more cost effectively.

Fig. 76 East Fife bonspiel, Kilconquhar Loch, January, 1962.

Fig. 77 The largest ice rink in the world. The Big Four Curling Club, Calgary, Alberta, has 48 sheets of ice for curling — on two floors.

Fig. 78   Ken Watson delivers a stone. Apart from showing a perfect sliding delivery by the originator of the slide, this photograph clearly shows the 'diamond pebble' which was made at the beginning of a competition and lasted until the end.

6

Delivering the Stone

Curling is a slippery game, and one of the problems that curlers through the ages have had to deal with is how to get a firm enough foothold on the ice to enable them to throw a stone.

There is no evidence at all as to the solution of the problem until about the end of the eighteenth century. Graeme, in his poem *Curling* (1771), has his 'steady youth' standing firm on 'cramp-bits.' At much the same period Davidson has the rinks of Bentudor and Glenbuck similarly accoutred:

> Wi' channel stanes baith glib an' strong,
> His army did advance —
> Their *crampets* o' the trusty steel
> Like bucklers broad did glance.

Such was Glenbuck's army, and Bentudor's men were also equipped 'wi' crampets bright.' The crampet was a foothold, attached to the shoe, as is clear from Glenbuck's exhortation to his men, in the same poem:

> Then tye your *crampets*, Glenbuck cries —
> Prepare ye for the speal.

The crampit was clearly one of the earliest types of curling footwear, though whether it was the first type, as Kerr asserts, is open to doubt, as there is just as clearly evidence for the use of triggers.

The crampit was a piece of iron with spikes on the under surface, attached to the shoe usually by straps or thongs. It was thus a dual purpose instrument, enabling the curler to get a foothold when throwing, and also when moving about the ice.

The disadvantages of such an implement are clear. The spikes must have punished the ice, and scattered debris far and wide. Nonetheless we find as keen a curler as Sir Richard Broun in his *Memorabilia* (page 51) expressing the view that an uncrampited curler was no curler and recommending an improved type of crampit which could be held on to the shoe by means of a screw attachment.

Some crampits fitted over the shoe like stirrups, some covered only part of the sole. Such can be seen on the feet of several curlers in Sir George Harvey's painting. Some were designed to cover the entire sole and heel of the shoe.

Penicuik Curling Club record in their minutes for 1818 the gift to Sir George Clerk, M.P., their patron, of a pair of brass crampits 'of as handsome a make as could be procured. The body to be of Brass. The Straps mounted with Silver Plate containing a suitable Inscription.' The crampits were duly bought and presented, and another pair put up for competition among the club members. In January 1823 the Peebles club appointed Mr Robert Brodie, a blacksmith, to be crampit maker to the club.

Despite the obvious disadvantages of crampits and in spite of the Royal Club's exhortations in favour of footirons, the crampit under the name of 'tramp' lingered on in Dumfriesshire until the remarkably late date of 1902, despite the unanimous adoption of a motion condemning their use in 1891:

DUMFRIESSHIRE CURLERS AND THE USE OF "TRAMPS".

A LARGELY attended meeting of the curlers of Dumfriesshire, called by advertisement, was held one day last winter. Mr. Johnstone Douglas, Comlongan Castle, was called to the chair, and he explained that the purpose of the meeting was to endeavour to promote more scientific play by discouraging the use of tramps on the ice. After some discussion, the Rev. John Gillespie, Mouswald, submitted a motion condemning the use of tramps and spikes, and it was unanimously adopted. In supporting his motion, Mr. Gillespie stated that his native parish of Johnstone was very enlightened in other things, but was in barbarism on this question. (Laughter). He had been brought up on tramps. (Laughter.) But he afterwards went to Ayrshire,

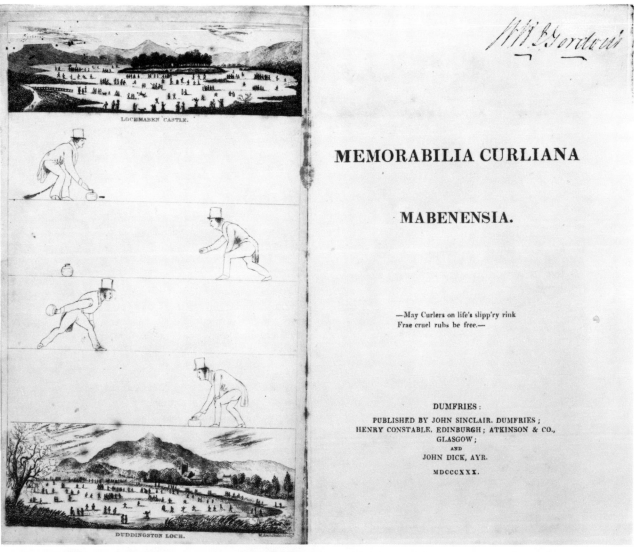

Fig. 79 Frontispiece and title page from Sir Richard Broun's *Memorabilia Curliana Mabenensia*, Dumfries, 1830. Sir Richard thus explains the frontispiece: 'Of the figures, the first represents the attitude of the player about to strike with force. The stone at the stretch of the arm in advance of the body — the feet close together, so as to admit, in delivery, of the player stepping out; thereby throwing the weight of his body into the arm.

The second figure represents the same player; when the stone has left his hand, and the step has been made.

The third figure represents the position of the player when the hack is used. The right foot is firmly fixed in the hack, and the left so far advanced as to bring the swing of the player's arm precisely to bear upon the level of the ice with full command of his stone. There is no difference of position for the different points of the game.

The fourth figure is the natural attitude of the player in all points of the game when great force is not required. The left foot is about fourteen inches in advance of the right — with which it forms right angles; the left hand rests slightly upon the knee; the eye steadily fixed upon the signal broom. The stone not further in advance of the body than the toe of the left foot.'

where he would have been thrown into the Atlantic — (laughter) — or at least put off the ice, if he had used tramps, and he had to unlearn the habit. Speaking from his own experience, he stated that you could play much stronger off the board — if any one doubted it he was ready to challenge him — and

you could also play much straighter. Rev. Mr. Paton, Penpont, stated that, after experience in Canada — where tramps were not used by Clubs of any standing — it was almost enough to drive him off the ice to find that he had to use them here.

(Annual, 1892)

Fig. 80 Silhouette of John Cairnie, delivering a very diminutive stone from his foot-iron. The punch marks on the surface, which were designed to give the shoe a good grip, can clearly be seen.

Fig. 81 Curling match between the Earl of Mansfield and the Earl of Eglinton on Airthrey Loch near Stirling, 16th January 1850. *Illustrated London News*, 26th January 1850.

Fig. 82   A classic crampit delivery. Note the right foot at right angles to the line of delivery, and the left foot set short of the front of the crampit. The stone would be lifted and swung mainly by moving the shoulders off the line of delivery. Braemar, Aberdeenshire, ca. 1900.

The Rev. John Kerr, writing a remarkably sour series of *Curling Reflections* in the *Glasgow Herald* of 21 May 1902, said: 'In the same tournament (viz. the Waterlow Cup at Lochmaben) I was much disappointed to see the antiquated and barbarous "tramps" still in use in a good many cases. These are bound to the feet, and their spikes, which, of course, are intended to keep the curler firm on his feet, do much damage to the ice. I thought it had been decided to forbid and forgo them altogether. They are what "C-B" would call "methods of barbarism", not worthy of civilised warfare.'

In the *Annual* for 1892 appeared an advertisement for what must be the crampit's final fling — a patent india rubber grip worn over the ball of the foot.

On 24 January 1855 the Linlithgow Town and Parish Curling Club were concentrating on yet another type of curling footwear. At their meeting on that date: 'Mr. Bartholomew [a member of the club] produced a newly invented *shoe* and explained in a clear and tradesmanlike manner the advantages of his invention, the principal of which was that the wearer of the shoe could at any time replace the iron outsole (which was run in on a groove and held in place by a pin) without being under the necessity of applying to a shoemaker.

'Doubts having been expressed as to the efficiency of the article exhibited the Meeting then adjourned to the Court Yard of the Hotel where Mr. Bartholomew put on the shoe and would have completely established the utility of his invention and the correctness of his statement had it not unfortunately happened that he was unprovided with a spare sole and that the pin of the shoe was lost. It was however unanimously resolved that an account of the invention be recorded in the books of the Club, with the opinion of the Meeting that Mr. Bartholomew is deserving of every encouragement in the carrying out of his Valuable discovery, which he stated

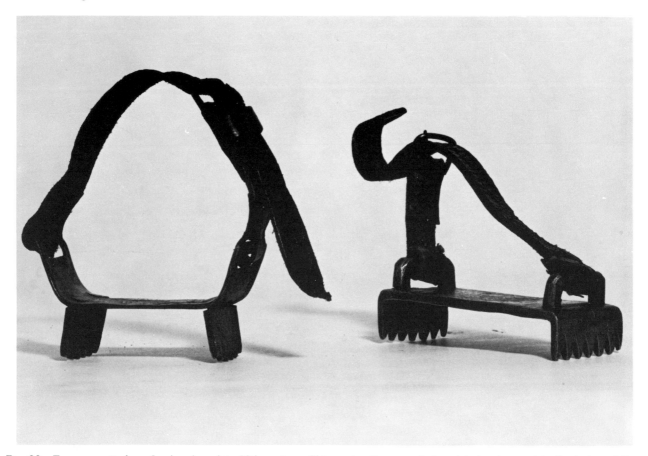

Fig. 83   Two crampits from Lochmaben, late 19th century. This contraption was designed to be strapped to the instep of the shoe. The serrated iron projections no doubt gave a sure footing, but at what cost to the surface of the ice!

was applicable either to a horse or to a·Man . . .' The tone of the minute suggests that the secretary, at least, had doubts about the efficiency of such a curling shoe.

But special shoes for curling did exist. The Duddingston Curling Club had a collection of curling curiosities, drawn upon by Arthur Henderson Bishop for the great Glasgow Exhibition of 1911. Among the exhibits borrowed from Duddingston were a 'wooden shoe sole with serrated metal plates on the bottom' and 'two ice boots, having on the sole iron plates with serrated edges.' The wooden sole and ice boots have disappeared, and with them all information as to their date and provenance.

Cairnie's opinion of crampits was forthright (page 43): 'Various are the footboards and fixtures which are in use on the ice, and we are sorry to say, that the almost barbarous custom of wearing crampits on the foot, in many places is still continued. They not only dirty and destroy the ice, but the wearer is as it were a *locum tenens,* and can scarcely move himself out of the way of a stone sent up the ice with a velocity comparable to that of

a steam carriage upon a fine railway. No person is admitted upon our ice who cannot use both legs and arms, and the most active and keen curlers will always be found the best sweepers. The only crampets we have seen which were passable upon a curling rink, were those at Ardgowan, which went over the shoe and fitted the foot very exactly, but whenever the player delivered his stone, he laid them aside . . . We cannot help remarking, that the crumping noise of piked crampets, which do so much injury to the ice, has a tendency to set the teeth on edge; and, we hope, that as they are perfectly unnecessary, they will be given up entirely, or deprived of their canine-looking prongs.'

In the parishes of Kilmarnock and Fenwick a more harmless form of footwear early found favour. In the 1st Regulation of Fenwick Curling Club it is enacted: 'Every member . . . when appearing on the Ice to play must have two stones of equal weight and direct round, a Besom and one Cloth shoe.' The sort of shoe is described by a Kilmarnock informant of Cairnie (page 73): 'Any player, who would venture on our ice accoutred with

OLD TRICKERS.

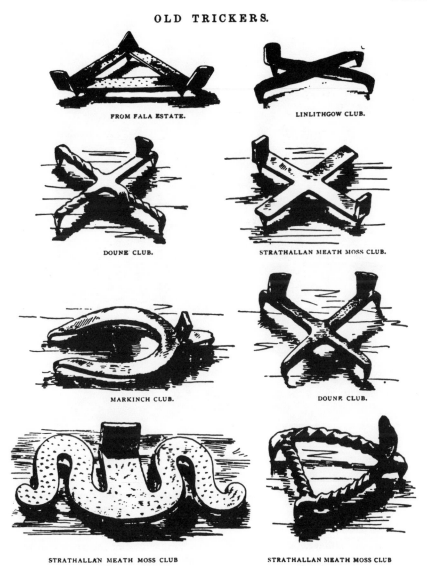

FROM FALA ESTATE.

LINLITHGOW CLUB.

DOUNE CLUB.

STRATHALLAN MEATH MOSS CLUB.

MARKINCH CLUB.

DOUNE CLUB.

STRATHALLAN MEATH MOSS CLUB

STRATHALLAN MEATH MOSS CLUB

Fig. 84 A collection of trickers reproduced from Kerr's *History of Curling.*

Crampets, would be saluted with an universal guffaw. We cannot conceive how a Crampetted player can attend to the sweeping of stones, with the *eident* care usual on our rinks, without so mangling the ice as soon to make it unfit for use. Shoes, and a kind of boots, made of carpet, dreadnought, or felt, are in universal use. With felt shoes a man may walk or run on the keenest ice, well assured that his "feet are from falling free".'

Examples of such boots are to be seen in the New Farm Loch painting and on the reverse of the Kilmarnock Morning Star Club medal. The writer has some photographs of about 1890 showing curlers at Ayr and Kilmarnock, still using the carpet boot.

It is evident from what Cairnie says that footboards were in use in some parts of the country. In others secure footing was obtained by the use of triggers. These, also known as trickers or crisps, were small metal platforms, usually triangular in shape, set into the ice on prongs, upon which the curler placed his foot. In some cases it would be possible to use only one, for the right foot, but the Muthill 'coat of arms' clearly illustrates the use of two triggers, one under each foot. Quite a number of old triggers have survived, and some of them are shown in figure 84.

In Kilmarnock a combination of trigger and felt boot was the custom. Cairnie's solution to the problem was his famous foot-iron, which he describes thus — (page 44): 'In place of footboards, or crampets, we invented what we call THE FOOT-IRON, which does not, in any way, injure the ice. This we recommended many years ago,

Fig. 85   Silver medal of Kilmarnock Morning Star Curling Club. On the obverse of the medal are engraved a pair of triangular trickers, a besom and a hair brush; and a pair of cloth boots which the Kilmarnock curlers used in place of crampits.

and it consists of a piece of strong sheet-iron, three feet nine inches in length, and nine inches broad. This iron is to be punched or well frosted on both sides, and turned up about one inch at the end. This frosting fixes the iron very completely to the ice without holding it: it is perfectly firm, and from having no pikes to move in an icy socket, there is little chance of its ever slipping. How often have we witnessed the blame of missing the mark attached to the piked foot-board, or to the crampets; the player bestowing on them, at the time, epithets of rather coarse abuse.'

Perhaps because of the Grand Club's strong recommendation in its favour, the foot-iron became universal in Scotland, and is still, for some inexplicable reason, used by many curlers when playing on outdoor ice. A very few, such as Scotch Cup skip, Willie Young, still throw from the foot-iron on indoor ice. By some curious linguistic quirk the common Scottish name for this accoutrement is now the 'crampit'.

A similar verbal transposition has resulted in the term for the present foothold. We in Scotland now call the small sloping platform from which most stones are thrown the 'hack'. The hack originally was a notch 'hacked' into the ice and, *pace* Kerr, it appears to the writer that this is likely from its very simplicity to have been the earliest form of foothold. One can see why it would lose favour. Curling in Scotland was often played on dangerously thin ice, and a hack would add appreciably to the danger.

Such considerations did not apply in the New World and the hack, a hollow set into the ice, is universal in Canada and the U.S.A. One reason why the raised 'hack' has been evolved in Scotland is that ice rinks are usually used for skating as well as curling: a series of hacks at each end of the ice sheet would be a hazard to skaters.

It is curious to think that such an apparently minor matter, like the foothold used, could have a radical

Fig. 86   Detail from funeral monument in the kirkyard of Tibbermore, Perthshire, dating from 1840. Apart from the pair of handsome decorated stones and a besom, there is depicted a pair of crampits. It can be seen that the sole of the crampit was composed of a rectangular piece of metal with a spike at each corner, and that it was held onto the foot by means of a broad strip of cloth or leather which passed over the top of the shoe, and was laced tight. See also fig. 183.

influence on the game, and yet it has. The Scottish delivery, whether it was from crampets, triggers, or a foot board or iron, was a stationary affair. The curler positioned his feet at the beginning of the throw, his hind foot at right angles to the desired direction, his body bent from the waist; and without moving his feet he swung and released the stone. It will be seen from figures 79 and 82 that the body was not at right angles to the line of delivery, and the tendency to swing the stone across the body must have been considerable.

The use of the Canadian-style hack, according to Ruth Howe, 'revolutionised the style of delivery in North America, because it changed the curler's position for delivering the stone. The toe of one foot was placed in the hack while the other foot supported the body. The placement of the hack provided a toe-grip which changed the body-angle for delivering the stone. Gradually, curlers who used hacks came to lower their centre of gravity by bending at the knees; later they began to move slightly toward the target as the stone was released. The toe-grip provided the back leg with thrusting power; consequently, in their follow through, curlers stepped or slid toward the target with the opposite or supporting leg'

(unpublished thesis, The Development of Curling in the United States, Indiana University, 1969).

Ken Watson, who is credited with developing the long sliding delivery, describes its evolution thus: 'The birth of the hack in curling made sliding possible. The old Scotch "crampit", which is still in use in some parts of Scotland, was a flat steel or iron plate similar in dimension to the "mat" used by lawn bowlers and as there was no opportunity for a toe-hold of any kind, it was imperative that the stone be delivered from a standing crouch position. The weight of a curling stone made it well nigh impossible to face the sheet squarely when delivering, thus the crouch stance with side-arm delivery was commonplace. Very rarely would a player take a step forward from the crampit to help synchronize the body movements while swinging the stone forward. The underfooting was too precarious to risk a bad fall to the ice. But with the advent of the hack a new era developed. The hack allowed a toe-hold. Now the player could swing freely, and with sure-footing began to throw faster rocks. The draw game gave way slowly to "chap and lie", and in some areas the "running game" became popular. Indirectly, when a curler began throwing faster stones the

Fig. 87 Otto Danieli, Switzerland's skip, delivers a stone at the Silver Broom, Perth, 1975, using the modern, sliding delivery. Rolf Gautschi and Uelli Muelli prepare to sweep.

first indications of the slide were noticeable as the greater arc of the stone, the weight of the stone, and the follow-through pulled him out of the hack even if only a foot or so. If he wore rubbers or overshoes, which he did, the flat of the sole of the rubber on the left foot caused enough friction to make the slide very short. Such was the case with the famous Bob Dunbar of the early 1900s. He had a smooth rhythmic swing and, according to tales of his prowess, he was the deadliest sharpshooter of them all. His running shots "smacked" opposition rocks with unerring accuracy. His secret was his perfect balance and follow-through which he practised by the hour. His follow-through only took him two or three feet out in front of the hack.

'Then along came Frank Cassidy, another name to conjure with in Western curling annals. Reportedly, Cassidy's swing was a pleasure to watch. His perfect symmetry of motion drew admiring comments wherever

he curled. Spectators noticed that he went further out from the hack in his follow-through than did Dunbar. In fact, he slid out on the side of his left foot an unbelievable distance to a point anywhere between the back of the eight-foot or twelve-foot ring. Cassidy had found that by such a delivery he could flatten out the arc of his swing and concentrate on throwing his whole body towards the broom.

'About 1913, a youngster named Gordon Hudson, started curlers' tongues wagging, and during the span of the next twenty years, the name Hudson brought dismay to those drawn against him. Here was a curler who out-Cassidyed Cassidy in his follow-through slide.

'By using his heel and the side of his left foot he could "glide" to the front ring with his sliding delivery. Along about the 1920s Gordon Hudson's name and style was a byword to those of us, who, as youngsters, loved to curl. We watched his every delivery and every move. We even

Fig. 88 The French skip delivers a stone at the Uniroyal World Junior Curling Championship at Aviemore, 1976. The sweepers are using cornbrooms.

imitated his mannerisms and his gestures. But his slide we couldn't imitate. All of us on our kid rink (averaging 18 years of age) were slim in build. Our ankles weren't strong enough to support a "side-of-the-foot" or "heel" delivery. Constant hours of practice failed to develop his slide for us. Then one night near midnight, after the evening games had been concluded, the four of us were out practising as usual when, to our amazement, Alex Chalmers, our lead, went skidding out crazily after a stone which he was delivering and ended up flat on his face somewhere near the hog line. The idea was born. Remove the left rubber and, presto! we could slide even further than the Great Gordon Hudson. What a thrill it was during the balance of that winter trying to keep balance and get the nose down to the handle of the stone at the same time!

'It seemed only natural to suppose that, by getting the eye immediately behind the extended right arm and hand and looking through the handle of the stone toward the broom at the other end, our marksmanship would be more accurate. It was just like sighting down a gun barrel. Believe me, it worked. The following year, 1926, we astounded ourselves more than anyone else in winning the Walker Theatre trophy in the World's largest bonspiel (Winnipeg).

'Fortunately for us, as the experience of later years proved, we had curled for three years before the amazing discovery of a "rubberless" slide. During those years we had developed a true basic swing so that the slide became only an exaggerated follow-through. Here is the mistake made by too many young curlers: they want to practise the slide first, so they never develop the swing along the line of direction. In the true sliding delivery, the stone is swung at the broom from the hack, and the slide simply follows the direction of the stone. The two together are synchronized into a smooth-flowing, effortless motion.'

To bring the position in footholds and footwear up to the present it is sufficient to say that in the New World the sunken hack is universal, whereas in Europe the raised hack is preferred. Where the sliding delivery predominates, the sliding sole is usually covered in some form of plastic, while the other sole consists of rubber.

It is a curious thought that even an ancient sport like curling has benefited from men's flights into space: had it not been for the necessity to develop a frictionless plastic coating for the nose cones of rockets, curlers would have been deprived of their favourite slippy sole, the plastic known as Teflon!

7

The Game

It is little to be wondered at that there are no early descriptions of the game: the players knew the rules by which they played; and no one else required to know the rules. The earliest prose description of the game in Pennant's *Tour* has already been quoted (page 11). This is a description which, from the point of the principle of the game, could scarcely be bettered, though in point of detail it leaves a lot to be desired.

The earliest actual description of the game occurs in *Curling: a Poem* by the Lanarkshire poet, James Graeme, which has already been quoted *in extenso* (page 10). The points of interest in the poem are that he describes the marking out of the rink:

> The goals are marked out; the centre each
> Of a large random circle; *distance scores*
> Are drawn between, the dread of weakly arms.

Thus we have the houses and the hog scores. We see that the Carnwath player stood on crampits and his stone was swept by 'full many a besom.' All the elements of the modern game are there.

The main difference between the eighteenth century game and that of the present day is in the size of rinks. Contrary to what one might expect from the modern size of rink, a team composed of four players each throwing two stones was the least common form. That was certainly the Duddingston rule, from the society's inception, and from there it was adopted eventually throughout Scotland and the rest of the curling world, but it is important to remember that in many — probably most — parishes, rinks consisted of from five to ten players each playing a single stone. The early evidence is sketchy but it is clear that in Muthill from 1739 each curler played one stone. As late as 1841 Muthill played Strathallan with 25 a side but by 1850, after they had joined the R.C.C., they had conformed to the four players per rink rule. In the parishes of Kilmarnock and Fenwich 4 × 2 prevailed, but in the neighbouring parishes of Mauchline, Tarbolton, Galston and Loudon 8 × 1 was the rule. In some parishes in North Ayrshire, and Renfrewshire, such as Paisley, Lochwinnoch, Dalry and Kilbirnie the usual complement of rinks was seven, and about 1830 in Beith there were two clubs, of which one played one stone each in rinks of seven, and the other played in rinks of four with two stones each.

Not unnaturally the early Scots who curled in Canada took their own parochial preferences with them as to numbers in rinks. James Bicket, secretary of the Toronto Curling Club, wrote in his interesting (and very rare — see Appendix B) little pamphlet, *The Canadian Curler's Manual; or An Account of Curling, as practised in Canada* (Toronto, 1840): 'The usual mode of playing the game is with 16 stones on a rink. This number is sufficient to impart interest to the playing, and more would towards the end of the head, crowd the ice. Sometimes these are played by four players on each side, playing two stones each, which mode may be preferable when a few only are exercising for practice; but in such cases the sweeping, which — unless the ice be very keen — is essential to success, can never be properly attended to, as the skip and player being sufficiently occupied by their own departments, only two brooms can be effectively employed at the same time. The most interesting game, therefore, is where there are sixteen players on a rink, with one stone each, eight players on each side . . .'

This was a matter about which the R.C.C. did not become positive until 1875. The first published rules, in the *Annual* for 1839, are silent on the matter. The amended rules in the 1840 *Annual* provide by implication for each curler's throwing more than one stone: Rule 5: 'In no case shall the same individual or party play two stones in succession; and *every player shall deliver both his stones* (alternately with an opponent, before any other of the same side or party play

Fig. 89   Woodcut from James Fisher, *A Winter Season*, Edinburgh, 1810. In this, one of the earliest pictures of curling, the stones closely resemble those in Pennant's descriptions. See p. 11.

one).' The rules were thoroughly revised in 1841: 'The adoption of a uniform system of playing, and the total abolition of local peculiarities, have been strongly recommended, for the purpose of preventing all sources of dispute,' says the writer of the preface to the 1842 *Annual,* and the rule therein printed: 'Every rink to be composed of four players a side, each with two stones, *unless otherwise mutually agreed upon,*' remained in force until 1874 when the italicised exception was removed and it became thenceforth illegal for member clubs of the R.C.C.C. to use the old system.

Each year from 1840 the R.C.C.C. *Annuals* contain reports of matches played for district medals given by the Royal Club. The reports are a valuable source of material as to the clubs that played, the number of rinks involved, the scores, the length of time of games, the ice conditions, and, until 1874 the number of men in each competing rink. It is interesting to note the gradual progress of the four-man system until by 1874 the non-conforming clubs were in a very small minority.

The Royal Club rules also influenced non-member clubs indirectly. For example, in 1851 Catrine Curling Society wrote in the following terms to their neighbours in Sorn and Auchinleck, neither of which clubs belonged to the Royal Club: 'Resolved 1st. That this meeting disapprove of the One Stone system of Curling, resolve to abandon it, and adopt the system of playing with two stones — according to the Royal Caledonian Curling

Rules — in all Matches, as well as in the Old established Parish Games. Resolved 2nd — That out of respect for their Sorn friends, as well as their neighbours of Auchinleck with whom they have had many a friendly game they will not refuse to play for the present Winter on the Single Stone system, if challenged, and an opportunity offers its self, but it will be the last season they will do so.'

Much of the regulation of early curling matches was left to *ad hoc* agreements between either the skips or the whole body of players. Even when there was a rule it was often not precise.

For example, the length of the rink at Duddingston (1804) was expressed this way: 'The usual length of a rink is from thirty-six to forty-four yards, inclusive; but this will be regulated by circumstances, and the agreement of parties. When a game is begun, the rink is not to be changed or altered, unless by the consent of a majority of players: nor is it to be shortened, unless it is clear that the majority are unable to make up.'

Lochmaben, in 1829, fixed the length of their rinks at 42 yards precisely, but, again, the rule was capable of alteration by mutual consent of parties. Moreover, 'the Rink shall be changed in all cases when, from the springing of water, the majority of players cannot make up. Neither the winning nor losing party having right to object; as all contests must be decided upon the fair and equitable principle of science, not of strength.'

Fig. 90 Curling, 1838. Detail from the silver inkstand shown in fig. 39. Note the tent on the shore of the loch.

Peebles, in 1821, left the length of rinks to the skips alone. And the Fenwick rules of 1814 provided for the longest rinks I have come across: 'Our rack shall be forty five yards betwixt Tee and Tee . . .' Since the Fenwick rules provided also for a small circle three yards behind each tee, 'and the tricker for the hind foot to stand within it', the length of a Fenwick rink was 48 yards, 6 yards longer than is established by the present Royal Club rules.

The size of the house seems to have varied markedly from place to place. Kerr says that it varied from two feet to ten feet in diameter. Though I have been unable to find any evidence for the latter size, there is evidence for remarkable variations. The Grand Club's house (1839) had a diameter of fourteen feet. The Peebles (1821) house was much smaller: 'the Cogees are to be circled with two rings, the one distant three feet, and the other a foot and a half'; and in Abdie (Fife) 'The Ring surrounding the Tee to be two feet in diameter, in playing one of the Cramps to be placed therein.' The Duddingston house used for points (1809) was only five feet across, as was the ordinary house in Toronto (1840).

In terms of the area which a curler had to hit with a draw, the Grand Club house was more than $7\frac{1}{2}$ times larger than that of Toronto; and no less than 49 times larger than the Abdie house!

The means whereby the length of a game was determined were also various. In some parts the usual method was to play for a certain number of shots, such as 21 or 31, the first rink to achieve that number being the winner. The difficulty in this mode of play was that there was no way of determining how long a game would last. Some 21-shot games were over in a couple of hours, others lasted for more than six. One wonders how long some modern striking rinks would take to achieve that total! In Canada too, according to Bicket, it was usual to play for shots, though games were often for as few as 7 or 15.

The Fenwick twist

The modern curler is so used to imparting a rotation to every stone he plays, by the in-turn or out-turn, that it must come as a surprise to discover that 'twisting' is a

Fig. 91   More detail from fig. 39.

comparative innovation on curling ice. 'Let it curl,' shouts the skip as a command to over-eager sweepers that they should stop sweeping; and everyone assumes that the name of the game derives from the curling course of the rotating stone, as it loses forward impetus. From the early books on curling, however, two facts are clear: first, that it was not until the beginning of the nineteenth century that 'twisting' was numbered among the curler's accomplishments; and, second, that, therefore, the 'curl' imparted by twisting cannot be the origin of the name of the game.

Broun (1830), at page 20, writes of giving a stone a slight out-sweep or in-sweep of the hand to counter biases, or unevennesses, on the ice. 'A stone thus thrown acquires a slight circular motion against the ice's inclination which, when skilfully imparted, provides for its direct course. This is not exactly pari passu with shooting round a corner — but is equivalent to allowing for the *lead* in the game of Bowls. Other curlers counteract the same by imparting to their stone, by a twist of the hand in delivery, a whirling motion which makes them in running

along the rink turn round against the bias.' Of all the informants who described curling in their areas for John Cairnie, only that of Kilmarnock even mentioned 'twisting', and remarked that it 'had been brought to high perfection here.' This observation elicited a whole paragraph of comment from Cairnie, at p. 138: 'We apprehend that straight lines are those that should be studied by the Curler, or if the advance in the science of twisting be such as to render it as certain as the play in general use, we are of opinion, that ice-bowling may come to rank amongst our winter amusements.'

It is clear from what both Broun and Cairnie write that in their areas straight shooting was the norm, and twisting was an extraordinary remedy for difficult ice. It is clear, too, that Cairnie would have regarded the modern game not as curling but bowls on ice!

The twist, however, spread in the next ten years as far as Largs, for in a letter of 27 January 1840 to the Vice-President of Kilmarnock Curling Club, Cairnie wrote: 'I have heard that with you you excel in turning the hand — I have but few players who attempt it and I only last year

Fig. 92 Curling at Duddingston, ca. 1860. Pen ink and water colour sketch by Charles Altamont Doyle, father of the novelist, Sir Arthur Conan Doyle. Charles Doyle seems to have had considerable interest in the game: he did illustrations for various curling publications, such as Taylor, *Curling: the Ancient Scottish Game*, Edinburgh, 1880; and Kerr, *History of Curling*, Edinburgh, 1890.

Fig. 93 Delivering a stone from a wooden footboard, Raith Lake, Kirkcaldy, ca. 1860.

began to practice it myself, so that I am rather an old scholar . . .'

Taylor, in *Curling: the Ancient Scottish Game*, includes a first-hand account of the origin of the Fenwick twist: 'We have been favoured by Mr John Fulton of Fenwick, an old, experienced and skilful curler, with the following interesting account of the origin of this scientific movement:

'If I recollect aright, and I am pretty certain on that point, the first year of the century was the year of its birth. That year was memorable for the length and severity of its winter. Curlers were more than satisfied with frost, and with the opportunities it afforded them for the practice of their favourite sport. In fact, they had played themselves out of games, and had mostly abandoned the loch in weariness. A few, however, of Fenwick curlers still held on. It is told that day after day, for a period of over six weeks, they were never absent from a small loch in this parish, on the farm of Meiklewood, then in possession of

a Mr Wm. Carse, who, being also a keen curler, was always one of their party. Here they met and amused themselves as best they could, playing every imaginable shot, or at 'points', as they are now termed.

'While thus engaged, they observed the effect of the rotatory motion a stone naturally takes on the ice on being delivered from the hand of the player. They saw that the stone always deviated or twisted from the straight line in obedience to that rotatory motion. They saw also that the rotatory motion was communicated to the stone by an involuntary, though natural, twist of the player's hand when he delivered it, and that all right-handed players gave the same twist to their stones, and all left-handed players gave an opposite twist. Having satisfied themselves of the truth of these observations, they felt assured that a discovery of importance to the game had been made, and that they had hit on a right principle, so they patiently set themselves to make it of practical value to curlers by acquiring the power to give to the stone the one or the other twist as they pleased, and from that time to the present all young curlers in Fenwick are taught the power of twisting as an element of first-rate value, and are so taught the use of it that they know at once from the skip's broom what twist is to be used.

Fig. 94   Raith Lake, Kirkcaldy, ca. 1860.

'It will be out of place here to write any panegyric on our peculiar style of curling as opposed to others. It is our own, and we are proud of it. We believe in it as the best and the surest for all sort of shots, especially on hard keen ice, where it undoubtingly tells to best advantage; and as by the practice of it in past years we have been more uniformly successful, and have gained more games from neighbouring clubs than many parishes can boast of. Besides, we think it a scientific style of play, requiring more skill than brute force, depending much more upon intelligent calculating judgment for success than on the strong arm. With good level ice and good curlers masters of the twist, it is very interesting and beautiful, and to a stranger wonderful, to watch the game and see how the stone twists into the desired place, ignoring guards as of no consequence. But to see the twist at its best it must be seen at Craufurdland Loch, which is perhaps the best conditioned curling pond in Scotland, and where the ice is always the best to be found anywhere. It is protected on all sides from sun and wind, and if the atmosphere is not positively thawish or damp, the ice remains hard. This favoured and lovely spot was, through the kindness of the late Wm Howison Crawford, Esq., of Craufurdland, and his son the present Colonel Craufurd, always at the free use of Fenwick curlers, and to such favourable conditions must no doubt be attributed some share in the success and good name which the twist has acquired.

'There was also another circumstance or state of things which helped to make the twist a success, which was this. At the time the twist was discovered, there were living in the village of Fenwick a number of as capable young men as could be found anywhere. Intelligent and moral, active and lithe of body and limb, full of spirit for sport of all kinds, they entered with zest into the new style of curling. They formed themselves into four rinks, in which they played always together, and thus acquired an esprit de corps, a confidence in each other which made them very formidable antagonists to all comers. They were known as the Fenwick "sixteen," and, like Wellington's invincibles, could have gone anywhere.'

Fig. 95 Craufurdland Loch, near Kilmarnock, ca. 1890.

In Scotland, the new form of play was by no means popular outside the parishes of Fenwick and Kilmarnock; in Canada in 1840 it was unknown: Bicket's description of how an end was played implies a straight-shooting style of play.

However, by 1850 the question of twisting had raised its head outside its native parishes, and got an airing in the press. A correspondent of the *Ayr Observer*, using the pseudonym 'Timothy Twist', discussed at length the merits and demerits of the new style of play in a letter which the Royal Club deemed important enough to reprint in full in the *Annual* for 1851.

'To shoot straight,' writes Timothy Twist, 'implies that the stone be launched from the hand "without any rotatory motion", and that it be directly aimed at its mark. No man can be a good Curler who has not learned to maintain these two conditions of straightness. The primary object always is to shoot straight at the mark; and when this is possible, no other track should be singled out. But whenever a stone, in leaving the hand, is made

to revolve on its own axis, on keen ice, it will not move in a straight line to the mark, but will proceed in a curve, deflecting to the right hand or the left, according to the twist which has been communicated to it when set down. If the elbow is turned out in playing, the outside or natural twist takes place; and if the elbow is turned in, the inside twist is the result. There are few players who can avoid twisting their stone; and this almost universal fault is the great cause of the ill success which attends their play. It is a fault, moreover, of the effects of which inexperienced Curlers are generally unconscious; and I have seen large parties of Curlers twirling their stones to the left hand, and complaining, with one voice, of the heavy bias on the ice, when the ice was perfectly level, and the disappointment of the players was to be ascribed solely to the rotatory motion of their stones. To guard against the habit of twisting is the first lesson to be learned by the young aspirant: and he who has learned to play a straight stone has already overcome one of the greatest difficulties of the art, for, in ordinary circumstances, this is

Fig. 96   A curling scene from the *Illustrated London News*, 5 January, 1889. One of a series of woodcuts on the Scottish New Year. Skaters were obviously a hazard that the curlers of old had to contend with.

the type of play which will tell most on the success of the game. But it cannot be denied that the ability to control the twist, and render that principle subservient to the will of the player, is a beautiful accomplishment in Curling, which vastly extends the interest and science of the game. The twist may be used on biased ice to keep the stone in a straight course; or it may be used when the ice is keen, to draw a calm shot past a guard, and to reach a point near the tee, wholly inaccessible to the player whose skill is limited to straight lines. This practice, however, requires to be resorted to with great caution and reserve. For many reasons, twisting will not always be successful against good straight play. It can only be employed on keen ice; and as the more ambitious and aspiring twister introduces new complications into the game, without a great preponderance of skill and practice he will not perform his many evolutions with the same accuracy that the plain practitioner will attain, on his simple and unvaried system. The latter will hit his mark oftener, when it is open to him, in his single way, than the former, who, by practising many devices, is less perfect in the execution of any one system. Those, even, who play always with an ugly, unscientific, natural twist, are often very efficient Curlers. By borrowing always on one side

and in one way, they attain to great accuracy in drawing to their mark, when the state of the ice and the position of the stones happen to leave it open to their hand, and you will see more accomplished and elegant performers exhibit much more science and count fewer shots. When any tolerable Curler begins first to try twisting, and acquires a taste for that system, his play will for a while greatly deteriorate, and he will be a much less efficient hand at a bonspiel than before. But when we speak of this game as a science, it may be justly said that no man can attain a place in the highest class of Curlers who cannot play straight, and also turn his hand out or in, with some degree of effect, when the state of the ice admits such displays of dexterity and skill. If good practical Curlers who know nothing of twisting often beat the higher and more scientific class of players, it is only because, like Paganini, they can perform better by long practice, on their one string, than the others can do with their more perfect instrument. But with experience and skill to avail himself fully of the additional power and advantages involved in his principle, the twister would, on keen ice, always defeat the player whose cunning is confined to a straight line, or to one uniform turn of his hand. As well might the combatant who has lost an arm

Fig. 97 Braemar, ca. 1900.

think to contend on equal terms with an adversary who has the perfect use of both — as well might an active rustic, who had no knowledge of boxing, expect to overcome, by sheer impetuosity and force, the accomplished master of the art of self-defence. It may be said of our Ayrshire Curlers in general that they are little conversant with the science of Curling; but the county abounds with capital players on the system which prevails amongst us. In Kilmarnock, where the Clubs are numerous and well organised, twisting is universally studied, and I conceive that in that place this system is carried to an exaggerated extent. The good old maxim 'shoot straight,' is almost entirely discarded, and you hear the skips issue their commands to turn the elbow out or in, when there is no occasion whatever for such an indirect course. At the same time, that town can boast a greater number of accomplished players than any other in Ayrshire; and whether the cause is to be sought in the big house besoms which they use, or in the knowing turn of the elbow, true it is that the Curlers of 'auld Killie' are kittle customers to meet with on a keen day. I am, Sir, with much respect, your obedt servt.

Timothy Twist
Ayr, 12th January, 1850'.

The early view was that twisting was suitable only on keen ice. Since the rotation of the stone takes more and more effect when the forward speed of the stone is progressively diminished, it is obvious that only on keen ice will the twist have maximum effect. The ice in Canada was generally much keener than in Scotland, and this probably explains why twisting became so early universal in Canada.

When Kerr's team returned home from their tour in Canada and the U.S. their worthy captain asked them all to contribute to his book on the tour, *inter alia*, their impressions of the curling. Almost without exception they remarked on the amount of twisting used, though by this

Fig. 98   Marking the rings. Coodham Loch, near Kilmarnock, 1977.

time 'twisting' was called 'handle.' Fairly typical was the observation of Alexander Campbell that 'the main distinction between our home game and theirs, lies in their giving every stone a turn of the handle, whereas we are accustomed at home to use the turn for the the most part to counteract a bias on the ice.'

Whether it be a direct result of the experience of these curlers in Canada, or of the keener ice that ice rinks in Scotland provided, or of a combination of both these factors, by 1914 J. Gordon Grant, in *The Complete Curler* (page 185), could include a whole section in his book on the scientific reasons for the 'curl' of the stone. In the course of this he says: 'A curling-stone, in addition to its forward motion over the ice (technically termed its motion of translation), possesses nearly always a twisting or 'curling' motion (termed its motion of rotation). This rotatory motion is sometimes set up by inequalities or other defects in the ice, but, as a rule, it is communicated to the stone by the player — often intentionally, sometimes unintentionally.' He goes on: 'To acquire

proficiency in playing the Kilmarnock twist practice alone will "make perfect." It looks easy enough on paper, but I have known many curlers who played *the old-fashioned straight game* [my italics] to perfection who acquired the "curl" with great difficulty.'

The writing was on the wall for the old-fashioned straight-shooting game; the more scientific 'twisting' game is now universal, and one of the first lessons given to the curling novice nowadays is how to deliver an out-hand and an in-hand.

The foregoing factual account of the mode of play gives little idea of the fervour of an actual game. The reasons for this fervour are not far to seek. Not only did the vicissitudes of a Scottish winter mean that the day's sport had to be snatched whenever the opportunity offered itself, but curling was the only activity in which one parish competed with another, and, because of the size of the competing teams, the result of the bonspiel affected everyone, directly or indirectly. In the 1830s and 40s, for example, it was usual for parishes such as New

Fig. 99 Marking the rings. Sketch by Charles A. Doyle, from Kerr's *History*.

Cumnock, Cumnock, Mauchline, Sorn and Auchinleck to take to the ice with teams of 162 curlers, composed of 18 rinks of 9 men. In these decades the population of Auchinleck parish was under 1520 souls. When allowance is made for disqualification of all the females on the ground of sex, and inability to curl through extreme youth and old age, one realises that in a parish match about half the able-bodied male population took part, with the result that every family in the countryside had an interest in the game. A good curler was an important parochial asset, as the rules of Tarbolton Curling Society graphically demonstrate: a member of the Society when called upon to play a parish game was 'bound to attend and play except he can give a satisfactory excuse that attendance will be to the hurt of himself or family.'

The towns, too, shared this fanatical attitude: any member of the Kilmarnock Townend Club 'not attending when warned to meetings to pay a fine of two pence if a resonable excuse be not given working not to be an excuse.'

All work yielded to curling: 'From "Sir John Frost's" lengthy visit it would seem,' wrote the secretary of the Kilmarnock club in the middle of a long frost in January 1841, 'that all are now frozen out, or at least *out* all must go, out of respect we presume to their much beloved and Illustrious visitor Ice, Ice, is all the cry, indeed to presume to be Buzy just now would only argue ones ignorance of Society.

'Every Idea of Business is totally frozen the Curling alone excepted, the truth is if you cannot talk frequently How to "Guard, or draw, or Wik a bore" To strike, to Twist, or Inwick, you are looked upon quite as an Ignoramus, One who has a great deal of the world to learn yet.—'

From such fanaticism military metaphors sprang with ease. Thus George Dun, secretary of the Abdie club,

which played on Lindores Loch, Fife, in February 1838: 'Sundry rumours reached Lindores about this time of a forthcoming challenge from the Cupar Club to be played, by some accounts on Lindores ice, by others on Biara; or elsewhere but no authentic intelligence having reached the office bearers, no preparations were made except warning the distant members to be in readiness in case of a declaration of war. Little was the peaceful natives of Abdie prepared for the invasion which was so soon to put their power to the test.

'When, on Saturday morning the 17th at half past ten o'clock, a multitude of the Cupar club (*all the Kingdom of Fife turn out*) were discerned on the ice, flanked by a double horse cart of stones, brooms, and other implements of war. Thus taken by surprise it was long ere Abdie could recover her scattered sons. One by one they began to arrive and at $\frac{1}{4}$ to 12 o'clock, twelve of the club had chanced to come forward besides five recruits; with such an array against them, various negociations were offered and finally there being Eighteen of the Cupar Club (all the flower of the flock) and only twelve of the Abdie (such as chanced to be present unconscious of the laurels which awaited them) it was agreed that the Cupar players should be balloted for, the twelve first drawn having to 'face the foe' — accordingly two rinks of twelve each entered the lists at twelve o'clock to fight till three . . . result at Three o'clock 1st Rink Abdie 17 Cupar 14 — 2nd Rink Abdie 24 Cupar 6. Often did the Cupar players complain of 'fortune's fickleness', in excluding some of their surest hands — but the merits of those they mourned were contested by some of the yearlings of the Abdie club who got up a fight about one o'clock . . . Result at 3 o'clock Abdie 11 Cupar 11. N.B. The four latter gentlemen of the Abdie club began their Curling career this frost!!'

For language of the battlefield the secretary of the Kilmarnock club, writing in 1841, surely wins the palm of victory: 'Met with Tarbolton Folks on Loch Fail today according to agreement. A beautiful Winter day when Gigs, Carrs, Sociables & Omnibusses of all descriptions were in great request for the transportation of the *Eighty* full equipped "Heroes of the Broom Cowe" all eager to meet the Enemy and join with ardour in the great icy Combat. Being formed of Five Companies [viz. the five curling clubs of the town] the first Grand Battallion of the season. At the approach to the Loch the Great Front of the Procession in full Battle array astonished the natives of the hills. When each 'Skip' marshalling his forces and with shouldered broom marched to the icy plain the 'Contest keen' began. And being a Parish Game the conflict was keen indeed it being long doubtfull which party were in the ascendency, success often fluctuating to both sides till within about an hour of the close when Tarbolton kept up a strong running fire And victory was ultimately declared in their favour by 58 shots . . .'

The Tarbolton secretary recorded the match with much less ardour: 'A Curling match took place betwixt 80 players of Kilmarnock, and 80 of Tarbolton on Fail Loch, two stones each player, which was gained by Tarbolton by 58 shots'.

8

Soup! Soup!

It seems likely that sweeping has always been an important part of the game. Its original purpose was no doubt to clear snow and other debris from the path of the stone.

In 1724, writes Allan Ramsay:

From ice with pleasure he can brush the snow,
And run rejoicing with his curling throw,

and Graeme in 1771:

. . . it glides along,
Hoarse murmuring, while, plying hard before,
Full many a besom sweeps away the snow,
Or icicle, that might obstruct its course.

It was soon discovered that hard sweeping could make a stone travel further, and so one of the most characteristic features of curling came about.

The earliest sweeping implements were bunches of broom tied with string. Curling poetry is full of references to such broom 'cowes'. For example, from a little-known poem, *A Game at the Ice*, by George McIndoe (Edinburgh, 1805), comes the opening quatrain:

When on the rink we take our stand,
Each with a broom-kowe in his hand,
We fix our cramps, our stane's arse clean,
We bend our knees, and raise our chin.

The next development was the straw besom (pronounced 'bizzom'), or broom.

In Kilmarnock, from at least the 1800s, the horsehair brush was used. Whether the use of the brush, as opposed to the besom, spread from Kilmarnock to other parts of Scotland I have been unable to determine, because curling literature is remarkably silent about it, but by the 1920s the brush had largely ousted the besom.

When John Kerr and his team of Scottish curlers made the first overseas tour of Canada and the U.S. in 1902-3,

they took with them a supply of broom cowes to be given away by the curlers to the natives in much the same way as early traders and explorers gave beads and trinkets to the original inhabitants of the New World. When the 1922-3 Scottish team followed them, the brush reigned supreme and the Scots found themselves involved in the beginnings of the cornbroom v brush controversy.

There can be little doubt that the sight of a pair of powerful sweepers noisily pounding the ice with corn brooms before a drawing 'rock' is more of a spectacle than a pair of brush sweepers bending low and silently over the stone; but the question as to which implement is more effective remains unanswered. As far as cost effectiveness is concerned, the brush beats the broom hands down. A hair brush will last even a powerful sweeper two or more seasons: powerful sweeping with a corn broom takes its toll to the extent of several brooms a season.

As I have said, the earliest implement was the broom cowe — depicted in many a picture. In its earliest form it can't have been much use for doing more than sweeping away surface dirt, for little pressure could be put on the ice. Such cowes can be seen in Harvey's *Curlers* and figure 73.

The corn broom was originally merely the household implement — broad and unwieldy. In Scotland, at least, it underwent some evolution. From being a flat bundle of fibres it became a smaller circular bundle. Many such brooms survive, the fibres tied neatly with coloured ribbon, and several presentation and prize brooms exist. Perhaps the first of these is a broom, the shaft of which is mounted with a silver and gold ducal coronet, which was given by the Dunkeld curlers to the Duke of Atholl in 1854 'In testimony of their respect and esteem.' From the same area of the country comes a prize broom, the shaft of which is surrounded from top to bottom by a continuous spiral of silver, upon which are engraved the donation by the Duchess of Atholl to the curling clubs of Atholl in 1853; the names of all the rinks which have won the broom; and, at the end, a note recording the Duchess's death in 1897.

In North America there was little evolution from the flat, 'household' shape until 1958, when the modern broom, a central bunch of long fibres surrounded by an outer skirt of shorter fibres, was patented by a Montreal inventor. Since then the North American corn broom has become a slim elegant implement, made in a bewildering variety of weights and sizes. The main disadvantage of the corn broom is its destructability: a rink of corn broom sweepers can leave a rink littered with the debris of broken fibres. In order to overcome this difficulty and to make brooms last longer, various synthetic materials have been used. In some the fibres are covered in a sort of knitted oversock, in others corn has been replaced with various forms of plastic.

The Atlantic is the great divide between the users of the corn broom and the brush, the curlers of North America greatly preferring the former, and the curlers of Europe and the rest of the world preferring the latter. Some of the younger rinks from Sweden and Switzerland, who have learned their curling from Canadians, use the corn broom to great effect, but there is no evidence that Scotland and Europe are giving up allegiance to the hair brush.

Whatever the correct view as to the relative merits of corn broom and brush, or 'push broom' as the North Americans have christened it — and it may be that each implement excels in some respects — there can be no dispute that to learn to sweep effectively with a corn broom is much more difficult than with a brush, and that effective sweeping with the corn broom takes a much greater toll of the curler's energy: no brush sweeper finds it necessary to protect his hands against calluses and blisters with surgical tape, or gloves.

The apparent power which is transmitted to the ice as a drawing stone is nursed along keen ice by corn brooms is highly suggestive of efficiency, but a brush can be used to sweep a stone right through a port too narrow to be negotiated with a corn broom, and with a brush a stone can be coaxed the whole length of its course to freeze against an opponent's winner.

The most curious development in modern sweeping is that some of Canada's best competitive rinks, such as those of Barry Fry, and Paul Gowsell, have taken to using the hair brush.

The rules as to sweeping have provided over the years an area for disagreement. The earliest rule, of which we have knowledge, is rule VI of the Duddingston Society. According to this rule a player could sweep his own stone the whole length of the rink, but his fellow curlers could

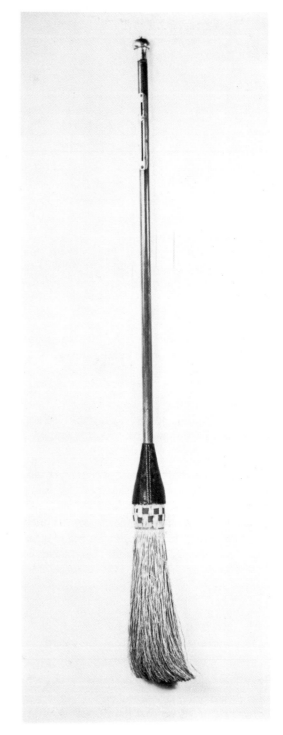

Fig. 100 Silver-mounted broom. At the top of the shaft is a silver curling stone. On each side of the shaft is a marker for recording the scores of both sides. The head of the broom is decorated with blue ribbon and protected by leather. It is a tradition within the family of the Earl of Mansfield that this is the broom which was used in the famous demonstration of the game to Queen Victoria and Prince Albert. See p. 116.

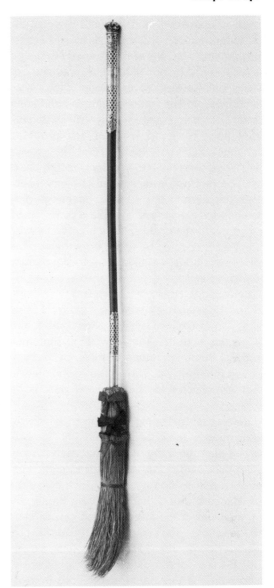

Fig. 101 'The Duchess's Broom'. Given to the curling clubs in Atholl by the Duchess of Athole in 1853, it records the names of winners until the death of the Duchess in 1897. The shaft is ebony, the mounting silver.

Fig. 102 Broom with wooden shaft mounted at the top with a silver and gold coronet and silver fretwork. Inscribed: 'Presented to John George Marquis of Tullibardine by the Members of the Dunkeld Curling Club on the Occasion of His Attaining His Majority as an Expression of their esteem and Best Wishes. 15th Dec. 1892.'

not sweep until the stone had reached the farther hogscore. The Lochmaben rules, printed in Broun, and confessedly incorporating the Duddingston rules, are identical, but the Grand Club in its first promulgated rules in the *Annual* for 1839 restricted the player to sweeping his own stone from the nearer hogscore, and his rink to sweeping from the farther hogscore, unless snow was falling or drifting, when tee to tee sweeping was allowed.

In other parts at this time it was obviously usual for the rink to sweep from tee to tee. On 25th January 1848, the day of the Linlithgow Grand Match, three rinks of Kilmarnock Townend curlers left Auld Killie at 4 a.m. to participate. None of them had ever travelled anywhere like as far in search of curling. No doubt they were full of expectation as they travelled, but they returned at midnight, 'and was very dissatisfyed, there was no sweeping the Stone till it was over the farthis *Colly* a thing scarcely know about Kilmarnock and never praktised.'

That each rink had been beaten by 14, 3, and 19 shots

by Penicuik, Kirknewton and Dalkeith respectively may to some extent explain the dissatisfaction, but they did not let the matter rest, for at the Annual Meeting of the Royal Club in 1850, a motion to allow sweeping from tee to tee was put forward by the Royal Club's secretary because of frequent applications made to him to have the law altered. Later that year the Kilmarnock Junior Club supported their Townend brethren and proposed the same change, being of opinion that 'the custom of sweeping from tee to tee is the ancient custom of all keen Curlers'. The proposal was remitted to all member clubs for their opinion. The 1851 meeting deferred consideration for a year, and in 1852 a compromise was reached. A middle line between the hog scores was to be drawn and a stone could be swept from there to the tee. In local competitions variation was to be permitted if every curler agreed.

It is interesting to consider the reasons why those who formed the original rules were in favour of restricted sweeping. James Ogilvy Dalgleish, then president of the Royal Club, wrote in the *Annual* for 1851 that the tee to tee proposal 'amongst many others *of a sweeping nature*', was maturely weighed by those who drew up the rules; but was rejected for the following reasons:

I. Because 'sweeping from tee to tee' gives a young man a most decided and unfair advantage over an old one, if the rule be that each person may sweep their own stone; And if their neighbours may also sweep it — then,

II. Because unless the ice be very strong, it yields to the weight of the sweeper, and can be biased in any direction, and advanced or retarded as he pleases.

III. Because of the difficulty of sweeping a stone, going with the velocity which it does immediately after leaving the player's hand, and for the first part of the rink, without *touching* or *moving* it, which, at such a distance from the tee-head, may be done without attracting the observation of the opposite party, or at least may give rise to disputes.

IV. Because of the injury done to the rink by sweepers running along it with a quick going stone.

V. Because science still being recognised as the

leading principle in Curling, that object is better promoted by letting a player attempt the shot prescribed for him 'with a fair field and no favour,' than by allowing himself, or his friends, to sweep and nurse his stone from the time it leaves his hand.

These reasons are as strong to my mind to-day, as when the rule was penned.

The only reasons I have heard urged for the change, are 'that it has been the practice in great part of the country,' and that the 'soup, soup,' makes one warm.

As to the first of these reasons, I well know how strong a partiality Curlers form for the particular mode of play to which they have been accustomed; but in forming a general code of regulations for our National Association, almost every locality has been necessitated to relinquish some ancient custom.

The practical question for all of us to consider is, which is most calculated to improve and raise the standard of science in our beautiful game.

As to the second proposition, it cannot admit of a doubt; but when it is remembered that only two can enjoy the 'soup, soup' at once, the other two, the skip and player being at work, I have always found that they had enough of it, if their only implement was a *broom besom,* betwixt the 'Hogscore' and the 'Tee-head,' and most certainly it is there that it is to be found warmest. If, however, there are any other reasons for the change, I hope some one of its supporters will publish them along with this, if the Committee admit it into the *Annual,* that Clubs in coming to a decision may have the whole subject before them, and may instruct their representative to support their views, when the subject comes to be discussed at next Annual General Meeting. I am, &c.

The middle line survived until 1896 when sweeping from nearer hog score to tee was allowed, and at last in 1976 the young men have won the day and sweeping is permitted from tee to tee.

The old arguments as to the science of the game, which involved a player in throwing a precise weight of stone, have given way to participation. Every curler can now play a part in the progress of every stone.

9

The Points Game

Curling has always been regarded primarily as a team game, and primarily, since the establishment of the four-man rink, as a game played by rinks of four players. However, it is only natural that a good curler should desire a means of proving (what he already knows!) that he is the most skilful curler of his club, or at any rate, better than the other members of his rink. The means adopted in 1809 by the Duddingston Curling Society of establishing individual prowess — the points game — has been more or less popular in Scotland since then.

The philosophy of the points game is to allow the curler a restricted number of throws at most of the typical shots of the game. The curler who scores highest is naturally the winner. The original Duddingston points competition consisted of only three shots — drawing, striking and

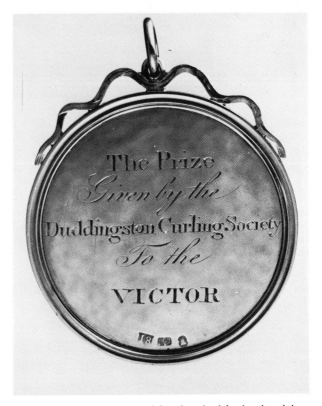

Fig. 103A   Gold medal of the Duddingston Curling Society, 1809. This, the first 'points' medal, subscribed for by the club in 1809, was missing for many years until rediscovered by chance in 1977. Obverse.

Fig. 103B   Reverse of fig. 103A.

Fig. 104 Medal Match of the Fingask Curling Club, 17th February 1853. The original caption in the *Illustrated London News*, 7th January 1854, deserves repetition: 'On occasions of this kind, each member of the club who competes for the medal, which is given by the patron or patroness of the club, plays, in turn, a variety of points in the game . . .

   In order to avoid delay, there are generally two rinks marked off on the ice; and each player takes, first, the one rink down with his curling stones, and immediately returns on the other rink. Thus, in the sketch, the principal figure to the left, who is standing on an iron cramp, is attempting to achieve one of the points of the game which is called "chip the winner;" the method of which is attempted to be shown in the rink on the right when the object of the player (who is out of sight), is to pass with his own stone, another half guarding the tee (the point aimed at), and displace the latter . . .

   The much-respected President of the Fingask Curling Club is Sir Peter Murray Threipland, Bart., of Fingask; and the medal which is competed for annually is the gift of his mother, Lady Murray Threipland, who is Patroness of the club. The Curling-lodge, or *Scottice* 'bothie', adjoining the pond, is used as a keep for the Curling stones, brooms, cramps, compasses, and apparatus proper to the game, as well as for the preparation on a field day of the excellent 'restoratives' of hot potatoes and whiskey punch. On the Medal Day an excellent déjeuner a la fourchette is given by the President to all present. A musician or two are generally in attendance; and the strathspeys and reels on the snow keep the lookers-on in exercise, and add to the amusement of the scene.'

inwicking — at each of which each curler had four throws. The Duddingston society provided by subscription a handsome gold medal for this competition in 1809.

   In 1836 the nearby Currie club instituted a much more comprehensive scheme of eight points, which was adopted by the Royal Club and encouraged by the award of 'local medals.' In this scheme each player played four shots at each of striking, inwicking, drawing, guarding, chap and lie, wick and curl in, raising, chipping the winner and, in the event of a tie, outwicking. To this has

been added, as a standard point, drawing through a port.

   Until 1888 the points player had to be perfect to score; for one mark only was allowed for each perfect stone; and naturally scores were low. In 1888 an attempt was made to popularise points further by making it easier to score, two points being awarded for a perfect shot and one for a stone that nearly makes it. The maximum possible score of 72 is seldom attained, any score in the 30s is considered good, and the best authenticated score in Scotland is 57 by James Stewart, Colmonell, at Ayr Ice Rink.

Fig. 105   Silver medal of Dundonald Curling Club, Ayrshire, 1850.

Fig. 106   Silver medal of Drummond Castle Curling Club, 1855, for points.

Fig. 107   Reverse of fig. 106, recording that John Marshall gained it outright, having five wins in succession.

Most clubs in Scotland have a points competition, and this form of the game remains quite popular. An interesting use of points occurred in some clubs in central Ayrshire. When a trophy such as a medal or a cup was won by a rink of four curlers, it obviously could not be held simultaneously by all of them. The present democratic practice is to allow each rink member to hold the trophy for three months of the year. But in Dundonald and other neighbouring clubs the winning of the trophy was succeeded by a points competition among the winning rink to determine who should keep it for the whole year.

10

The Royal Caledonian Curling Club

Until the nineteenth century communications were such that there was no scope for travelling far in search of curling competition: parish played contiguous parish. However, the first decades of the century saw a marked improvement in roads, and the beginning of railways. It thus became possible to look further afield for competition.

One result was the county match. The first of these was a match between Midlothian and Peebles in 1823. Dr Renton of Penicuik, pleased with the success of the first match which he was largely responsible for arranging, sought to arrange a second in 1825 with fifteen rinks on each side of seven players and one stone each. Having received no reply to his letter, he went to Peebles and met some of the curlers there, 'and found them more anxious to start obstacles to retard it, Than arrangements to forward it. In order to eliminate all objections started, Mr Renton in the pure spirit of Gallantry, proposed for the accommodation of all Parties, to commission a Steam Packet to convey the whole curlers to Iceland where unless they were disturbed with a shower of fire and sulphur from the burning Mount Hecla, they would find ice 4000 years old in readiness for them, And they might return with the pillars of a former world for Curling Stones, Viz, the fine Stupendous Basaltic Column of Iceland.' (Penicuik Minutes. 1 Dec. 1825.)

Apart from the extravagant language, this passage does show us how far curlers' horizons were widening. According to Kerr, Dr Renton had already, in 1824, suggested a National Curling Association.

Cairnie (page 139) tells us that Broun had suggested an Amateur Curling Club of Scotland to him, particulars of which would, he hoped, be furnished in a second edition of *Memorabilia*. The second edition never appeared but details of a prospectus for an Amateur Curling Club of Scotland, in 1834, are preserved *in extenso* in the Douglas Curling Club minute book. Again no action followed.

A further suggestion of a convention formed of 'secretaries, or some accredited office bearers of the principal initiated clubs of Scotland' was made in his pamphlet, *Laws in Curling,* by Dr Arnott in 1838. This had a result. The following advertisement appeared in the *North British Advertiser* of 26 May 1838:

'TO CURLERS. — In consequence of what is suggested at p. 11 of the *Laws in Curling* (a pamphlet just published by Maclachlan & Stewart, Edinburgh), it is hoped that the *initiated Curlers* in Scotland will depute one of the Brethren of their Court to meet in the Waterloo Hotel, Edinburgh on Wednesday, the 20th June next, at eleven o'clock, A.M. for the purpose of making the mysteries more uniform in future, and, if requisite, to form a Grand Court, to which all the provincial ones shall be subject, and to elect a Grand President, with other office-bearers. It is hoped that all Brethren who see this notice will direct the attention of their President or Secretary to it without delay. — 16th May, 1838.'

The response to this advertisement, though disappointing, was sufficient to encourage those present to take matters a step further, and they inserted a second notice in the same newspaper:

'TO CURLERS. — In consequence of an advertisement which appeared in the *North British Advertiser* of 26th May, 1838, a meeting of Curlers was held in the Waterloo Hotel, on the 20th instant, John Cairnie, Esq. of Curling Hall, Largs, in the chair. Deputations from various Clubs appeared, who approved generally of adopting a uniform set of regulations, applicable to the whole of Scotland, assimilating the technical terms, forming a court of reference, &c.

'But anxious for a fuller representation of the different Clubs throughout the country, in order to perpetuate and connect more closely the brotherhood in this ancient national game, they adjourned to Wednesday, 25th of July next, at twelve o'clock, in the Waterloo Hotel, when they hope the different Clubs of Scotland will make a point of sending Deputations.

                    JOHN CAIRNIE, Chairman.'

Kerr (pages 232-234) deals at length with the identity of the person or persons who inserted the advertisement. The only information that can be added to what he writes is contained in a letter written by Cairnie himself to the Vice-President of Kilmarnock Curling Club and dated 1st July 1840. In that letter Cairnie says, 'You are mistaken if you think I had any hand in the getting up of the Grand C. Club — it was from some anonymous notice that I attended in Edinburgh. I believe the author was a Kinross man, and I think the formation will look better yet — The rules etc. require much improvement.' This letter is one of a hitherto unknown group between Cairnie and the Kilmarnock Club which were sold at a stamp auction in Glasgow in March 1979. In another letter of the group Cairnie writes, 5th March 1840, 'I certainly think I should get at least a vote of thanks for my improving the sport.' The tone of this remark, and the fact that he wrote his *Essay* to vindicate his claim to the invention of artificial ponds, make it unlikely that if he had been the author of the advertisement he would have claimed anonymity for it.

Be that as it may, the result of the meeting of 20th June 1838, of which Cairnie was elected chairman, was a further meeting on 25th July, at which representatives of 36 clubs were present, and a resolution was passed 'That this meeting do form itself into a club, composed of the different initiated clubs of Scotland, under the name of the "Grand Caledonian Curling Club." '

The following report of the meeting comes from the *Edinburgh Evening Courant* of 30th July 1838:

'A numerous and highly respectable Adjourned Meeting of Curlers, from all parts of Scotland, took place in the Waterloo Hotel on the 25th instant.

'This, the first, as it may be called (the previous one being small), of, we hope, a long series of such meetings, has commenced most auspiciously. The various deputations (representing nearly 40 Curling Clubs from different parts of the country), included

Fig. 108   Grand Caledonian Curling Club District Medal. This design was used by the Grand/Royal Club from 1839 until 1878. Thousands of examples survive.

many zealous and well-known cultivators of this ancient game. John Cairnie, Esq. of Curling Hall, was unanimously appointed Chairman, who, in a short, but comprehensive address, explained the objects of the Meeting, which were generally to assimilate the ceremonies and mysteries of "initiation," as also the rules and laws of the Curling Clubs of Scotland; and to form a general and central court of reference, to consist of one or more Representatives from the initiated Curling Societies who had that day met, and of those who shall afterwards concur in the objects of the Association — the general heads of which will be seen in the advertisement of the proceedings.

'The Chairman, in stating his views to the Meeting, eulogized this ancient and national game as one which, independently of its own intrinsic merits as a noble and manly recreation, was well calculated to form a bond of kind and elevated feeling, identified as it is with much that is good in our national sympathies and habits.

'The Meeting, at the suggestion of Dr. John Renton of Penicuik, agreed that the Association should be called the "Grand Caledonian Curling Club:" and it was no small proof of the feeling which existed in the Meeting, that little, if any, difficulty occurred in passing the various resolutions, in the framing of which, the Chairman, James Ogilvy Dalgleish, Esq. Lindores, Dr. Renton, and John W. Williamson, Esq. of Kinross, took an active and efficient part.

'Among the company we observed the author of a useful work, *Laws on Curling* (M'Lachlan & Stewart, Edinburgh, but originally published at Kinross), in

Fig. 109 Royal Caledonian Curling Club District Medal. This design, originally struck in silver but now in bronze, has been used in great numbers from 1878 until the present day.

which publication the suggestion of this Association first appeared, though we learn that the same idea had been also entertained by several other gentlemen.

'A few improved Curling Stones were exhibited, and among the rest a specimen of what is supposed by many to be the *original* Curling Stone. This, and about thirty others, were found in the water after the partial draining of Lochleven. These stones, from six to ten inches in diameter, are evidently of artificial make; and from the known antiquity of the game in that neighbourhood, the probability of their having been used in the original game of Bowls on the ice is certainly much increased.

'Not the least interesting part of the proceedings was the description, by the Chairman, of the scientific application for the freezing of extended surfaces of water, by which a lead or rink may be formed in three or four hours, even where the thermometer is little, if at all, above the freezing point.

'Thanks were voted by acclamation to the Chairman, and to James Skelton, W.S. now appointed Secretary to the Association.

'Previous to the Anniversary Meeting on the 25th July, next year, it is expected that the necessary arrangements for the proper constitution of the

Association will have been completed. Apologies were received from various gentlemen, and among others from the well-known author of the *Memorabilia Curliana* of Lochmaben, at present in London.

'A party afterwards dined together in the same hotel, at which Mr. Ogilvy Dalgleish presided, whose admirable conduct in the Chair contributed not a little to the hilarity of the evening. The "Court" was constituted in due form by a member of the Kinross deputation, according to the most ancient usage, and afforded to those who were not acquainted with that ceremony great interest and amusement.'

The first constitution adopted by the Grand Club had as two of its objectives the encouragement of inter-club competition; and improvement of skill in curling. The first objective was to be achieved by district medals, to be competed for in a bonspiel by at least two clubs at a time; and the second by local medals to be competed for at points by the individual members of a club.

District medals have been awarded annually by the club since that date, and many a club is able to display at its annual supper a visible proof of its curling success in a collection of such medals. Indeed the writer of the preface to the *Annual* for 1842 waxes lyrical: 'When the great facilities are taken into account which steam power affords, by means of rail roads, for *transporting* Curlers and their curling stones, it *seems* impossible at present to limit the extent to which Curling contests may be carried. What a hitherto unapproachable field for rival competition will be laid open!! The Curlers of the mother country may soon be expected to rival those in the New World, who are reported to go from one to two hundred miles to play a game.'

It will be seen that in the account of the meeting of 25th July 1838 a resolution was passed that a committee be formed '. . . for the purpose of considering the mysteries and ceremonies, and also the rules and laws of the Curling Clubs of Scotland, and to prepare a mode of initiation . . .' At the festivities which followed the formal meeting, a 'Court was constituted in due form by a member of the Kinross deputation, and afforded those who were not acquainted with that ceremony great interest and amusement.'

In this way also the Grand Club sought to engender a national feeling among curlers by encouraging brotherhood, in a somewhat Masonic manner. The committee reported 'that the only purpose designed by a form of Initiation is, (as this Club is intended to unite the whole kingdom into one brotherhood of the Rink) to enable members to recognise each other as such, though personally unknown, and thereby to ensure them, when visiting distant Clubs, a participation in their game, which, owing to the numbers who resort to the ice (particularly near large towns) it would be impossible to extend to strangers indiscriminately', but that explanation is only part of the truth.

The Committee were also 'most desirous for the adoption of a Uniform Club Button', but decided to postpone its adoption. A fine design for such a button appeared on the title page of the first four *Annuals*.

The constitution and rules were changed repeatedly in the first few years, as more and more clubs joined. Royal patronage was sought and obtained. When Queen Victoria and Prince Albert were on a visit to Scotland in 1842 the club sought the patronage of Prince Albert and, as an inducement to His Royal Highness, presented him with 'a splendid pair of Curling Stones, made of the finest Ailsa-Craig granite, most beautifully finished and ornamented, the handles being formed of silver, and bearing an appropriate inscription.' The presentation was made on behalf of the Grand Club by the Earl of Mansfield, their president, at his residence, Scone Palace, near Perth. The well-known circumstances of the presentation are best told in the words of the *Annual* for 1843: 'Her Majesty inquired particularly respecting the game of curling, and with a view to illustrate the explanations that were given to Her Majesty by Lord

ANNUAL

OF THE

ROYAL

Grand Caledonian Curling

CLUB,

FOR 1844.

PRINTED FOR
THE ROYAL
GRAND CALEDONIAN CURLING CLUB,
BY THE PERTH PRINTING COMPANY.

Fig. 110   Title page of the *Annual* of the Royal Grand Caledonian Curling Club for 1844.

Mansfield, the polished oaken floor of the room was summarily converted into a "rink", and the stones were sent "roaring" along its smooth and even surface. And we have reason to know that her Majesty herself "tried her hand" at throwing the stones, although they proved to be too heavy for her delicate arm. Both her Majesty and the Prince expressed surprise when informed as to the usual length of a "rink" and appeared to imagine that it must require a very great degree of strength to propel the stones to such a distance.' Searches at Windsor Castle, Balmoral Castle, Sandringham, and Buckingham Palace have, unfortunately, failed to discover Prince Albert's stones.

The resulting title, 'The Royal Grand Caledonian Curling Club', was too cumbersome, and by 1846 'Grand' had been dropped.

Even before achieving royal patronage the Grand Club saw its influence spreading beyond the seas, for in July 1841 the Montreal Club was admitted 'by acclamation.' The hopes of the founders of the club were quickly realised. By 1848 there were 187 clubs and 8000 curlers, of which two, Montreal and Stadacona, were Canadian. By the end of the club's second decade, there were 349 clubs, including eight in England, one in Ireland, twenty-three in Canada, and three in the U.S.A.

Each year since 1839 the Royal Club has published an *Annual,* which contains the names of the office-bearers and members of each club, a report of the annual meeting of the Royal Club, and articles of interest on curling. In the *Annual* year by year is recorded the history of the game: the importance of the publication cannot be overemphasised. A modest financial loss on production of the *Annual,* which occurs in some years, is a small price to pay for such a comprehensive record of history as it is being made. It is, however, a matter of regret that in recent years the formal material has not been supplemented by general articles on curling and reports on the outdoor activities of clubs. A series of mild, open winters during the late '60s and early '70s in Scotland has been followed by many spells of fine curling weather. The outdoor game has taken on a new lease of life. It is a pity that some of the many bonspiels and matches played during this period have not been chronicled in the *Annual.* The curler will look in vain in the *Annuals* for the interesting fact that in the winter of 1978-79 Broomhall Club played on their pond in the estate of the Earl of Elgin in Fife for the record period of eight weeks, although the curlers on the last day had to play in water almost up to their knees to achieve the record!

That a national curling association should have been formed so early in Scotland is a remarkable occurrence: other national sports associations did not begin to appear for nearly another fifty years. That it did so at a time when the game was taking off in Canada was particularly fortunate, for it meant that the nation which was destined to become the most important curling country in the world in terms of innovations and numbers was still open to the influence, if not latterly directly subject to the jurisdiction, of the mother club.

In the twentieth century the role of the Royal Club has increased in importance despite the formation of autonomous national associations. The present constitution provides for the representation of all affiliated clubs and associations by the election of their presidents as Vice-Presidents of the Royal Club. Thus in 1980 the Vice-Presidents of the Royal Club represent Canada, U.S.A., Sweden, Switzerland, New Zealand, Norway, France, Germany, Denmark, Italy, England, Holland, Wales, and Finland.

Within Scotland the Royal Club is responsible for organising the national competitions which have increased in number and importance since the end of the last war. In the international sphere the Royal Club has the duty of organising international tours to and from Scotland. Moreover, office-bearers of the club have selflessly devoted much time and energy in the encouragement of the game in countries where assistance was requested.

But it is in the context of world curling that it has played its most important part. But for the initiative of the Royal Club, the Scotch Cup/Silver Broom would not have emerged, and as a result of its active encouragement similar world events for the under-25s and the ladies have been instituted.

SCOTTISH CHAMPIONS
Since the inception of the Scotch Cup
(with a note of the Ice Rink out of which they played)

Year	Skip	Third	Second	Lead
1959	Bobby Young (Falkirk)	Jimmy Scott	John Pearson	Willie Young
1960	Hughie Nielson (Glasgow)	Watson Yuill	Tom Yuill	Andrew Wilson
1961	Willie McIntosh (Perth)	Andrew McLaren	Jim Miller	Bob Stirrat
1962	Willie Young (Perth)	John Pearson	Sandy Anderson	Bobby Young
1963	Chuck Hay (Perth)	John Bryden	Alan Glen	Jimmy Hamilton
1964	Alex Torrance (Glasgow)	Alex Torrance	Bobby Kirkland	Jimmy Waddell

Year	Skip	Third	Second	Lead
1965	Chuck Hay (Perth)	John Bryden	Alan Glen	David Howie
1966	Chuck Hay (Perth)	John Bryden	Alan Glen	David Howie
1967	Chuck Hay (Perth)	John Bryden	Alan Glen	David Howie
1968	Chuck Hay (Perth)	John Bryden	Alan Glen	David Howie
1969	Bill Muirhead (Perth)	George Haggart	Derek Scott	Murray Melville
1971	Jimmy Sanderson (Edinburgh)	Willie Sanderson	Iain Baxter	Colin Baxter
1972	Alex Torrance (Hamilton)	Alex Torrance	Bobby Kirkland	Jim Waddell
1973	Alex Torrance (Hamilton)	Alex Torrance	Tom McGregor	Willie Kerr
1974	Jim Waddell (Hamilton)	Jim Steele	Bobby Kirkland	Willie Frame
1975	Alex Torrance (Hamilton)	Alex Torrance	Tom McGregor	Willie Kerr
1976	Bill Muirhead (Perth)	Derek Scott	Len Dudman	Roy Sinclair
1977	Ken Horton (Glasgow)	Willie Jamieson	Keith Douglas	Richard Harding
1978	Jim Sanderson (Edinburgh)	Iain Baxter	Willie Sanderson	Colin Baxter
1979	Jim Waddell (Hamilton)	Willie Frame	Jim Forrest	George Bryan
1980	Barton Henderson (Aberdeen)	Greig Henderson	Billy Henderson	Alastair Sinclair
1981	Colin Hamilton (Gogar Park)	Mike Dick	David Ramsay	Richard Pretsel

11

John Cairnie of Curling Hall

John Cairnie, the first president of the Grand Club, was born at Dunipace about the year 1769. Not much is known about his antecedents. He was educated in the University of Glasgow, and obtained his diploma as surgeon in Edinburgh. In 1791 he made a voyage to China and in the subsequent year entered the service of the Honourable East India Company with the rank of assistant surgeon. After some years in Ceylon he was promoted surgeon in 1802 and attached to the 2nd Madras Native Cavalry, but he resigned his commission in 1805 and returned to Scotland. While in India he lost his left arm as a result of 'an accident with gun powder,' though whether that was the cause of his return to his native land is not known. By 1813 he had decided to settle at Largs on the North Ayrshire coast and there he built Curling Hall, a comfortable villa overlooking the Firth of Clyde, designed by David Hamilton, one of the fashionable architects of the day. At Largs he spent the last 30 years of his life as a gentleman of leisure, frenetically devoting all his energies to his favoured pastimes of sailing and bowls in the summer and curling in winter.

In a letter to a Kilmarnock correspondent in 1840 he says of himself: 'I do believe the generality of people here think I am demented, for what betwixt Curling bowls and boating I am ever on the qui vive for the last 40 years.' It was he, as he proudly boasts, who introduced the game to Largs, where it was taken up with enthusiasm. The first club to be formed there was the Noddle Curling Club, so called from a burn of that name which ran through the town. By a lucky chance the minute book of the Noddle Club has survived, although the club itself has long since vanished. The volume chronicles the feats of the club from 1814 until 1824. Until December 1819 Cairnie was president. Thereafter he was elected Secretary for the season 1819-1820, and used the minute book as his curling diary, inserting not only highly personal and lively accounts of games, but notes on the weather, some lines

of verse, and a curious testamentary writing. Cairnie mainly refers to himself in the third person as 'Mr Carnie' or 'The Secretary,' and displays no false modesty.

This volume has not been available to any previous writer on curling, and since it contains practically the only surviving autobiographical material on Cairnie, excerpts from the season 1819-1820 will be interesting, as illustrative of the man. Curling began on Monday 13th December, 1819:

'Four most excellent games one of 21[1] — two of 13 and one of 7 were decided this day on the ice . . .

'Two bottles were emptied upon this occasion. Mr Carnies' party gained all the four games and were in high spirits at their having shewn such good play to players supposed inferior to few.

'Upsett a stone moving several others with The Driver'[2]

14 Dec. 1819: 'Two keen contested games took place in which the play in general was good on both sides, — fortune again favouring Mr Carnie's party, who gained the day and Mr Carnie gained one bottle of whisky from Mr Cracknell the party consuming one bottle more upon the Ice. It was beginning to get dark when they broke up —'

15 Dec. 1819: 'A hard and keen contest . . . Two bottles of whisky part of a bett gained by Mr Carnie were produced and another bottle of common whisky for the use of the Club —'

'. . . looking like change of weather — . . .'

During a temporary thaw on 17th December 1819 Cairnie's thoughts remained on curling. He engrossed a copy of his Will into the minute book:

---

1 It was often the custom to play for a certain number of shots, as is still the way with bowls. The first rink to score the agreed number of shots were winners. See p. 95.
2 The name of one of the stones. See other named stones under 17 December, 28 December, 29 December, 30 December, 10 January

Mr CARNIE'S WILL.

I will and bequeath as follows —
For the use of the Noddle Club
2 Stones marked J.C. excellent as leaders upon keen ice —
1 Stone The Glasgow for the Preses use
1 d°   The Haco for the use of the Vice
1 d°   The Secunder (amissing) for
            Secretary's use — since found —
1 d°   wooden handle for a weak player
that is to say provided in the event of my death the above stones may be in my possession, this obligation not preventing me from disposing of them in any way I may hereafter think fit —
— if they become the property of the Club they are to be kept in charge by the Preses for the time being.

John Carnie
Secy.

Curling resumed on 27th December: 'The ice this morning the finest on the D.M.P. possible . . . played 2 games both gained by Mr Carnies sides. emptied the bottles'

28 Dec. 1819: '. . . a hard contested game was played and gained by Capt. Morris side being 21 to 18 — This is the first game the Secretary has lost this season . . .'
'in the play today The Driver stone upsett another this must be owing to the shape'

29 Dec. 1819: '. . . — a bottle of rum from Mr Craig (a bett) was consumed & a bottle of whisky from Mr Cracknell . . .'
'. . . The Young Tinkler & the bonnet were roughly handled — the young Tinkler being put hors de Combat & the bonnet lost a part of his stern frame — John Bull stood well on his legs, and gave and received many hard blows & snatches — the owner of bull promising to be a first rate player — played till 5 p m'

30 Dec. 1819: After 2 hard contested games — 'The appearance of the weather is that of sett in frost and threatening snow — Mr Cracknell's new stone the Caledonia was launched this day upon the ice and had the worst of the day, but promises fair to be a credit to the owner — played till 4 p m — N.B. Mr Carnie's side last game were all young players, who had got the first lessons from the Secy. J.C.'

31 Dec. 1819: 'Victory again crowned the side of the Secretary . . .
A *slam* was the produce in this game Arthur's side being 8 Shotts to 0 — alias nothing —
It was agreed (the Ice being mostly covered with snow) that it be cleared immediately and orders to that effect

Fig. 111 Portrait engraving of John Cairnie, which appeared as a frontispiece to the *Annual* of the Royal Grand Caledonian Curling Club for 1844 to accompany an obituary.

were given — A bottle of Radical Whisky was consumed, and the party with the Secretary left the ice at ½ past 3 leaving a side to practice — . . .
The weather was severe the play not inferior to that described in the Societys book of Songs.
— this year has afforded more sport, than the 5 previous years put all together — sic dicat

J. Carnie Secy'

1st Jan. 1820: 'The Secretary being unable to form a proper party this night (with the assistance of a fine moon etc.) he sent a challenge to John Bull who did not appear in time, but 3 of the Members . . . after the clock struck 12 had several curls with the stones on the frost — who should play farthest —

J.C. Victor

hard & frosty looking —
  2 a m

J.C. Secy.'

1 Jan. 1820: '. . . bad play all day, partly from the bias on the ice, but more so from seeing in the new year —
— 2 bottles one of Rum the other of Whisky old betts were consumed on the ice, & parliament cakes in abundance

— Capt Morris & Mr Carnie paired off at 3 O clock —
leaving the rest of the Club picking a new side —
— It is pleasant to think tomorrow is a day of rest for my
bones and back and all feel sore and out of order —'

'Jany 3. 1820
Mr Cracknell and Mr Carnie this day decided a bett upon
the ice and 2 bottles of whisky were given the lookers on
— Mr Carnie gained — 2 other games were played
before The Secretary left the ice, one of which was lost
the other won by the party on whose side the Secretary
played — Mr Cracknell & Mr Carnie played 7 stones
each, it was a hard contest and kept up a copious
determination towards the surface — It snowed and
many hoggs were seen during the fall — Orders were left
for Cleaners to clean the ice — this day I found Secunder
the missing stone —'

On 4th January it was 'Threatening thaw, wind SE —
no report from the D M P[1] — this day very tired & stiff,
allowed as a day of rest . . . The Secretary's opinion is
that the thaw wont last long.
J.C. Secy.'

'Jany 5 — 6 — & 7 — We had thaw — at 8 p m
appeared frosty —
Jany. 8. last night we had frost — the old ice on the
Secretary's inspecting it was capital and 4 players soon
after were on and played — . . .
N.B. this day — no drink.
J.C. Secy.'

'8 Jany. 1820 —
The Secretary wrote Mr Brown of Beith inviting him and
his party to fix the day for meeting the Club on the
D.M.P. Mr Cracknell Honorary Member was also wrote
to, to play John Bull & Caledonia if need be, at least that
we shall have the use of the handles in the Secretary's
possession.
"Q.F.F.Q.S." '

On the 10th several games were played, marred by a
bit of altercation on the ice, which elicited from The
Secretary the comment:

'Every dog should have his day.
But let both sides have whats fair play . . .

'The ice was soft and not keen but many superior shotts
were played on both sides, and the Secretary offered to
play any of the opposing party as first picked & give some
of them odds —
. . . A bottle & pocket pistol[2] were fully consumed; had
there been two bottles more we would have seen them
Ended.

---

1 The DMP was Dead Man's Pond, one of the curling ponds
in the vicinity of Largs.
2 Hip flask of whisky.

— The Curlers left the ice about the dusk, the weather
still looking dull & doubtfull —
I with the Driver and Belle Poule
The Glasgow and far famed Secunder
With Caledonia and John Bull
Shall beat the Club or shall knock under
And just that we may wet our throttle
I'll lay of rum a single bottle.'

'Jany. 11 & 12 softish — no play — at Hunterston
13 Jany 1820.
— Messrs Lang Craig & The Secretary were at the ice
and had hard work sweeping — They were engaged
practising and getting The Secretary's lessons when after
a few heads Wm Jamieson & Mr Underwood came up
and with them young Willy —
A Game was played Mr Carnie taking the weak side
having the beginners . . .
— Some good shotts were made and had it not been for
the snow The sport was excellent — The Secretary's
pocket pistol was consumed — Weather threatening
change or more snow —'

On 14th January, having lost two out of three games,
the last by 7 shots to 0, Cairnie wrote: 'this shows the race
is not to the quick or the battle to the strong.
— Many fine shotts were taken
'. . . — Mr Orr was admitted & paid 5 shillings and as he
is a left handed player it was agreed he should forfeit One
Gill every time he forgot to shift the board — he played
some very superior Shotts — 2 pocket pistols that
appeared were quickly consumed —'
15th January: 'Some showers last night, but icicles
appear at 9 a m & altho' now soft enough to course the
weather has all the appearance of frost — The Secretary
coursed at Skelmorie & killed 2 hares
9 p m. frosty — Aurora Borealis in the North
— promising fair for good ice on Monday'
Jan. 17 1820: '. . . The Secretary would not have
chosen the side he played on . . .
. . . The game was gained as in The Secretary's opinion
might be expected by Mr Andersons party being 21 to 17
it was however hardly contested, some good and some
very bad play was shown —'
18 Jan 1820: '. . . A challenge from the Comrate[1]
people was sent and should the day answer it will be

---

1 Comrate is a Cairniean adjective from Cumbrae: The Large
Cumbrae is a small island off the Ayrshire coast near Largs. It
is said that a minister there was wont to pray for the
prosperity of the inhabitants of the Cumbrae, and also of the
inhabitants of the neighbouring islands of Great Britain and
Ireland.

further reported upon tomorrow — A paper inviting persons to lay meal on the Curling was also left — it stated that when 4 Bolls[1] were subscribed the Curlers would pick sides
— The Secretary subscribed One Boll. —
— at 2 p m east wind very cold —
— last night the frost was very severe
— A Cart for the stones to be up at 3 p m —'
19 Jan: 'Strong wind at E. and very severe frost —'
20 Jan: 'This day the following party went to Cumbraes to play the players in that quarter — . . .
— It was past 12 O clock before any thing was fixed or ready for play and before beginning it was agreed in presence of many persons betwixt The Secretary and Mr Wishart[2] that the game should be 21 — . . .
An equal number opposed them with stones quite unfit to appear on any rink of Curlers, some were oval, some triangular and only one of them fit for Muster —
On the ending of the game the members were 21 to 12 — in favour of the Noddle or Largs — here as Mr Wishart *forgot* the number fixed on The Secretary left the ice resolved not to play with that person again upon any terms — The Secretarys pocket bottle, and an odd bottle gained by him from Mr Ewing together with the bett for a pint & Cheese & Bread were consumed — The Secretary left his party who he doubts not would do their duty of which a report shall be made.

N.B. Should I ever play those Curlers again, I shall take care their stones shall be agreeable to those in our & in all other Clubs, had that been the case it is in my opinion doubtful if the Comrate party would have reckoned one in the game.

J. Carnie Secy.

At leaving off I learn the Comrate party were 5 to Largs 4 —
The play was as bad as possible on our part, but the Ice was excellent.

J.C.

I anticipate from drink and fatigue that we shall certainly loose if we play vs Kilburnie tomorrow.'
21 Jan. 1820: 'A trifling bett for pyes and drink was taken on by Mr Daroch with 6 other players from Kilburnie reckoned the very best including Mr Jamieson of Kilburnie Place ag' Mr Carnie and his side
As follows —

---

1 A boll was a measure of meal, generally equivalent to 6 imperial bushels.
2 A Cumbrae curler.

Mr Carnie   last 2 stones ⎫
  Wilson   ⎪
  Jameson   ⎬ with one Stone
  Dayer   ⎪
  Snodgrass   ⎪
  Craig   ⎪
Mr Jas Lang   1st leader   ⎭

a pleasant and hard contest commenced the Kilburnies leading till they got up to 14 when they were led by the Largs players, and it was fixed before beginning that the game should be over when 4 O Clock came for which purpose several watches were set. At that hour The Secretary had the satisfaction of gaining his bett the numbers being
     Largs 27   Kilburnie 22
The Secy. treated the party to 2 bottles & 14 pyes @ 4d . . .'
22 Jan: 'Mr Cracknell Honorary Member came down to get a lesson and went up with the Secretary when they found only 3 players on the ice . . .
No pocket pistol appearing a glass of grog refreshed some of the party on coming down the hill at 3 O Clock —
Barometer falling'
24 Jan: 'It appears from the accounts above that at least (various games) in all not less than 49 have been played this season, and much amusement has been afforded upon the D.M.P.
— We can also boast of beating the Kilburnie picked side and of a trifling victory over a sett of beginners upon the Comrate —'
  Thus did the Secretary sum up a successful curling season.
  Cairnie's main claim to fame is as the inventor of artificial curling ponds. In his *Essay on Curling and Artificial Pond Making* (1833) he informs us that he had first communicated his ideas about such rinks to the Secretary of the Duddingston Curling Society upwards of twenty years before. Although the Noddle minutes record that in 1820 'Mr Cairnie is making a curling pond in his hare park', the pond appears not to have been completed and it was not until late December 1827 that he put his ideas into operation by building a clay-lined shallow pond beside Curling Hall. (The mode of construction is described elsewhere.) He was immensely, and rightly, proud of his invention, for it immediately quadrupled the number of days on which curlers could enjoy their sport. He formed a club, the Thistle, or Cairnie's Own, with a membership restricted to ten, and he summoned the club by flying a red flag at the mast head when there was ice. Throughout his life he extolled

the virtues of his artificial ponds and tried to encourage curling clubs to build then. When he appeared at that seminal meeting in the Waterloo Hotel at which the Grand Club was formed, he was carrying copies of his *Essay* under his one arm, no doubt with a view to spreading the gospel about artificial ponds.

In January 1840 Cairnie was involved in correspondence with the Kilmarnock Clubs about their joining the Grand Club. 'With my Curling rink at Kilmarnock,' he writes, 'I am certain you would have every year nearly 3 months Curling.'

On 5th March 1840, in another letter, he says: 'I cannot refrain from giving your Club some account of my success in making sport for the Curlers — On my artificial rink I have this day had *in succession* 15 days of the finest ice possible for Curling — . . . I certainly think I should get at least a vote of thanks for my improving the sport, and have thoughts of having a second Edition of my book published.'

In August 1840 he returns to the fray, inviting the Kilmarnock Clubs and their opponents to play a Grand Club Medal Match on his pond: 'I wish to mention that I think as you will be certain of ice, and that too *the best ice,* the matches should be played on my pond, to which you the Ayr & Mauchline Curlers will be made welcome.' As it happened, the Kilmarnock curlers did not accept his invitation, though his letter is referred to in the Kilmarnock Club's minute book, which the present writer has recently rediscovered.

Cairnie's other contribution to curling was his famous foot iron, which, under the name of 'crampit', served the Scots curlers for over a century.

While Cairnie had been successfully constructing his clay risk in the west, the curling minister, John Sommerville of Currie, had been experimenting with a paved rink in the east. Cairnie's polemical *Essay* was written to vindicate his invention against Sommerville's rival claim. From two points of view the *Essay* is important. First, it did encourage curlers to build artificial rinks; and second — and more important for the historian of curling — it is a storehouse of information as to curling, gleaned by Cairnie from various parts of Scotland.

Cairnie's *Essay* and Broun's *Memorabilia*, both published within the space of three years, played their part in creating the conditions in which a National Curling Club was possible. They brought the attention of a wider public to the game; they enabled curlers to see beyond the bounds of their own and the neighbouring parishes.

In the Addenda to his book Cairnie speaks with approbation of Broun's suggestion of an Amateur Curling Club for Scotland. He proposes that in connection with this club it should be recommended 'that every Curling Society in Scotland should correspond, and give in a list of their Office-bearers, the number of Curlers, matches played, and any matter connected with the game that was interesting'. Six years later, the first *Annual* of the Grand Caledonian Curling Club gave physical form to this recommendation.

It was fitting that Cairnie should have been elected first president of the Grand Club formed on that momentous July day in 1838. He had 'done more to elevate and excite the popular feeling in favour of the "roaring play" than any man of his time; and "Cairnie's rinks" were familiar as household words to every knight of the broom and channel stane . . .'

When the Grand Club held an adjourned meeting at Kilmarnock Town Hall in October 1841 the club secretary, Mr Ritchie, said: 'It is with great pleasure that I rise to propose the health of a gentleman present, who is unrivalled in the annals of curling — Mr Cairnie of Curling Hall, Largs. No sooner did that gentleman retire from the service of his country, than he came among us to take the lead as the Father of the Great Caledonian Curling Club. I am sure that there is no individual in Scotland better entitled to that honour. I would simply give that gentleman's health in connection with the club, as its parent. There is not a name more deservedly celebrated for curling. I believe he is far in advance of any of us, and too fast for nature herself, for with ten minutes of keen frost he can turn out a band of curlers on his own pond.'

Cairnie, in reply, said simply and touchingly: 'I am now an old curler, and very unable to speak as I should: but I am a keen curler: the spirit is willing, but the flesh is weak. I think I shall curl to the last . . .'

The season of 1841-42 was his last: Cairnie died on 27th October, 1842, in his 73rd year, and was buried in the old graveyard at Largs on 2nd November. The famous flag flew at half mast over his famous rink on the day of the funeral:

Why droops the banner half-mast high,
And curlers heave the bitter sigh?
Why throughout Largs the tearful eye,
So blear'd and red?
Oh! listen to the poor man's cry!
John Cairnie's dead!

While winter's breath as waters freeze,
Lays waste the fields and bares the trees,
Or well-rigged yachts in joyous breeze
For prizes ply,
Cairnie, thy name by land or seas
Shall never die.

A more practical testimony to the esteem in which Cairnie was held was provided by the proprietors of the *Lady Brisbane* steamer, who, according to the *Glasgow Courier*, hearing of the numbers of mourners who intended to travel from Glasgow to the burial, and 'with a view of "throwing a stone to the cairn" ' of their departed friend, announced that 'all who proceed to Largs on this sorrowful but interesting mission, will be carried down and brought back to Glasgow the same day free of charge'.

12

The Grand Match

In 1963 the *Observer* newspaper described curling's largest outdoor bonspiel as 'sport's greatest non-event', a comment not without an element of truth in it, for although preparations have been made for the match in most years since the first at Penicuik in 1847, the event has taken place outdoors on only 33 occasions.

The reasons are not far to seek: a vast concourse of two and a half thousand curlers, their stones, their spectators — a nation at play — require six inches of good black ice. To achieve this on a deepwater loch needs a hard frost of over a week's duration, and Scottish winters, cold and nasty though they be, seldom provide such a prolonged spell of frost.

When the weather conditions are right, however, the experience of playing in a grand match is so exhilarating, the spectacle so magnificent, the stories that circulate at curling dinners so enticing, that it is the ambition of every Scottish curler to play in at least one Grand Match before he dies. The Grand Match is to the Scottish curlers what Mecca is to the devout Muslim!

Such is the present enthusiasm for the Grand Match, and such was the enthusiasm in the century before the Second World War, that it is strange to read in the *Annual* for 1950 the view of a Royal Club President that the event should be given up for ever.

The origins of the Grand Match, in which the North of Scotland plays the South (the boundary between North and South being drawn from time to time in different

Fig. 112 Grand Match, Carsebreck, 1897 or 1899.

Fig. 113   Grand Match, Carsebreck, 1935.

places to suit the relative prowess of the curlers in each division of the country) are to be sought in the inter-county matches of the early nineteenth century. In 1843 a match between Perthshire north and south of the river Tay was organised to coincide with a meeting of the Royal Club.

More national matches were arranged for 1844 and 1845 but the weather did not permit them, and the first Grand Match took place on 15th January 1847 on the upper pond at Penicuik House, Midlothian. Only twelve northern rinks appeared, and the surplus southern rinks were arranged into inter-county matches.

The second Grand Match was arranged to take place on Linlithgow Loch, and on 25th January 1848, 35 northern rinks met an equal number of southern rinks, the 100 surplus southern rinks playing matches amongst themselves. Including spectators, 6000 persons were present.

In 1850 the arranged venue was Castle Semple Loch, Lochwinnoch, Renfrewshire. The proprietor of the Loch, however, belatedly refused permission for the match and a neighbouring proprietor had to flood 200 acres of Barr Meadow to allow the match to take place. With 127 rinks a side and several thousand spectators, the match proved a great success.

The truly patriotic feelings displayed by John Campbell Shairp, Principal of the University of St Andrews, in his poem, *The Lochwinnoch Bonspiel,* written just after the event and first published in the *Annual* for 1851, are proof that the Grand Match had fulfilled the hopes of its organisers in uniting Scots from all the airts into a national 'brotherhood of the rink':

THE LOCHWINNOCH BONSPIEL.

January 11th, 1850.

Keen and snell is the weather, ye Curlers, come
gather,
    Scotland summons her best, frae the Tweed to the
Tay,
It's the north o' the Clyde 'gainst the southern side,
    And Lochwinnoch the tryst for our Bonspeil to-
day.

Ilk parish the've summoned, baith landward and
borough,
    Far and near troop the lads wi' the stanes and the
broom,
The ploughs o' the Lothians stand stiff i' the furrow,
    And the weavers o' Beith for the loch leave the
loom.

The blithe shepherd blades are here in their plaids,
    Their hirsels they've left on the Tweedside their
lane,
Grey carles frae the moorlands wi' gleg e'e and sure
hands,
The bannet o' blue, and the auld farren stane.

Fig. 114   Grand Match, Lochleven, 1959.

And the Loudons three, they forgather in glee
   Wi' townsfolk frae Ayr, and wi' farmers on Doon,
'But over the Forth' come the lads frae the north
   Frae far Carse o' Gowrie, and palace o' Scone.

Auld Reekie's top sawyers, the lang headed lawyers,
   And crouse Glasgow merchants are loud i' the
play.
There are lairds frae the east, there are lords frae the
west,
   For the peer and the ploughman are marrows today.

See the rinks are a' marshalled, how cheerly they
mingle,
   Blithe callants, stout chields, and auld grey-
headed men,
Till their loud roaring stanes gar the snowy heights
tingle
   As they ne'er did before, and may never again.

Some lie at hog score, some oure a' ice roar,
   'Here's the tee,' 'there's the winner,' 'chap and lift
him, twa yards,'
'Lay a guard,' 'fill the port,' 'now lads! there's nought
for't
   But a canny inwick, or a 'rub at the guards,'

It is done — we maun part — but fair fa' each kind
heart!
   Wi' the auld Scottish blood beating warm in the
veins;

Curlers! aye we've been leal, to our country's weal,
   Though our broadswords are besoms, our targets
are stanes.

We are sons o' the true hearts, that died wi' the
Wallace,
   And conquered at brave Bannockburn wi' the
Bruce,
These wild days are gone, but their memories call us,
   So we'll stand by langsyne, and the gude ancient
use.

And we'll hie to the spiel, as our fathers before us,
   Ye sons o' the men whom foe never could tame!
And at night round the ingle we'll join the blithe
chorus,
   To the land we loe weel, and our auld Scottish
game.

One incidental by-product of this match was a litigation
between the proprietor of Castle Semple Loch and the
curlers of Lochwinnoch, in which it was, unfortunately,
decided by the Court of Session, in Edinburgh, that no
matter for how many years the curlers of a locality had
curled on a loch, they had acquired no legal right to play
their sport upon it. Having established this legal principle,
the owner of the loch seems to have been satisfied, for
two Grand Matches in 1864 and 1878 subsequently took
place on this loch.
So popular were the early Grand Matches in terms of
players and spectators, so huge the numbers on the ice,

Fig. 115   Grand Match, Lake of Menteith, 1979.

that the dreadful prospect of a drowning disaster presented itself to the Royal Club, and a committee was established in 1851 to secure a 'piece of ground which could be flooded for the purpose of affording a safe sheet of ice for the Grand Matches'.

The efforts of the committee produced Carsebreck, a site of about 63 acres in Perthshire, conveniently situated for the Scottish Central Railway line and nowhere more than six feet deep when flooded. Until it was abandoned by the Royal Club after the Second World War, Carsebreck was the main venue for Grand Matches, and 25 matches took place there, the last of which, and biggest of all with 2576 curlers, took place in 1935. Charles Martin Hardie's painting of the Carsebreck Grand Match gives a good idea of the site, on a wide fertile strath, surrounded by sweeps of low grassy hills.

The ravages of the Second World War, during which sluices and bridges were unattended and unrepaired and railway sidings lifted to be turned into tanks and guns, meant the abandonment of Carsebreck. After the hesitation already alluded to, the Royal Club once more affirmed its faith in Grand Matches on natural lochs; and each year since 1950 the large Grand Match Committee has gone to work, though its efforts have been blessed with success on only three occasions.

Since the Match is meant to be the national bonspiel, it must be played on a centrally situated loch. Such are

Loch Leven at Kinross, Lindores Loch in Fife, the Lake of Menteith near Stirling, and Stormont Loch between Perth and Blairgowrie. Every year a draw is made and sent out; every year as frost sets in hopes begin to rise; nearly every year the hopes are dashed again. Entries are restricted to 300 clubs from the North and 300 from the South, not from any lack of enthusiasm for the event, but only from the logistical necessity of speed in preparing 300 rinks on natural ice in the shortest feasible time.

When a suitable frost has set in, club secretaries are postcarded to be in readiness: if the frost lasts and the match is to come off, the final announcement is broadcast by the British Broadcasting Corporation, but before then the bush telegraph has done its work and preparations are already under way. Stones are being dug out of cupboards, or rescued from sheds, or attics or gardens, and cleaned and polished. Stones are begged, borrowed or stolen by improvident curlers; rusty crampits are scraped down. Brushes, besoms, ropes, lifebelts, are looked out. Whisky is purchased. Private transport arrangements are finalised — for no one now relies on the railway.

Stones are set out in the frost to freeze them down ready for play. Every curler goes to bed with a silent prayer that the thaw will stay away long enough to allow the match to be played *this year*.

On the day of the Match curlers are up early and

proceed to the loch in private car, in lorry, in bus. Many a curler is well refreshed with whisky long before the loch is reached.

At the loch, final preparations are being made. Each of the 300 rinks is numbered, public address lines are strung along the ice, the Royal Club Secretary and Grand Match Secretary establish themselves in their headquarters in a local hotel, prepared for a long hard day.

The police arrive — to direct traffic into frozen fields on the lochside used as car parks. Curlers begin to arrive; stones, which have been happed up in the backs of cars to protect them from the warmth, are quickly put on the ice. People scurry to and fro finding their rink and their opponents. Long trains of roped-together curling stones are pulled, for all the world like faithful puppies, out onto the loch. The camp followers follow with the food. All is bustle and activity. Greeting is piled on greeting, as curling friends from all quarters of Scotland meet. Hands are shaken; drams are drunk.

When the right rink is found, it is swept and tidied. Coloured tassels are tied onto handles to distinguish rink from rink. Introductions are made; toasts are drunk.

The Royal Club President arrives — in 1979, in a helicopter on to the ice of the Lake of Menteith, which was so keen that the downdraught sent spectators involuntarily slithering across the ice.

So great is the din that his greetings over the loudspeakers go unheard by the majority. The unheard preliminaries over, the Earl of Elgin, past President, fires off an ancestral cannon at 11.30 a.m., and in response to this signal the match begins. At once the din of exuberant curlers is muffled by the roar of hundreds of stones, simultaneously gliding over the ice,

Till their loud roaring stanes gar the snowy heights tingle,
As they ne'er did before, and may never again.

The time allotted to the match is three hours. Some games have consisted of eighteen ends; some, from frequent stoppages for refreshment, a mere eight. Some stones, having lain outdoors for years, are quite unsuited to the task, and never cross the hogscore. Others are so keen that they scarcely can be persuaded to stop in the house. Some games are closely fought. In others results like 44-1 are achieved.

The match is brought to an end by another report from the cannon. Score cards are totted up and taken to the secretary's office. No one knows whether North or South has won. No one cares. Winning is not important. To have been there is the thing. Tomorrow's newspapers will carry the result.

Tired, but exhilarated, curlers leave the ice; they have made their pilgrimage, and are happy to have been united through participation in the Grand Match 'in one brotherhood of the rink'.

A statistical footnote on Grand Matches

There have been 16 matches in January, 9 in December, 7 in February, and 1 in November.

The earliest date on which a match has been held was 24th November, in 1909; the latest, 15th February, in 1853, both at Carsebreck. In only one year, 1880, has the match been held twice, in both January and December.

The smallest match was the first; the largest, in 1935, consisted of 322 rinks aside.

The south has beaten the north on 24 occasions, though it must be said that in the 6 matches held since 1925 the north has been victorious in 5 and the south's only victory was gained by the paltry margin of 11 shots.

The total number of shots scored by the northern curlers in all Grand Matches is 79,835; the south's grand total amounts to 86,352. Since the total number of rinks on each side amounts to 5,552, it will be seen that the average northern score is 14.38 while the southern chiels scored 15.55. This average, however, like all averages, disguises grosser figures: in the 1979 match the highest up rink was Edzell, who vanquished their opponents by 44 shots to 1!

What cannot be quantified statistically is the enjoyment generated by a Grand Match. All present on 7th February 1979 will surely agree that fun was the main point of the day's proceedings, and that that was enormous!

13

Curling in the New World

Whatever doubt enshrouds the origins of curling in the Old World, there is no doubt that it was the Scots who carried the game to the New, though even here the beginnings are legendary rather than historical fact.

The received story is that it was Fraser's Regiment, the 18th Highlanders, who first played the game in Canada. After the fall of Quebec in 1759 the Scottish troops, it is said, had time and ice in plenty on their hands and so, having no granite curling stones with them, 'someone conceived the idea of melting down cannon balls' and thus forming ersatz curling stones.

This story has some superficial plausibility about it, explaining, as it appears to do, the origins of iron-play in Lower Canada, but it does seem strange that a regiment from the Highlands of Scotland, to which curling had certainly not yet penetrated from the Lowlands, should have felt the lack of stones so greatly as to invent an iron substitute.

Nonetheless, iron 'stones' did find favour in Lower Canada, and caused considerable cultural shock in a French-speaking farmer, on seeing for the first time Scottish iron-players energetically engaged in their favourite sport. His uncomprehending reaction is recorded in the minute book of the Montreal Club and was given publicity by being printed in Cairnie's *Essay*: 'J'ai vu aujourd'hui une bande d'Ecossois, qui jetoient des grandes boules de fer, faites comme des bombes, sur la glace: après quoi ils crioient "Soupe, soupe"; ensuite ils rioient comme des foux. Je crois bien qu'ils sont vraiment foux!' 'Today I saw a band of Scots, who were throwing large balls of iron, made like kettles, on the ice, after which they shouted "Soup, Soup!" Then they laughed like madmen. I do believe that they really are mad.'

With the establishment of Montreal Curling Club in 1807 we pass from legend into historical fact. The Montreal club, which consisted of twenty members, was composed of Scots, who engaged to meet, play and eat every fortnight on a Wednesday. It is reported that their stones tended to break on impact, and therefore recourse was had to cast-iron stones. A model for these was constructed of wood by a cooper in the lower town of Quebec and sent to the forges of Trois Rivières where the finished iron stones were made.

The war of 1812-1814 inhibited the game, but, in 1821, a few years after its close, we find a second club being formed at Quebec, and four or five years later a club was formed at Halifax.

Despite these early foundations, curling, it appears, had a very precarious hold on Canada until about 1836. In fact John Mactaggart, the compiler of the *Gallovidian Encyclopedia*, (see p. 22), who was in Canada from 1826 until 1828, wrote, 'Notwithstanding the number of lakes and rivers which abound in Canada, and all the intensity of the winter frost, still the game of curling, the great ice amusement of Scotland, is *unknown*. [My italics]. There was a curling club formed in Montreal some time ago but it seldom attempted the game. The weather is too cold even for the keenest curler to endure and the ice is covered very deep with snow. The curling stones, 'if I may use this expression', they have constructed of cast-iron; but as iron is a great conductor of heat, they were not found to answer well, as they stuck into the ice. The surface of the lakes, too, is never what a person knowing the game would call true, that is, level; let no Scottish emigrants then, as heretofore, conceive they will be gratified with plenty of this amusement. Thus it does not follow, that where there are plenty of men, water, and frost, there will be curling.' (*Three Years in Canada*, London, 1829.)

Despite Mactaggart's observations Broun tells us, at page 44, that in 1829, 200 pairs of Ailsa Craig stones had been shipped for Canada; and there was certainly sufficient interest in the game for a challenge to issue from

Fig. 116   Curling match at Montreal, January 1855. The scene was sketched by Mr Duncan, 'the clever artist of that city.' *Illustrated London News*, 17th February 1855.

Quebec to Montreal for a match at Trois Rivières halfway between the two towns in the winter of 1835-36. In fact the enthusiasm must have been considerable, for the two towns are 180 miles apart, and the idea of such a sporting challenge, involving a journey of such a distance, was unprecedented not only in Canada, but in the rest of the world.

The match took place on 10 January 1836, and in order to be there on time the Montreal curlers had had to leave in various conveyances on 7th and 8th January. Moreover they, being the losers, had to pay over £3 each for the dinner that followed the game, but nothing daunted by the expense of the journey and the dinner, the parties agreed to play the match again in January 1837; and in the next year the Montreal club constructed a wooden rink under cover near the Lachine canal, which was probably the first covered rink in British North America.

In Upper Canada the large influx of Scottish immigrants, encouraged by the Canada Land Company, managed by John Galt, the Scottish novelist, gave rise to the foundation of curling clubs at Kingston (1820), Fergus (1834), West Flamborough (1835), Toronto and Milton (1836), Galt and Guelph (1838), and Scarborough (1839).

James Young, the historian of the town of Galt, writes that the first game in that part took place in 1836-37 among some Scottish residents, who 'made blocks out of the maple tree, putting in pieces of iron as handles, and, although labouring under some disadvantages, the survivors describe it as a jolly and long-to-be-remembered meeting.'

The wooden 'stones' used by the Galt curlers were commonly resorted to in Upper Canada, until conventional stones could be procured. They were usually cut from the solid trunk of a maple or birch tree and shaped. To prevent splitting, and to add weight, a band of iron was fastened around the middle.

Soon the more enterprising curlers turned to making their stones from 'ice-borne boulders of whinstone or granite called hard-heads' which were removed from ground being cleared for cultivation, and an early example of entrepreneurial initiative is shown in the following advertisement which appeared in the *British Colonist*, Toronto, in 1839: 'To Curlers — "Geluque Flumina Constiterint Acuto" — Horace. Curling stones may be had on application to the subscriber who has taken great pains to collect a number of blocks of the most excellent grain. Several members of the Toronto Club have already been supplied, and specimens may be

Fig. 117   Curling on the Don River, Toronto, ca. 1860. Water colour. Public Archives, Canada. C11234.

seen on the Bay on Playing Days or on application to Mr McDonald at the City Wharf, or to the subscriber at his residence, 16 New Street. The price of the stones is eight dollars per pair, according to handles and finish. Peter McArthur.'

On February 12, 1839 a bonspiel took place on the Don River between 24 curlers from outside Toronto and 24 from the Toronto Club. The Governor-General and Lieutenant-Governor of Upper Canada were among the spectators.

In 1840 there was another bonspiel between Quebec and Montreal Clubs. On this occasion each club sent a rink the whole way to the opponents' town and the matches were played on the same day. Curling was augmented in 1842 by the formation of the Montreal Thistle Club, and the 71st Regiment at St Jean played in the early 1840s. The *Montreal Gazette* reported a match between Montreal and the 71st on the St Lawrence River in 1841 at which there were thousands of spectators,

including the Governor-General, in attendance during the whole of the play which lasted from 11 o'clock until 6 p.m.

In the 1840s clubs were formed in Upper Canada at Barrie, Paris, Woodstock, London, Hamilton, Dundas, Ancaster and Whitchurch. In Lower Canada in the same period clubs were formed at Chambly, Stadacona and Cameron in Quebec, and in Nova Scotia there is reference to curling at Albion Mines and Pictou and in Newfoundland the Avalon Club was formed at St Johns in 1843.

As has already been noted, Montreal Club was admitted a member of the Grand Caledonian Curling Club in 1841 'by acclamation'. The *Montreal Gazette* said of this event on 24 August 1841, 'This favour, as generous as it was unexpected, will, we doubt not, have a favourable effect in giving a new incentive to the exertions of the numerous admirers, in Montreal, of the healthful and manly game of curling.' Despite the

Fig. 118 Curling in the High Park, Toronto, ca. 1860. Water colour. Public Archives, Canada. C11233.

Montreal and Quebec curlers' appetite for travel, the isolation of most curling clubs and the difficulties of travel meant that most play was local, for medals given by the Royal Club, or other donors.

George Denholm, president of the Toronto Club, gave a medal for competition. In 1843 it was won by William Reynalds, a *Canadian*. The *Toronto Colonist* commented: 'Curling may now be considered in this Province, a Canadian, rather than a Scottish game.'

That Canadians, as opposed to Scots immigrants, were taking up the game, is shown by the spread of the game by the 1850s to Ayr, Hamilton, Ancaster, Dundas, Newcastle, Darlington, Coburg, Burlington, Bayfield, Peterborough, Ottawa, Buckingham and Almonte.

In Galt Club, where the rivalry against the Paris Club has been described as 'positively ferocious', skill was encouraged by having practice days, and fines were enforced against members not attending for practice.

A most important event in the development of the game in Canada was the formation of the Canadian Branch of the Royal Club in 1852. The Montreal, Thistle, Quebec, and Stadacona clubs were original members, and from Upper Canada, Coburg and Bytown joined in the same year. Hamilton joined in 1854, Kingston, Toronto, London, Paris and West Flamborough in 1855, and Burlington in 1857.

In 1858 an invitation was sent to the Royal Club to send out a rink to Canada, but although the idea appealed to the Scots, the seed then sown did not bear fruit for another 44 years!

By the 1850s communications had improved and large bonspiels were possible. 1858 saw the first Grand East-West Bonspiel held in Burlington Bay when 32 rinks competed. In 1859 the numbers had increased to 42 rinks, and on the Don River at Toronto rinks from Montreal, Bowmanville, Newcastle, Scarborough,

Fig. 119   Curling on the lakes near Halifax, ca. 1870, from Henry Buckton Laurence, *Sketches of Canadian Sports and Pastimes,* London, 1870. Public Archives, Canada. C8774.

Darlington, Toronto, Burlington, Paris, Bayfield, Dundas, Ancaster, London, West Flamborough, Fergus, Guelph and Hamilton played against each other.

In 1852 also a Nova Scotia Branch of the Royal Club was formed with, as initial members, Halifax, Pictou, Thistle and Portsmouth.

The great expansion of the railway system in Canada after 1850 not only made new settlement possible, it put hitherto isolated communities in touch, and permitted the beginnings of the development of a provincial attitude to the game. By 1867 there were 2000 miles of railway joining up the major towns of Ontario and Quebec and the Maritimes.

In Canada the organisation of the game closely paralleled the settlement pattern. The first organisation, the Canadian Branch, was formed in 1852, with its headquarters in Montreal. Although by 1875 it comprised a fairly large number of clubs, it had not fulfilled the hopes of its founders by uniting all curlers under its banner.

One reason was the great distance between the main area of population growth, southern Ontario, and Montreal. Before 1875 communications were not sufficiently good to enable all the Ontario member clubs of the Canadian Branch to attend meetings, and there was a strong feeling that their point of view was not being heard.

The other reason was the Canadian Branch's insistence on playing the iron stone, which gave rise to continuous difficulty because of the different techniques and strategy required. In 1861 Toronto and Stadacona (Quebec) played for a Royal Club district medal at Montreal on the rink of Montreal Thistle Club. The Stadaconans insisted on playing their irons. On this occasion a compromise was reached: it was agreed that one of the two rinks on each side would play with the unfamiliar stones. The result could have been foreseen: the stone players who had to play with irons lost, as did the Stadaconans who had to use 'granites.' Thus neither side drew satisfaction from the compromise. The result

Fig. 120   Prince Arthur opening the Caledonia Rink at Montreal, 1870. *The Graphic,* 21 May, 1870. This shows how large and spacious indoor rinks with natural ice had become in the few years that had elapsed since Canadian curling first went indoors.

was, however, close: Toronto, 39, Stadacona, 44. Nonetheless the governor-general, speaking at the dinner after the match, remarked that he was sure that if the Royal Club only knew that the members of the Stadacona Club had travelled 340 miles, and those of the Toronto Club to meet them 666 miles to play for a Royal Club medal, double the number of medals would be sent to Canada next winter.

By 1873 stone-playing clubs in the Branch outnumbered the iron playing by 33 to 6. Political events suggested a solution. In 1867 the former colonies in Canada were joined together in a confederation by the name of the Dominion of Canada, with representation at federal level based on population. Ontario curlers saw in this a pattern for the future development of the organisation of curling in the Dominion. In 1872 J.S. Russell of the Toronto Club proposed a motion at its

annual general meeting which would have initiated discussion with the Montreal and other clubs with a view to forming a Dominion Curling Association. The motion failed for lack of support, but Russell had sown the seed, and in 1874 at the Toronto club's meeting the following resolution was unanimously passed:

That, whereas on account of local distance and for other reasons, there has not been and there is not likely to be any great amount of intercourse in curling matters between the several provinces of the Dominion of Canada and, that while there are in the Province of Ontario many more curling clubs than in any of the other provinces, still for the reasons before named, only a few of them are in connection with the Royal Caledonian Curling Club; and believing that it is desirable that every club should be

Fig. 121   The opening of the Thistle Curling Club Rink, Montreal, 1871. *Canadian Illustrated News,* 14th January 1871. Public Archives, Canada. C54213.

connected with this, the parent club, and that this object would be largely secured by a Branch of the Royal Club for the Province of Ontario, with its headquarters in Toronto: further that the co-operation of the other affiliated clubs in the province for this end be urgently requested and that, if possible, the matter shall be so arranged as to take effect before the publication of the next annual of the Royal Club, and that the President and the Secretary, together with the mover of the resolution, be appointed a committee to see that the provisions of the resolution are carried out.

The result of this resolution was a decision to form an Ontario Branch of the Royal Club, on the same lines as the Canadian. The new branch was duly admitted in 1874. Only eleven clubs which retained their preference for iron stones — Arnprior, Renfrew, Pembroke, Belleville, Kingston, Montreal, Montreal Caledonia, Montreal Thistle, Quebec, Ottawa, and the viceregal Club at Rideau Hall — remained in the Canadian Branch, and until in 1947 the iron players finally gave up

their insistence that everyone was out of step except them, relations between the Canadian branch and the rest of Canada were restricted.

In 1882 the Royal Club, on the petition of the Ontario Branch, agreed 'in the interest of curling in the Ontario District, to allow the Ontario Branch to be a *corresponding* association, no longer subordinate or contributory to the Royal Club . . .' Thus the Ontarians were the first to sever formal relations with the Mother Club, although they emphasised that independence did not mean any lessening of filial attachment to the mother club.

The pattern established by the Canadian, Nova Scotia, and Ontario Branches was continued as settlement and, with it, curling spread westwards across the continent. In fact the Ontario Branch reported to the Royal Club in 1882: 'The large emigration from our Province to the new Province of Manitoba and the North West Territories has thinned the ranks of many of our curling clubs; but the emigrants are everywhere carrying with them the love of the game, and already about half-a-dozen clubs have been organised in that land so eminently adapted for

Fig. 122   Curling bonspiel, Toronto, 1875. *Canadian Illustrated News*, 13th February 1875. Public Archives, Canada. C62554.

curling: so we who remain are calmly awaiting our fate, when these curlers, perfected by six or seven months' daily practice every year, will come down and "scoop us out", not giving us a shot; soutering, is, I believe, the proper term.'

The writer of this report was correct: the long dry winters of the prairies proved ideal for curling and it is no surprise that today the centre of gravity of world curling lies in Calgary, Regina and Winnipeg.

The part played by the railways in the expansion of the game in eastern Canada has already been noted. The second half of the nineteenth century in Canada was dominated by the completion of the first transcontinental railway, the Canadian-Pacific.

Gerald Redmond, in an unpublished thesis on *The Scots and Sport in nineteenth century Canada*, submitted to the University of Alberta for the degree of Ph.D. in 1972, says of the railway: '. . . it had permanently shaped the map of Canada as it created and developed

the communities that stretched across the Prairies . . . As it shaped the geography and life of the new nation; so it also formed the future of Canadian sport, including curling.' One way in which curling was actively promoted is recorded thus: 'Almost every railway town in Western Canada early in its history erects a commodious building, which is flooded on the interior ground and forms an ice sheet which lasts with some additions, for three or four months.'

It has been written that the first curling in the province of Manitoba took place about 1812, the time of the first settlement there. 'Then the men of Kildonan used to go out onto the frozen Red River and throw their home-cured "rocks" made from knotty burr oak, soaked and frozen in water, down the ice.' The settlers' first governor recorded playing at 'hurls on the ice' during the winter of 1812-13. And later when the settlement of Kildonan grew up and extended from the forks at Winnipeg to St. Andrew's and beyond, these burly men, toughened by

Fig. 123   Curling on the St. Lawrence opposite Montreal, 1878. Public Archives, Canada. C14512.

Fig. 124   Making ready for curling at Quebec. Public Archives, Canada. PA46026.

Fig. 125 Montreal Thistle Curling Club, 1905. This indoor rink, with natural ice, where play went on in the evenings under artificial light, was the sort of building which excited the envy of the first Scottish team to tour Canada in 1902-3.

their work in wresting a living from the land, guiding York boats, or manning the fur presses of the trading company, used to cast rocks weighing fifty pounds or more down the ice. (79th Annual Bonspiel, 1967, Canada's Centennial Year, Winnipeg, The Manitoba Curling Association.)

Whether that account is fact or fancy, 1876 saw the formation of the first organised curling club in the province. The Winnipeg Club had an auspicious beginning with seventy members and a newly constructed rink which, within a brief space, arrangements were in hand to illuminate with artificial light. The winter climate of the Prairies was ideal for the sport, with the result that in a very few years the centre of Canadian curling moved from southern Ontario to Manitoba.

Other curlers followed the lead of Winnipeg, and clubs were founded in quick succession at Emerson and Portage la Prairie in 1880, Winnipeg Granite in 1881, Brandon in 1883, and Stonewall in 1884. A Grand Provincial Bonspiel, which was destined to become the largest indoor event in the world, began in 1884.

It was not long before the Manitoban curlers attained independence from Ontario by forming in 1888 the Manitoba Branch of the Royal Club, and under its auspices the Bonspiel prospered: an entry of 62 rinks in 1888 had grown to a mammoth list of 454 rinks by the year of the Branch's jubilee in 1948.

When the Scottish Team arrived in Winnipeg in 1903 at about the time of the Bonspiel, John Kerr was moved by the experience to write superlatives: 'If Canada be the chosen home of Scotland's ain game, where it can be enjoyed with a fulness that is out of the question in the Old Country, then undoubtedly Winnipeg is the very fireplace or hearth of the game in the Dominion. In the Annals of curling there has been no place like Winnipeg, and no one can foretell the future that awaits the game at that great centre . . . We have, at home, our Grand Match, North *versus* South in Scotland, where more than 2000 curlers annually assemble in battle array, but that is simply a one-day gathering. At Winnipeg, 800 or so, accompanied by their wives and daughters and sweethearts, take up residence for a fortnight. For the time, as Athens was given over to idolatry, Winnipeg is wholly given over to curling. What St Andrews is to golf, so is Winnipeg to that other royal and ancient game.' He concluded that 'Winnipeg was the summit and acme and climax of all.'

That Manitoba has continued to be 'the very fireplace or hearth' of the game in Canada can be seen in the results of Canada's national curling championship, the Brier. Since its inception in 1927, rinks from Manitoba have won on no fewer than 21 occasions!

In 1908 the Manitoba Branch sought and obtained independence from the Royal Club in the form of the Manitoba Curling Association.

Fig. 126   Curling in the High Park, Toronto, 1914. This photograph provides an interesting comparison with the same location in the water colour, fig. 118. Public Archives, Canada. PA60877.

Fig. 127   Crude wooden blocks and an even cruder broom show how deep the interest in the game had gone. Public Archives, Canada. PA99885.

In Saskatchewan curling became organised with the formation of the Assiniboia Branch of the Royal Club in 1904, before which time the clubs there had come under the jurisdiction of the Manitoba Branch. The first three clubs, formed in the 1880s, of which we have notice, are the Prince Albert, Rosthern and Battleford. In 1889 curling began in Regina; and in 1890 at Qu'Apelle and Indian Head. Soon the province could boast more clubs than any province in the Dominion, and it maintains that predominance today.

The first recorded clubs in Alberta are Lethbridge in 1887, Calgary and Edmonton in 1888, Macleod in 1898, Anthracite and Banff in 1899 and Medicine Hat in 1900. These and other clubs formed the Alberta Branch of the Royal Club in 1904, but rivalry between Calgary and Edmonton led to the creation in 1917 of the Alberta Curling Association with jurisdiction over the Edmonton region. Although the climate of the Pacific coast was much less propitious, curling began in the province with the formation of a club at Kaslo in 1895. In 1898 the Kookenay Curling Association was started to regulate curling in the province; in 1906 it changed its name to the British Columbia Curling Association and became affiliated to the Royal Club.

Thus the years between 1852 and 1906 saw the whole of Canada associated to a greater or lesser extent with the mother club of curling. The formation of all the provinces of Canada into a national association took longer. Even J.S. Russell, who had first publicly mooted the idea of a Dominion Association, realised that there were difficulties in the way. In the report from the Ontario Branch, which accompanied the Ontarians' request for independence from the Royal Club in 1882, Russell wrote: 'And in reference to the formation of a grand Canadian Curling Association, co-extensive with the Dominion, they desire to report: That although such an Association of the Curling Clubs existing in the several Provinces of Canada is desirable for many reasons, yet considering the vast area over which the Clubs are spread, the different materials of which the curling stones used in the various Provinces are made,' — no doubt a dig at the iron players of the Canadian Branch — 'and their different sizes, shapes, and weights, and that for these reasons there is no possibility of any except the most casual intercourse taking place between them, they are of opinion that it is not desirable to take any further steps in the matter for the present.'

The beginning of the Brier in 1927 brought the matter once more under discussion. At the conclusion of the second Brier in 1928, Senator Haig of Winnipeg,

Fig. 128   The rink at Rideau Hall, Ottawa, ca. 1872-78. Lord Dufferin and party. Successive Governors of Canada gave their patronage to the game. Public Archives, Canada. PA8498.

chairman of the Brier Trustees, raised the question of forming a Dominion Curling Association, which was necessary, he said, for two purposes, the formulation of general rules, and the supervision of Canadian-Scottish curling tours. All the representatives, except those of the Canadian Branch, were in favour of the proposal, and it was decided to postpone a decision, which was not reached until 1935. At a meeting held in the Toronto Granite Club in March of that year a constitution for a Dominion Curling Association, duly affiliated with the Royal Club, was adopted, and the Royal Club gave its blessing. In Canada's Centennial year, 1967, the name was changed to the Canadian Curling Association.

One can reasonably suppose that curling came to the United States along with Scottish immigrants in just the same way as it did to Canada. In fact the border for many purposes existed only as a line drawn on a map, and settlers came and went across it practically as they pleased. In any event, when documented curling in the United States begins with the formation of the Orchard Lake Curling Club in 1832, the Scots were there. According to the *Annual* of the Grand National Curling

Club of America for 1880-81, 'a group of Scottish immigrant farmers and sheepmen headed for Chicago by boat were wrecked on the shores of Lake St Clair.' They decided to remain where Providence had put them, and 'in foraging the countryside for survival, they came upon Orchard Lake, liked the country and soil, and established themselves there.' The climate was propitious for curling and, according to an account by one of the founder members, 'The Orchard Lake Curling Club was organised at the house of Dr Robert Burns, January 2, 1832, and the first game played by the Club was played on Orchard Lake on Saturday, January 7, 1832, with hickory blocks, each player playing one block . . .'

David Foulis, secretary of the Grand National Club, writing in 1899, says: 'The game was played some eighty years ago in New York City, where the busy thoroughfare of Canal Street is now. It was there the members of the St Andrew's Society would go for an afternoon's pastime, when they could get so far up town.' Milwaukee saw the beginnings of curling in the 1840s, and in 1845 it was formally organised by the foundation of a curling club whose founder members' names

Fig. 129 Curling in the Rockies. Public Archives, Canada. C14082.

proclaim their Scottish origins: James Murray, David Ferguson, John W. Dunlop, Robert Gunyon, Findlay McFadyen, Archie McFadyen, Thomas Kinney, and Alexander McFarland. By the early 1850s there are notices of curling at Portage, Caledonia and Dekorra in Wisconsin.

The *Standard Guide to Chicago* for 1892 reports that: 'Curling was introduced to Chicago in 1854. At the start, the Chicago Club was composed exclusively of Scotsmen, but since that time it has grown and extended its membership, including several Americans and members of other nationalities.'

From 1864 Chicago and Milwaukee have played annual matches, and to them falls the distinction of playing in 1892 the first games on artificial ice in North America.

The 1850s continued to see expansion, clubs being

formed in 1855 at Philadelphia, New York (Thistle and Caledonian), Boston-New England in 1856, Boston City in 1858, The Paterson Club of New Jersey in 1860 and Detroit in 1865.

Scottish influence remained strong. It was in the *Scottish American Journal* that an advertisement was published, calling a meeting of curlers interested in forming a national association; and it was in the rooms of the Caledonian Club in New York City that delegates met in June 1867 and formed the Grand National Curling Club of America. Within a year twelve clubs had joined, and in succeeding years clubs from Minnesota and Wisconsin had become members.

As in Canada, and for the same climatic reasons, the Mid-West soon became the centre of the nation's curling. By 1892 clubs situated there outnumbered the others and a new North Western Curling Association of America was founded, with its headquarters in St Paul, Minnesota and as its area of influence, the states of Wisconsin, Illinois and Minnesota.

Though the game continued to expand and prosper in the North West Club's jurisdiction, it did not enjoy the same success in the east, where the climate was much less suitable. In the first decades of the twentieth century a series of mild winters coupled with the economic Depression brought curling in the east almost to its knees, but improvements in the economy and the advent of artificial ice rinks saved the day.

At present the game is played in all the border states, as well as in Alaska and some central states.

A national men's championship had its inception in 1957. As in Canada again, it was the national championship which gave rise to the national Association, for in 1958 the United States Men's Curling Association came into being.

By the 1850s both in Canada and the United States curlers were evidently avid for competition from further afield than their own back yard: in 1858 the Canadian Branch issued a challenge to the Scots curlers to come and play them on Canadian ice. A more practicable proposal was made in December of that year in the *Scottish American Journal*, New York. The writer, obviously a Scot, remarks on the facilities for practice making perfect that existed in the United States. 'This,' he says, 'is calculated to make good players, eight hours a day for three or four months in the year can scarcely fail to do so: and the New York Caledonian Club can accordingly turn out some hands as good as any that ever threw a stone.' He points out that there is also the New York Thistle, and the likelihood of two more clubs in New York, plus one club in Boston, two in Philadelphia and one in Cleveland, and he therefore proposes a Match between Canada and the United States. 'New York is but a day's journey from Montreal, Kingston, Toronto, and Hamilton, at all of which places there are strong clubs; and we have no doubt our friends at Boston, Philadelphia, Cleveland, and elsewhere on this side of the line, would be glad to come to try their skill with their countrymen from the North. The Caledonian Club here will this winter have the use of a spacious pond in the new Central Park, where any number of rinks could be accommodated. The idea is a feasible and attractive one.'

Whether inspired by this article or not, the Toronto curlers came part of the way to New York in 1864 and played a successful bonspiel against United States curlers at Buffalo. So successful was the match that the next year saw 23 Canadian and 23 U.S. rinks participating in an international match on Lake Erie at Black Rock near Buffalo. Canada won by 658 to 478. This led to a series of international matches for the Thomson-Scoville Medal from 1866. This was replaced by the Gordon International Medal in 1884 'to be played for at Montreal and the United States alternately under the direction of the officers of the Canadian Branch of the Royal C.C.C.' Curling relations between the two countries have continued to be of the most cordial.

Curling is now a nationwide sport in Canada. The big competitions attract rinks from all over the country. They attract them with large money prizes, a practice that began in Saskatchewan where in 1947 motor cars were first put up as prizes. This has engendered a professional attitude to the game among some curlers and, in fact, an association of quasi-professionals. It is natural that sportsmen who excel in their sport should wish to compete at the highest level. It would be impossible for many rinks to compete unless they were able to finance their travel — not to mention loss of income — by winning money prizes. Hence the paradox. Without large prizes competition and standards of play would fall. Yet the necessity to win breeds a win-at-all-costs attitude to the game which is contrary to the centuries-old tradition of sportsmanship. The rules of curling are brief. Play is largely self-regulating. This is the spirit of curling. The umpire is seldom resorted to.

Professionalism in Canada has recently given rise to a paper which was considered by the rules committee of the Canadian Curling Association at a meeting at the Brier in Calgary in March, 1980. The paper contained suggestions for discussion, such as that penalty shots for infractions of the rules should be introduced: for example, in the event of a serious breach, or series of breaches, the innocent skip should have a free draw to the house and could score an extra shot for that end. There was even a proposal that an offending player should be 'sent off'. Happily, the proposals were rejected out of hand in favour of the continuation of self-regulation in the spirit of curling. Most curlers will be glad at the outcome, but appalled that the proposals could ever have been seriously made.

The Brier

Nowhere in the world is there such a depth of curling skill as in Canada. The ubiquity of the game, and the vast numbers who play, have given rise to conditions in which competition of the highest order can exist.

This was recognised as early as 1927 with the establishment of a Canadian Curling Championship for the famous Macdonald's Brier Tankard, now known simply as 'The Brier'. From 1927, when the first round robin competition was held at the Toronto Granite Club,

Fig. 130 The Richardson rink returning home with the Scotch Cup, 1959.

until 1932 the competing rinks played under the title of their home towns. In that year the competition became truly national by the establishment of provincial representation. Until 1940 Toronto Granite Club was the invariable venue of the event, but then the important decision was taken to move the championship from place to place so that different provinces might be hosts. This factor, perhaps more than any other, has contributed to the success of the championship, for venue vied with venue in making better and better arrangements for the curlers and spectators. At first spectators were few, but since the last war the event has attracted large numbers of spectators, and extensive coverage on TV and film.

The Brier has now established itself as the most important event in the curling world as far as numbers are concerned. The competition during Brier week is the culmination of thousands of qualifying games, the participating rinks being the champion rinks of their province. In order to win the province championship, a rink has first of all to win out of its own club. There follow weeks of district qualifying bonspiels, until the provincial winner emerges.

Until 1979-80 the format of the competition was the round robin in which each rink plays all the others. There is much to be said for this form of play, for it undoubtedly gives the palm to consistent players. In 1980, however, under a new sponsor, the Brier took a new form, and henceforth the round robin will be succeeded by semi-finals and a final. The advantages of this format are the maintenance of spectator interest to the very end of the contest, and — what I feel is regarded by the sponsors as more important — the fact that it enables the mass media to be sure of maximum interest during the final. The winners of the Brier represent Canada at the World Curling Championships, which take place about two weeks later.

Among the many notables who have won the Brier are Gordon Hudson, of Strathcona C.C., Winnipeg, twice winner in 1928 and 1929; Ken Watson, of the same club in 1936, 1942, and 1949; and Ernie Richardson, Regina, who won in 1959, 1960, 1962, 1963.

The table of winners below discloses most significantly where the centre of gravity lies. The western provinces of Manitoba (21 wins) Alberta (13 wins) and Saskatchewan (7 wins) have dominated the Brier.

Table of winners
(Rinks are listed in the order of skip, third, second, and lead)

1927
Nova Scotia
Halifax Curling club
Murray Macneill
Al MacInnes
Cliff Torey
Jim Donahue
Record: 6-1
Site: Toronto

1928
Manitoba
Strathcona Curling Club
(Winnipeg)
Gordon Hudson
Sam Penwarden
Ron Singbusch
Bill Grant
Record: 9-2
Site: Toronto

1929
Manitoba
Strathcona Curling Club
(Winnipeg)
Gordon Hudson
Don Rollo
Ron Singbusch
Bill Grant
Record: 9-0
Site: Toronto

1930
Manitoba
Granite Curling Club
(Winnipeg)
Howard Wood Sr.
Jim Congalton
Victor Wood
Lionel Wood
Record: 8-2
Site: Toronto

1931
Manitoba
Strathcona Curling Club
(Winnipeg)
Bob Gourley
Ernie Pollard
Arnold Lockerbie
Ray Stewart
Record: 8-1
Site: Toronto

1932
Manitoba
Granite Curling Club
(Winnipeg)
Jim Congalton
Howard Wood Sr.
Bill Noble
Harry Mawhinney
Record: 6-2
Site: Toronto

1933
Alberta
Royal Curling Club (Edmonton)
Cliff Manahan
Harold Deeton
Harold Wolfe
Bert Ross
Record: 6-1
Site: Toronto

1934
Manitoba
Strathcona Curling Club
(Winnipeg)
Leo Johnson
Lorne Stewart
Lincoln Johnson
Marno Frederickson
Record: 7-0
Site: Toronto

1935
Ontario
Thistle Curling Club (Hamilton)
Gordon Campbell
Don Campbell
Gord Coates
Duncan Campbell
Record: 6-1
Site: Toronto

1936
Manitoba
Strathcona Curling Club
(Winnipeg)
Ken Watson
Grant Watson
Marvin MacIntyre
Charles Kerr
Record: 8-1
Site: Toronto

1937
Alberta
Royal Curling Club (Edmonton)
Cliff Manahan
Wes Robinson
Ross Manahan
Lloyd McIntyre
Record: 9-1
Site: Toronto

1938
Manitoba
Glenboro Curling Club
Ab Gowanlock
Bung Cartmell
Bill McKnight
Tom McKnight
Record: 9-0
Site: Toronto

1939
Toronto
Granite Curling Club
(Kitchener)
Bert Hall
Perry Hall
Ernie Parkes
Cam Seagram
Record: 9-1
Site: Toronto

1940
Manitoba
Granite Curling Club
(Winnipeg)
Howard Wood Sr.
Ernie Pollard
Howard Wood Jr.
Roy Enman
Record: 9-0
Site: Winnipeg

1941
Alberta
Calgary Curling Club
Howard Palmer
Jack Lebeau
Art Gooder
St. Clair Webb
Record: 8-1
Site: Toronto

1942
Manitoba
Strathcona Curling Club
(Winnipeg)
Ken Watson
Grant Watson
Charlie Scrymgeour
Jim Grant
Record: 8-1
Site: Quebec City

1943-1944-1945
*No Briers held due to Second
World War*

1946
Alberta
Sedgewick Curling Club
Billy Rose
Bart Swelin
Austin Smith
George Crooks
Record: 9-2
Site: Saskatoon

1947
Manitoba
Deer Lodge Curling Club
(Winnipeg)
Jimmy Welsh
Alex Welsh
Jack Reid
Harry Monk
Record: 9-0
Site: St. John, N.B.

1948
British Columbia
Trail Curling Club
Frenchy D'Amour
Bob McGhie
Fred Wendell
Jim Mark
Record: 8-1
Site: Calgary

1949
Manitoba
Strathcona Curling Club
(Winnipeg)
Ken Watson
Grant Watson
Lyle Dyker
Charles Read
Record: 9-0
Site: Hamilton

1950
Northern Ontario
Kirkland Lake Curling Club
Tom Ramsay
Lenny Williamson
Bill Weston
Bill Kenny
Record: 7-2
Site: Vancouver

1951
Nova Scotia
Glooscap Curling Club
(Kentville)
Don Oyler
George Hanson
Fred Dyke
Wally Knock
Record: 10-0
Site: Halifax

1952
Manitoba
Fort Rouge Curling Club
(Winnipeg)
Billy Walsh
Al Langlois
Andy McWilliams
John Watson
Record: 10-0
Site: Winnipeg

1953
Manitoba
Dauphin Curling Club
Ab Gowanlock
Jim Williams
Art Pollon
Russ Jackman
Record: 9-2
Site: Sudbury

1954
Alberta
Granite Curling Club
(Edmonton)
Matt Baldwin
Glenn Gray
Pete Ferry
Jim Collins
Record: 9-1
Site: Edmonton

1955
Saskatchewan
Avonlea Curling Club
Garnet Campbell
Don Campbell
Glen Campbell
Lloyd Campbell
Record: 10-0
Site: Regina

1956
Manitoba
Fort Rouge Curling Club
(Winnipeg)
Billy Walsh
Al Langlois
Chuck White
Andy McWilliams
Record: 9-2
Site: Moncton

1957
Alberta
Granite Curling Club
(Edmonton)
Matt Baldwin
Gordon Haynes
Art Kleinmeyer
Bill Price
Record: 10-0
Site: Kingston

1958
Alberta
Granite Curling Club
(Edmonton)
Matt Baldwin
Jack Geddes
Gordon Haynes
Bill Price
Record: 9-2
Site: Victoria

1959
Saskatchewan
Civil Service Curling Club
(Regina)
Ernie Richardson
Arnold Richardson
Garnet Richardson
Wes Richardon
Record: 10-1
Site: Quebec City

1960
Saskatchewan
Civil Service Curling Club
(Regina)
Ernie Richardson
Arnold Richardson
Garnet Richardson
Wes Richardson
Record: 9-1
Site: Thunder Bay

1961
Alberta
Alberta Avenue Curling Club
(Edmonton)
Hec Gervais
Ron Anton
Ray Werner
Wally Ursuliak
Record: 9-1
Site: Calgary

1962
Saskatchewan
Regina Curling Club
Ernie Richardson
Arnold Richardson
Garnet Richardson
Wes Richardson
Record: 9-2
Site: Kitchener

1963
Saskatchewan
Regina Curling Club
Ernie Richardson
Arnold Richardson
Garnet Richardson
Mel Perry
Record: 9-1
Site: Brandon

1964
British Columbia
Vancouver Curling Club
Lyall Dagg
Leo Hebert
Fred Britton
Barry Naimark
Record: 9-1
Site: Charlottetown

1965
Manitoba
Granite Curling Club
(Winnipeg)
Terry Braunstein
Don Duguid
Ron Braunstein
Ray Turnbull
Record: 9-1
Site: Saskatoon

1966
Alberta
Calgary Curling Club
Ron Northcott
George Fink
Bernie Sparkes
Fred Storey
Record: 9-2
Site: Halifax

1967
Ontario
Parkway Curling Club
(Toronto)
Alf Phillips Jr.
John Ross
Ron Manning
Keith Reilly
Record: 9-1
Site: Ottawa

1968
Alberta
Calgary Curling Club
Ron Northcott
Jim Shields
Bernie Sparkes
Fred Storey
Record: 9-1
Site: Kelowna

1969
Alberta
Calgary Curling
Ron Northcott
Dave Gerlach
Bernie Sparkes
Fred Storey
Record: 10-0
Site: Ottawa

1970
Manitoba
Granite Curling Club
(Winnipeg)
Don Duguid
Rod Hunter
Jim Pettapiece
Record: 9-1
Site: Winnipeg

1971
Manitoba
Granite Curling Club
(Winnipeg)
Don Duguid
Rod Hunter
Jim Pettapiece
Bryan Wood
Record: 9-2
Site: Quebec City

1972
Manitoba
Fort Rouge Curling Club
(Winnipeg)
Orest Meleschuk
Dave Romano
John Hanesiak
Pat Hailley
Record: 9-1
Site: St. John's, Nfld.

1973
Saskatchewan
Regina Curling Club
Harvey Mazinke
Bill Martin
George Achtymichuk
Dan Klippenstein
Record: 9-1
Site: Edmonton

1974
Alberta
St. Albert Curling Club
Hec Gervais
Ron Anton
Warren Hansen
Darrel Sutton
Record: 8-2
Site: London

1975
Northern Ontario
Fort William Curling Club
Bill Tetley
Rick Lang
Bill Hodgson
Peter Hnatiw
Record: 9-2
Site: Fredericton

1976
Newfoundland
St. John's Curling Club
Jack MacDuff
Toby McDonald
Doug Hudson
Ken Templeton
Record: 9-2
Site: Regina

1977
Quebec
St. Laurent Curling Club
Jim Ursel
Art Lobel
Don Aitken
Brian Ross
Record: 9-2
Site: Montreal

1978
Alberta
Medicine Hat Curling Club
Ed Lukowich
Mike Chernoff*
Dale Johnston
Ron Schindle
Record: 9-2
Site: Vancouver

*skipped and threw third rocks

1979
Manitoba
Deer Lodge Curling Club
(Winnipeg)
Barry Fry
Bill Carey
Gordon Sparkes
Bryan Wood
Record: 10-1
Site: Ottawa

1980
Saskatchewan
Nutana Curling Club
(Saskatoon)
Rick Folk
Ron Mills
Tom Wilson
Jim Wilson
Record: 11-1
Site: Calgary

1981
Manitoba
Assiniboine Memorial Curling Club
(Winnipeg)
Kerry Burtnyk
Mark Olson
Jim Spencer
Ron Kammerlock
Record: 10-3
Site: Halifax

14

Curling Elsewhere

Robin Welsh's recently published *Curling Map of the World* shows that the game is presently played in four continents: in North America, Europe, Australasia and Africa, to list them in descending order of numbers of players. As one might expect, a game of ice and winter has but a precarious hold on the Dark Continent, but contrary to one's expectations it has been established there in the least likely place, at Abidjan on the Ivory Coast in equatorial West Africa. The one ice rink there supports a small number of devoted French, supplemented by a fair number of prosperous Swiss curlers who think nothing of flying down to Africa for a bit of sunbathing and curling at the week-end.

Although there was some curling for a period in an ice rink built at Melbourne in Australia and a club was established there between 1933 and 1939, the game did

Fig. 131 Curling at Croxteth Hall, near Liverpool, the residence of the Earl of Sefton. The Earl was president of the Royal Club in 1862-63. *Illustrated London News*, 5th March 1853.

Fig. 132   Curling on the outdoor rinks at Mürren, Switzerland, overlooked by the Eiger. A 'dolly', or tee-marker, lies on its side at the foot of the picture. Swiss outdoor ice is very smooth and unpebbled.

not take on, and the only remaining curlers of the Southern Hemisphere are to be found in the South Island of New Zealand. In June 1934 four members of the Curling Club of Australia left Melbourne to visit the curlers of New Zealand. On their way they played at the glaciarium in Sydney, where 'a large crowd of exiled Scots turned up to watch the game,' encouraging hopes that a club would 'ere long' be formed in Sydney, but it seems that the 1934 game was the first and last played in New South Wales.

In New Zealand the four Australians played 23 matches, of which they won eight, lost eight and drew five. One of the Australians was the wife of I. M. Moffat-Pender, the prime mover of curling in Melbourne, and he records in the *Annual* of 1934-35 that she was the first lady ever to appear on New Zealand ice. In the province of Otago there in the months of July and August small numbers of curlers play on frozen ponds and dams, some of horrifying depth! Curling was taken to New Zealand by Scottish immigrants as early as the 1870s and the game

survived with little contact with the mother country beyond the reading of Royal Club *Annuals* year by year, for in 1886 a New Zealand Province of the Royal Club was established. In the same volumes the Scottish curlers were kept in touch with the doings of their antipodean brethren, by annual reports from curling's furthest flung outpost. Because of the isolation of New Zealand from the rest of the curling world, the game was uninfluenced by all the Canadian innovations which have transformed the game in Europe. The style of play was old-fashioned: Moffat-Pender records, 'They play very quickly, too, losing no time in any unnecessary palavers, and their well-observed rink routine, added to their great keenness, enables them to play two matches during a single day — and each match of 21 ends! The number of ends played in a day is regularly 42. This may sometimes even be exceeded.'

In 1971, the Royal Club, or to be more precise, some members of the Royal Club, including Willie Wilson, the president, brought this isolation to an end by making a curling pilgrimage, at their own expense, to New Zealand. They arrived two days too late to participate in the big province bonspiel but were able to play some games on indifferent, and dangerous, ice. Willie Wilson gave the New Zealanders their first demonstration of the sliding delivery. A pleasant sequel was the first tour of Scotland by a New Zealand team in 1973. At a time when many Scottish curlers were getting worried at what they saw as the commercialisation of curling because of Canadian influences, the style of play and attitude to the game of the New Zealand curlers was an inspiration. None of them had played on anything but natural outdoor ice; most of them had never heard of the in-turn or the out-turn; their tactics were unsophisticated; to some of us who had the good fortune to play against them, the experience was like a breath from the past. They personified the simple virtues of friendship and brotherhood, both on and off the ice, which we had been brought up to believe were the hallmarks of curling, but which to some seemed threatened by the win-at-all-costs philosophy which tough competition and big prizes engender.

Asia has never proved fertile ground for the game, though we find accounts of curling in Manchuria, and in Tientsin, in China, in *Annuals* from 1890 to 1941. An exotic addition to the *Annual* for 1938-39 was part of the rules of curling in Chinese! (See fig. 134).

There have been several attempts by American and Canadian curlers to introduce the game to Japan, but so far the game has not taken root.

Before the last decades of the nineteenth century, curling was unknown on the continent of Europe. If the

Fig. 133   Willie Wilson, President of the Royal Club, directs on New Zealand ice, August 1973, while members of the New Zealand Branch look on.

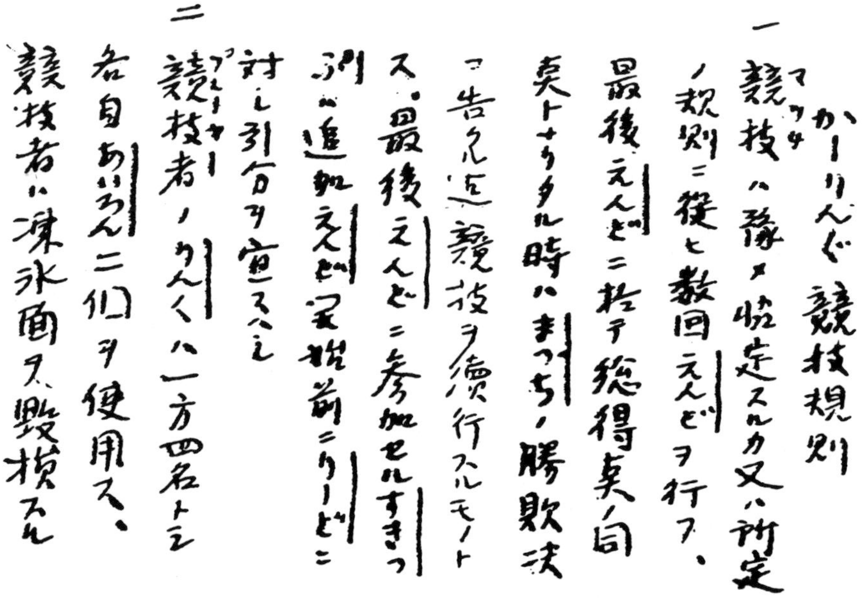

一

競技ハ豫メ臨定スルカ又ハ所定
ノ規則ニ従ヒ數回えんどヲ行フ、
最後えんどニ於テ總得點ノ自
喪トナリタル時ハまっち゛ノ勝敗決
「告之近」競技ヲ續行スルモノト
ス・最後えんどニ参加せルすきっ
別ニ追加えんどヲ聲掲前ニリードニ
対し引合ヲ宜スヘし
プレーヤー
競技者ノ刈人ハ一方四名十二

二

各自あいりん二仍ヲ使用ス、
競技者ハ凍水面ヌ嬰掦スル

かーりんぐ 競技規則
マッチ

Fig. 134   Specimen of the rules in what is said in the *Annual* for 1938-39 to be Chinese, but is, according to a consulted Chinese scholar, Japanese. It includes references to rinks and stones.

Fig. 135   St Moritz, Switzerland, ca. 1910.

stations, such as St Moritz, Zermatt, and Mürren were composed almost entirely of Scots and English who went to Switzerland for curling holidays: the natives only participated in small numbers. The same situation obtained in the Alpine resorts of France, Germany and Italy. It was not until the building of artificial ice rinks that nationals of these countries began to participate in any numbers.

Of all the European curling countries, it is Switzerland that has experienced the most outstanding growth of the game in recent years. In 1950 there were only six indoor artificial rinks; in 1979 there are over one hundred. The decision to hold the Silver Broom in Switzerland in 1974 contributed greatly to the expansion. The vast ice arena at Bern not only witnessed the largest crowds ever to spectate at curling matches on the continent of Europe, but saw an upsurge of interest in the game throughout the competition, due largely to the exciting performance of Peter Attinger and his young rink from Dübendorf near Zürich, who won all their round robin games in a highly stylish and polished manner. The press and television fanned the flames of enthusiasm, and great was the chagrin of the Swiss crowd when Attinger lost the semifinal to the ultimate winner, Bud Somerville of the U.S.A., after two extra ends. Swiss enthusiasm was further increased next year when Otto Danieli and his rink won the Silver Broom for Switzerland for the first time at Perth, Scotland.

Curling is now played in Denmark, Germany, Austria, Italy, Holland, France, Finland, Norway and Sweden.

The policy of holding curling's premier international

game, or something like it, was played in the sixteenth century in the Low Countries, it had long since been forgotten. Even in mountainous parts of Europe, like the Alps, where there was lots of snow and ice, curling was unknown. When the British discovered the winter attractions of the Swiss mountains, and introduced skiing there, they flocked to the mountain resorts and their hotels. No doubt some of the skiers from Scotland realised that in the Alps their ain game of curling could be added to the delights of skiing, skating, sledging and tobogganing; and played in conditions unobtainable at home, under clear sunny skies on ice that could be relied upon not to disappear overnight.

Most of the early curling clubs in the high Alpine

Fig. 136   Buxton, Derbyshire, is one of the highest towns in England, and therefore an eminently suitable place for curling.

Fig. 137   Curling on the River Avon, Warwickshire, near Leamington, ca. 1900.

championship, the Silver Broom, at venues on the continent of Europe as well as in Scotland and in North America not only marks the advance in curling in the countries where it is held, but actively stimulates that advance, with the result that Canada has won the trophy since 1972 only once.

In Sweden which, with a curling population of about 10,000, is very similar to Switzerland in numbers, curling has an older history, and the growth of the game has been less explosive. It was, of course, a Scot, William Andrew Macfie of Greenock, who introduced the game, in 1846. Sweden was the first country in Europe from which a Scottish curling tour was made in 1923.

That curling has never taken vigorous root in England is at first sight surprising; but since the games people play are an expression of the national psyche, and since the relations between the Scottish and English peoples were bitterly hostile for many centuries — and certainly not cordial in the first century after the Union of 1707 — the reluctance of the English to adopt the national pastime of their old enemy becomes more understandable. It has been argued that climatic factors are the reason for the game's failure to spread south but, it is submitted, the reasons are primarily cultural. No doubt the English have adopted with enthusiasm Scotland's other national game, golf, but in doing so they have transformed it: in Scotland

golf is a game played by every section of the community, just as curling is, whereas in England golf tends to be played by a social élite. It may be that the egalitarianism of curling was uncongenial to the English spirit. The cultural divergence worked in the opposite direction, too, for the English national game, cricket, has found the soil of Scotland less than congenial.

The first mention of curling in England occurs in Ramsay's *Account* (page 22): 'It has made its appearance in some of the northern counties of England; and within these few years has even found its way to the capital of the British Empire. There, the first essay was made upon the New River; but the crowd of spectators, attracted by such a novel spectacle, becoming very great, the ice threatened to give way, and the curlers were with reluctance compelled to desist.' In 1847 a game on the Serpentine between two Scottish Members of Parliament, Sir William Gibson-Craig and the Hon. Fox Maule, later Earl of Dalhousie, was still such a curiosity that the press of spectators forced the Parliamentary curlers to abandon the game. It was in the northern half of England that the game was played, as the list of the 32 clubs affiliated to the Royal Club in 1890 shows. In 1868 the Royal Club held its annual meeting at Liverpool, no doubt in recognition of the support given to the game by the Earl of Sefton, president of the Royal Club in 1862, and

Fig. 138   The Glaciarium, Southport, Lancashire, 1885. For several years, the only artificial ice in Great Britain. *Illustrated London News*, 1 August, 1885.

whose pond at Croxteth Hall near Liverpool was the venue of many a curling match between Liverpool and Manchester.

The glaciarium at Manchester has already been mentioned, but although it afforded ice for curling, the enthusiasm it engendered was insufficient, and the venture collapsed after a few years. It is ironical that England should be the first place where curling was played on artificial ice.

The next location chosen for an ice rink was Southport. The glaciarium there flourished for about 10 years from 1879 and attracted many Scottish rinks to its competitions. In 1885 the Royal Club held its annual meeting at Southport and the curlers attending were able to enjoy the novel experience of playing for the Holden Shield in *July*!

After the collapse of the Southport venture curling suffered a setback in England, and enthusiasm waned. Small bands of curlers, mainly expatriate Scots, continued to cultivate the game, but there have been only three ice rinks in England where curling has taken place: from 1910 the Manchester Ice Palace; from 1965 to 1973 the Ice Drome at Blackpool; and from 1951 to 1980 Richmond Ice Rink at London.

Curling in England is now organised by the English Curling Association, founded in 1971 by the two provinces, the First English and the London, each of which has eight clubs. It is hoped that the game will be given a boost by the building of a projected ice rink complex in Manchester.

The establishment of a leisure complex at Deeside in North Wales resulted in the establishment of a Welsh Curling Association in 1974, the members of which make up for their fewness with their keenness.

15

Youth

In bygone ages, when youth was expected to be seen and little else, it was not too surprising that there was little scope for the participation of youngsters in the game.

The clubs which made provision for the training and encouragement of youth in the skills of the game were few in number: the commonest method of learning was by absorption, and not instruction. (The ungainly, inefficient deliveries one sees every day in every Scottish ice rink show that absorption is still the main Scottish method!)

There were, however, exceptions to the general rule. Dunfermline Curling Club included in their list of office bearers for publication in the *Annual* of the Grand Club for 1842 a 'Professor of Curling'. The Grand Club's secretary having declined to include this functionary, the secretary of the Dunfermline curlers wrote to him as follows, and recorded his letter in the minute book: 'I shall feel much obliged by your causing an asterisk being placed at the word Professor . . . and inserting the following remarks as a footnote in the Annual . . . *In diverging from a regulation of the G.C.C.C. it may be proper to state, that our Professor holds no sinecure office, his duties being the instructing and superintending the play of our young members; it may interest keen curlers to know, that he has been sixty three years an eminent and keen keen curler, and though numbering eighty one winters is still an active hale old gentleman.' Despite this special pleading the *Annual* was published without Dunfermline's professor.

Sanquhar formed a 'corps de reserve,' presided over by an experienced officer, and boys' bonspiels were played between the parishes of Sanquhar, Kirkconnel and New Cumnock in the early nineteenth century.

In Kilmarnock, too, there existed, from the late 1820s, a club whose members were exclusively young men. The Kilmarnock correspondent of Cairnie's *Essay*, at page 75, describes it thus: 'We may not pass unnoticed, of comparatively recent origin though it be, the Morning Star Club — a school for training the youth of our town at once to the habits of early rising, and the mysteries of the curling craft. Their hour of assembly is seven in the morning; and, foul or fair, there is commonly a respectable muster. At eight, they partake of coffee, and enjoy the sport till ten, when they return to business, that their seniors may take their place at "auld Scotia's manly game". The existence of such a club, at such hours, with such refreshments, is ample evidence, that the olden fire of enthusiasm for the game, is neither becoming dim in the breasts of the rising generation, nor in need of the stimulus of "strong drink", to keep it alive "in the morning early", even although it should be that

> "Cauld blaws the wind frae north to south,
> And drift is driving sairly." '

At Wanlockhead, the lead mining village situated high in the Dumfriesshire hills, there was formally instituted in 1883 the Wanlockhead School Curling Club, though the schoolboys had played for forty years before then for a pewter medal commemorating the visit to Scotland of Queen Victoria and Prince Albert in 1842. The instigator of the club was the village schoolmaster, John Edmond, who referred in a poem to the boys' use of wooden stones.

> We've seen wee *callens*[1] 'fore the doors
> Their *wudden ice-stanes*[2] fling;
> The same *tee totums*[3], men grown, place
> Three stane stanes in the ring.

---

1 boys
2 wooden curling stones
3 wee lads

156

It was not until 1929 that a competition specifically designed for younger curlers was instituted in Scotland. A handsome silver trophy was donated by T. B. Murray of Biggar (President of the Royal Club in 1936-7) for this national competition for curlers under 25 years of age. The competition languished, however, after only a few years. In 1959 Edinburgh Ice Rink Curling Club, who had inherited the trophy, presented it to the Royal Club and it reverted to its former purpose as the national junior trophy. The Murray Trophy is now keenly fought for among growing numbers of young curlers under the age of 21.

Two interrelated factors have contributed to the growth of junior curling in Scotland. In the early 1950s school curling began in Glasgow; in the 1960s Edinburgh and Perth followed suit; and the growth of new ice rinks has spawned many Young Curlers' Clubs. The phenomenal popularity of curling amongst the youngsters of Stranraer resulted in the success of Andrew McQuistin's rink at the 1980 Uniroyal World Junior Curling Championship at Kitchener, Ontario, and of Peter Wilson's at Megève in 1981.

In Canada the possibilities for children's curling were much greater. Children did not need to spend money to emulate their seniors. A constant supply of ice in each back yard or open space gave rise to 'jam can' matches in which large tin cans, filled with concrete, took the place of genuine stones. It was not long before the jam can curlers were formed into school leagues.

Although the numbers playing the game in the newer curling countries were comparatively small, there was sufficient enthusiasm for young curlers to take up the game. There can be little doubt that the Canadian sliding delivery and noisy cornbroom attracted many who had hitherto thought of curling as a game for old men. Proper coaching in the European countries produced many teams of first-class technique. In fact, at the Silver Broom at Bern in 1974 the representatives of Norway were a rink of diminutive schoolboys. The contrast in size between Sjur Loen, the 16-year-old Norwegian skip and 'genial giant' Hec Gervais, of Canada, gave the photographers a field day.

With so many youngsters playing the game on both sides of the Atlantic it was natural that they would wish their own version of the world championship. At the East York Ice Rink in Toronto in 1975 this wish materialised. Young curlers from nine nations (Scotland, Norway, France, Sweden, Canada, the U.S.A., Switzerland, Germany and Italy) competed for the first time for the Uniroyal World Junior Curling Championship. Once again the results showed the vincibility of Canada, for in the final it was the Swedish rink, skipped by Jan Ullsten, who beat their Canadian opponents. In the three following years the Canadian favourites won, but in 1979 and 1980 it was the turn of the U.S.A. and Scotland respectively.

Since sponsorship has been assured until 1985, the Uniroyal seems certain to go from strength to strength.

16

The Ladies

'Ladies do not curl — on the ice,' wrote the Rev. John Kerr in 1890. He went on to demonstrate his male chauvinism by writing: 'The Rational Dress Association has not yet secured for them the freedom that is necessary to fling the channel-stane, and like Her Majesty at Scone, the majority find the curling-stones too heavy for their delicate arms.'

No doubt when Kerr wrote, a curling lady in Scotland was a rarity (and yet only five years later the first all-ladies club, Hercules Ladies, of Elie, Fife, was admitted a member of the Royal Club, without, it seems, a murmur, or even a raised eyebrow), but the scales must have fallen from his eyes when he captained the Scottish team in Canada in 1902-3, for on three occasions the Scottish curlers not only found examples of these *rarae aves*, lady curlers, but were soundly beaten by them, at Quebec, and at Montreal, by both the Ladies Montreal Curling Club and the St Lawrence Ladies' Curling Club. So much for the ladies' 'delicate arms'!

Kerr does recount, though, in a footnote, some anecdotes which, he says, are exceptions to the rule: 'About fifty years ago a ladies' bonspiel was played on Loch Ged in the parish of Keir, two rinks of the maidens of Capenoch against two rinks of the maidens of Waterside, with skips of acknowledged skill presiding over them. An enormous concourse of spectators assembled, and the sun in honour of the occasion shone out brightly upon the scene. The ice was bad, and, according to our informer, the maidens had to play the match "fetlock-deep in water;" but great skill was displayed on both sides, the curling-broom being handled as dexterously as the domestic one, and channel-stanes, which female arms are supposed to be unable to cope with, being whirled with all the ease of the distaff. After a keen contest the maidens of Capenoch were victorious by a single shot. In his History of Sanquhar Club (p. 46),

Mr Brown records a match between the wives of Sanquhar and Crawick Mill.'

'On 10th February 1841 the married ladies of Buittle challenged the unmarried, and the match came off at Loch-hill, twenty ladies a side, and a gentleman skipping each team. So novel a scene attracted such a crowd that the players were compelled to shift the rink several times. The game was carried out with the determination peculiar to the sex, and resulted in the defeat of the married party, who declared that there had been treachery in their camp. That they had some ground for their suspicion was proved by the fact that soon afterwards the skip of the married ladies was united to a young widow who had played on the unmarried side, and had cast sheep's eyes over the hog-score all the time of the match.'

To Kerr's 'exceptions' can be added two attractive sketches of ladies curling at Penicuik in 1847, done by Jemimah Wedderburn, who also painted the first Grand Match there; and Rule 3rd of the Peebles Club (24 December 1821) shows that ladies there had shown an interest in the game a generation before that: 'When Ladies come near the Rink and are disposed to play, the skips shall have the privilege of instructing them to handle the stones agreeable to the rules of the Game.'

The earliest recorded all-female match is to be found in the pages of *The Dumfries Weekly Journal* of 7 January, 1823, where a match at Sanquhar 'within these very few years' is noted in which 'the sides were pretty numerous, and composed exclusively of women — the wives against the lasses.' After the match the curleresses retired to a tavern: 'How the husbands relished this unusual display of masculine prowess, and convivial dispositions, on the part of their wives, need not be enquired into. A similar occurrence has not happened since.'

Kerr would undoubtedly have approved of the tone of the account of a subsequent all-ladies match, which was

Fig. 139 Surely the first picture of a lady skip. The Countess of Eglinton, 1860, on one of the ponds at Eglinton Castle. Note the initials and coronet on the stone, and the hair brush, which was usual at this time in central Ayrshire. Water colour sketch by A.A.A.

printed in the same newspaper in January, 1826: 'On Tuesday last, 28 blooming damsels met on Dalpeddar loch, in the parish of Sanquhar, to play a friendly *bonspiel*. They formed themselves into two rinks, and although wading up to the ancles in water, seemed to enter into the spirit of the game, and to contest it with as much intense anxiety as if the question that the losing party should all die *old maids* had depended upon the issue. At the conclusion of the game neither party became victors, the number of shots having been equal. Many individuals of the other sex were attracted to the

scene of action; and as the *ladies*, like true curlers, had resolved to adjourn to the toll-house, where a *het pint* had been ordered, they kindly invited the gentlemen to accompany them. It soon, however, became a matter of doubt if this was of sufficient potency to counteract the bad effects resulting from wet feet, and as *tea* could not be expected to prove more efficacious, our heroines resorted to whisky toddy, and through its inspiration, and owing perhaps to some remains of dampness still adhering to their shoes, a dance was ultimately proposed, in order to put all matters into proper sorts;

Fig. 140   Lady Egidia Montgomerie, from the same group of water colour sketches.

and the ball was kept up with great vigour until far into "the wee short hours o' the morning". It may be true that there is no good reason why females should not have their hours of recreation as well as men, but it seems advisable that these recreations which they do engage in should be of a character befitting their sex. Ice playing is certainly not a game of this description — it has nothing *feminine* pertaining to it either in theory or practice. If, therefore, prudence and propriety are to be consulted, the fair maidens of the lower end of Sanquhar parish will not again resort to the same expedient for obtaining a day's relaxation and enjoyment.'

The first occasions on which ladies are shown playing in purely ladies' matches occur in 1859 and 1860. They are recorded in a number of sketches preserved in a scrap book belonging to the Dowager Countess of Eglinton. The 13th Earl of Eglinton (1812-1861) was a keen sportsman who indulged in all manner of sporting activities but was particularly fond of curling. In the policies of his castle at Eglinton, Kilwinning, Ayrshire, he had no fewer than four artificial ponds, three of which are depicted in the sketches. In one, his countess is skipping a rink, which includes their daughter Lady Egidia Montgomerie. (See fig. 140). In another the ladies are

Fig. 141 A group of ladies on Eglinton ice, 1859. Water colour sketch.

sweeping a pavement rink, preparatory to play, in a manner that suggests that brushes were not too familiar implements in their 'delicate' hands. (See fig. 66).

That these games were not isolated occurrences is shown by the following portion of an account in the *Ayr Advertiser* of the contest for the Eglinton Jug in 1864/5: 'Nor was Lady Eglinton forgotten in these cheers; for whilst this game had been going on, her ladyship too had been curling, having brought her own rink and curling stones with her — beautiful pieces of workmanship, of about 15 lbs each. Besides herself, there were Lady Egidia Montgomerie, Miss Montgomerie of Annick Lodge, and Miss Noaker. She was opposed by Mrs Craufurd, yr. of Craufurdland, and three Master Fairlies of Coodham. This game was an object of great attraction, from the picturesque dresses of the ladies and the dazzling colour of their brooms, which were painted in the most brilliant hues; but, alas! the pitiless storm soon drove the fair curlers from the Loch.'

The Ladies' Branch of the Royal Montreal Curling Club, whose members confounded John Kerr in 1903, had been formed in 1894 under the title of 'The Ladies' Montreal Curling Club.' In the first year the club had 25 members.

When the ladies did not, or were not permitted, to curl, they were not, according to the *Ayr Advertiser,* forgotten:

'4 Feb. 1830

AIR CURLING CLUB BALL
"When snaw lies white on ilka knowe,
The ice stane and the guid broom cowe
Can warm us like a bleezin' lowe".

The long continuance of the frost has afforded to the lovers of the manly game of curling in the west country a vast deal of amusement this season; and the members of the Air Club resolved, at a recent meeting, that, while they were enjoying themselves in many a well-contested *bonspiel* the ladies should not be forgotten. Accordingly,

Fig. 142   A lady tries her hand at throwing a stone at Rozelle, Ayr, ca. 1895.

they gave a splendid Ball in the County rooms, on Friday evening last, to a party including themselves of about two hundred, amongst whom were many names of "high degree," and many ladies "bright and fair". The floor of the ballroom was chalked off in regularly formed rinks, with tees and hogscores, and, over the door opposite that by which the party entered were placed two curling stones. — The members of the club mostly wore a sprig of "the guid broom cowe," with a roseate ribbon on their breasts; and, in many instances, the ladies did the club the honour of displaying the same characteristic emblem of the national game amongst their adornments.'

Not to be outdone, the Kilmarnock curlers held a ball the next year: 'The room was very tastefully decorated. At each end were placed several curling stones with immense broom *kowes* covering them with their ample umbrage. The floors were chalked into rinks, with colleys, tees, rings, stones, and players. Several of the figures, both of the curlers and skaters, were happily hit off; and the anxious or triumphant attitudes of some of the former created much merriment among the fair dames.'

From the beginning of the twentieth century, and particularly since the institution of indoor artificial ice, the numbers of women curling have continually increased. The ladies are now a firmly established, and important, part of the curling scene: were it not for the ladies, who fill the ice during the day when most of the men are at work, it is clear that many an ice rink and many a curling club would find itself in financial difficulties. In most curling countries there are now national ladies', and, indeed, national mixed, championships.

17

The Silver Broom

The most prestigious trophy in the curling world is undoubtedly the Air Canada Silver Broom, played for each March at the annual World Curling Championship by the champion rinks of ten countries.

In only twenty years this event has grown from an annual, and unequal, tussle between the champion rinks of Canada and Scotland, to an event of truly international dimensions. Wherever curling is played the best rinks keep their sights on a place in the Silver Broom.

The beginnings of the competition were modest. In 1959 Robin Welsh, Secretary of the Royal Club, put in print the idea of initiating a competition between the champion rinks of Scotland and Canada. Thitherto, international competition between the countries had been restricted to periodic curling tours, which were social rather than competitive. The idea immediately struck a chord with Jock Waugh, a member of the Scotch Whisky Association. When he put the suggestion to the Association, they readily responded, and presented the Scotch Cup.

Having won the Brier in Quebec in 1959, Ernie Richardson and his rink travelled to Ayr, Perth, Falkirk, and Edinburgh to play the rink skipped by Bobby Young of Airth. The Richardsons' 5-0 victory in the series heralded the beginning of a new era in Scottish curling. The Scots and their drawing game could not withstand the onslaught of the accurate, hard-hitting, long-sliding Canadians. Perhaps symbolic of the difference between the old world and the new was the fact that the Scots skip still played off the crampit. The older, more conservative Scots were aghast at the Canadian style of play, though they had to admire their shot-making skill, particularly when they switched, as occasion demanded, to the drawing game, and still out-curled the Scots. The younger curlers saw in this exhibition of top-flight Canadian curling the direction in which the future of the competitive game lay.

The original plan did not envisage a large contest among all the curling nations of the world, but the idea behind it, that it should be the *champion* rinks of the participating countries that should compete, was of great importance: this was the germ from which developed the great competition we have today.

It was not long before the original limits were broken: in 1961 the U.S.A. was added to the list of competitors, and in the following year Sweden joined as well. The European rinks, hitherto used to playing the drawing game, were no match for the North Americans. Ernie Richardson and his family rink, from Regina, who played in four Scotch cups between 1959 and 1963, lost only one game in that period. Their take-out precision, and sliding delivery, overwhelmed the Scots and the Swedes; but both countries were not slow to learn and in 1963 Chuck Hay and his young Perth rink surprised their compatriots by adopting for the first time a Canadian running style of play.

1964 marked a new chapter in the history of the Scotch Cup: two more European nations, Switzerland and Norway, entered the competition, and, for the first time, the event took place outwith Scotland, in Calgary. That the young Scots skip, Alec Torrance (Hamilton), took Lyall Dagg (Vancouver) to an extra end before falling in the final, seemed to show that the Canadian stranglehold was loosening. In Perth next year, to the jubilant acclaim of the curling world, a non-Canadian rink, skipped by Bud Somerville, won the event for the first time. At Vancouver in 1966 Ron Northcott won back the trophy that most Canadians regarded as their own.

1967 was another important milestone. In that year was seen the first all-European final. In order to get there Sweden had vanquished the U.S.A. in one semi-final, and Chuck Hay, playing in his home rink of Perth, had routed Canada by 8 shots to 5. Hay returned the same score against Woods of Sweden to win the title.

Fig. 143   The Scotch Cup, Scotland, 1959. The winning rink, Canada. Left to right, Wes Richardson (1), Garnet Richardson (2), Arnold Richardson (3), and Ernie Richardson (skip). Ernie's rink won again in 1960, 1962, and 1963.

By this time the complement of competing nations had risen to eight by the addition of France in 1965 and Germany in 1967. Canada had twice failed to win the competition, and Canadian curlers had begun to regard the world championship less as a pleasant postlude to the Brier and more as a serious competition, victory in which would have to be fought for.

At this stage the Scotch Whisky Association, perhaps feeling that the competition they had begat was growing, cuckoo-like, uncomfortably large, announced to an astounded Royal Club that they were giving up the sponsorship.

Some months of anguished searching by the Royal Club produced a new sponsor: on 15th January 1968 the Royal Club and Air Canada announced simultaneously on their respective sides of the Atlantic that Air

Canada would sponsor the world championship under a new title and for a new trophy, the Air Canada Silver Broom.

It was fortunate that an organisation which daily spans the Atlantic with its jet planes should undertake the support of a competition which had done so much to strengthen sporting ties across the same ocean. In fact, the concept of a world curling championship was really a product of the age of air travel. It must be remembered that all curlers are amateurs with a living to earn. It is important therefore that they should be able to travel to the world event in the shortest possible time. Who better than an airline to solve the logistical problems of transporting ten rinks from different countries, cheaply and swiftly, to the championship?

Since 1968 Air Canada has sponsored the competition

Fig. 144   The Scotch Cup, Vancouver, Canada, 1966. The winning rink, Canada. Top to bottom, Fred Storey (1), Bernie Sparkes (2), George Fink (3), Ron Northcott (skip).

Fig. 145   The Scotch Cup, Scotland, 1967. The winning rink, Scotland. Left to right, John Bryden (3), Alan Glen (2), David Howie (1), Chuck Hay (skip).

in various ways. The choice of venue has always been a matter for Air Canada and the Royal Caledonian Curling Club.

The actual arrangements for the competition are made by a local committee in consultation with representatives of Air Canada. The local committee will often decide on a local or national theme. For instance, when the Silver Broom returned in 1975 to Perth in Scotland, the theme chosen was the history of the game in its homeland, and a comprehensive historical exhibition was mounted by the Royal Club in Perth Museum and Art Gallery; and Chuck Hay, Scotch Cup Winner of 1967, to open the proceedings, threw the first stone, which on this occasion could be none other than the massive 119 lb Jubilee Stone; and Chuck and his 1967 rink, resplendent in the old red, blue, and tartan uniforms of Dunkeld Curling Club, swept the stone to the tee with historic silver-mounted brooms. (Chuck afterwards confessed that lest

the ice were damaged by the gigantic stone, he and his rink had fixed a plastic sole on it!)

Spectator interest, particularly among North Americans, runs high, and Air Canada are also responsible for transporting spectators to and fro across the 'Pond', as they call the Atlantic. As far as the participants are concerned, Air Canada provides their transportation *gratis* and, in addition, allows them expenses to cover board and lodgings during the competition. The idea is that no curler should be out of pocket, nor should he profit by his participation.

Since Air Canada has taken over, the competition has grown in popularity, both with players and spectators, and in scope. Denmark and Italy became participants in 1973.

The format has always been a round robin, in which each team plays every other team once. Thereafter the arrangements have differed: at some Brooms the winner

Fig. 146   Air Canada Silver Broom, Perth, Scotland, 1969. Winning rink, Canada. Left to right, Fred Storey (1), Bernie Sparkes (2), Dave Gerlach (3), Ron Northcott (skip). The new trophy is clearly seen in this picture.

of the round robin became one of the finalists, and the rinks placed second and third played a semi-final to determine the other; in other Brooms the top four rinks after the round robin were the semi-finalists, top playing fourth, and second playing third.

As far as European curling is concerned, the Scotch Cup/Silver Broom series of World Championships has given a great impetus to the game. Not only has the World Championship been played in Europe: at Perth, Scotland, in 1969 and 1975; at Megève, France, in 1971; at Garmisch-Parten Kirchen, Germany, in 1972; at Bern, Switzerland, in 1974 and 1979; and at Karlstad, Sweden, in 1977 — and the curlers thereby been enabled to see top-quality curling on their side of the Atlantic — but the results achieved by European rinks have spurred on young curlers to emulate their successful

compatriots. The result has been an explosion of interest in curling in countries such as Switzerland and Sweden, particularly among young people, and it is the Canadian style of play, the take out game, that they have adopted.

The most remarkable feature of the Silver Broom series since 1972 has been the eclipse of Canada. The improvement in European standards has not only meant that the competition is much more open, but has resulted in Canada's failure to win the Broom since 1972 except in 1980. The U.S.A. has produced four winning rinks, Sweden and Switzerland two each and Norway one. The success of Norway is remarkable. The curling population of the country is tiny and yet Kristian Sorum and his rink, runners up in Winnipeg in 1978, were winners in Bern in 1979.

The spectacular European results since 1972 have not

Fig. 147 Air Canada Silver Broom, Megève, France, 1971. Winning rink, Canada. Left to right, Rod Hunter (3), Jim Pettapiece (2), Bryan Wood (1), Don Duguid (skip).

Fig. 148 Air Canada Silver Broom, Garmisch-Partenkirchen, Germany, 1972. Winning rink, Canada. Left to right, John Hanesiak (2), Pat Hailley (1), Orest Meleschuck (skip).

Fig. 149   Air Canada Silver Broom, Regina, Canada, 1973. Winning rink, Sweden. Left to right, Kjell Oscarius (skip), Bengt Oscarius (3), Boa Carlman (1), Tom Schaeffer (2). The first continental rink to win.

happened by chance. A policy decision was taken by Air Canada in 1968 that they would assist the emerging curling nations as far as possible. They offered free transport to eminent Canadian curling coaches to any country which requested their assistance. The Swedes, the Swiss and the Norwegians availed themselves of this offer and were coached by Ray Turnbull, Wally Ursuliak, Warren Hansen, and Don Duguid.

Thus have the newer European curling nations been enabled to adopt the game-winning style of play of Canada; all youngsters, and others, taking up the game are taught the basics of a good sliding delivery and the strategy of the take out game. In Scotland, where the game had evolved in depth in a different direction over many generations, there were problems: large numbers of older curlers were hostile to the Canadian game and chauvinistically resented the idea that Canada had anything to teach them about their own game. The lesson has been learnt, however, and Chuck Hay has been appointed National Coach, by the Royal Club, with the result that modern ideas on the game are being imparted under his direction throughout the country.

M

LIST OF WORLD CHAMPIONS

SCOTCH CUP

Year	Played In	Champion	Skip	Third	Second	Lead	Won-Lost
1959	Scotland	Canada	Ernie Richardson	Arnold Richardson	Garnet Richardson	Wes Richardson	5-0
1960	Scotland	Canada	Ernie Richardson	Arnold Richardson	Garnet Richardson	Wes Richardson	5-0
1961	Scotland	Canada	Hector Gervais	Ray Werner	Vic Raymer	Wally Ursuliak	4-2
1962	Scotland	Canada	Ernie Richardson	Arnold Richardson	Garnet Richardson	Wes Richardson	6-0
1963	Scotland	Canada	Ernie Richardson	Arnold Richardson	Garnet Richardson	Mel Perry	5-1
1964	Galgary	Canada	Lyall Dagg	Leo Hebert	Fred Britton	Barry Naimark	7-0
1965	Scotland	U.S.A.	Bud Sommerville	Bill Strum	Al Gagne	Tom Wright	6-1
1966	Vancouver	Canada	Ron Northcott	George Fink	Bernie Sparkes	Fred Storey	8-0
1967	Scotland	Scotland	Chuck Hay	John Bryden	Alan Glen	David Howie	7-2

AIR CANADA SILVER BROOM

Year	Played In	Champion	Skip	Third	Second	Lead	Won-Lost
1968	Pte. Claire	Canada	Ron Northcott	Jimmy Shields	Bernie Sparkes	Fred Storey	7-1
1969	Perth	Canada	Ron Northcott	Dave Gerlach	Bernie Sparkes	Fred Storey	7-1
1970	Utica	Canada	Don Duguid	Rod Hunter	Jim Pettapiece	Bryan Wood	8-0
1971	Megève	Canada	Don Duguid	Rod Hunter	Jim Pettapiece	Bryan Wood	9-0
1972	Garmisch Partenkirchen	Canada	Orest Meleschuk	Dave Romano	John Hanesiak	Pat Hailley	9-0
1973	Regina	Sweden	Kjell Oscarius	Bengt Oscarius	Tom Schaeffer	Boa Carlman	9-2
1974	Bern	U.S.A.	Bud Somerville	Bob Nichols	Bill Strum	Tom Locken	8-3
1975	Perth	Switzerland	Otto Danieli	Roland Schneider	Rolf Gautschi	Ueli Mülli	8-3
1976	Duluth	U.S.A.	Bruce Roberts	Joe Roberts	Gary Kleffman	Jerry Scott	10-1
1977	Karlstad	Sweden	Ragnar Kamp	Hakan Rudstrom	Björn Rudstrom	Christer Martensson	10-1
1978	Winnipeg	U.S.A.	Bob Nichols	Bill Strum	Tom Locken	Bob Christman	9-2
1979	Bern	Norway	Kristian Sørum	Morten Sørum	Eigil Ramsfjell	Gunnar Meland	
1980	Moncton	Canada	Rick Folk	Ron Mills	Tom Wilson	Jim Wilson	10-1
1981	London, Ontario	Switzerland	Jürg Tanner	Jürg Hornisberger	Patrick Loertscher	Franz Tanner	8-3

Fig. 150   Air Canada Silver Broom, Bern, Switzerland, 1974. Winning rink, U.S.A. Left to right, Bob Nichols (3), Tom Locken (1), Bill Strum (2), Bud Somerville (skip). The performance of the Swiss rink contributed greatly to the increase in popularity of the game in Switzerland.

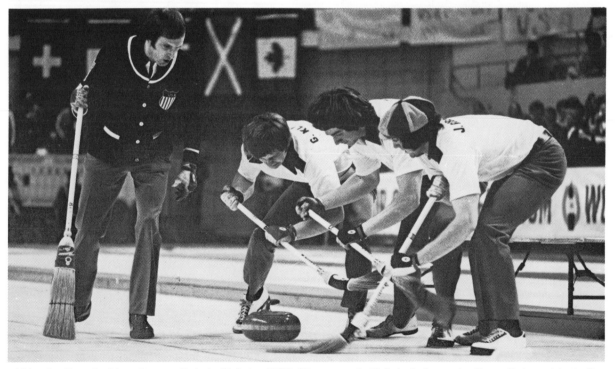

Fig. 151   Air Canada Silver Broom, Duluth, U.S.A., 1976. Winning rink, U.S.A. Left to right, Bruce Roberts (skip), Gary Kleffman (2), Jerry Scott (1), Joe Roberts (3).

Fig. 152   Air Canada Silver Broom, Karlstad, Sweden, 1977. Winning rink, Sweden. Left to right, Bjorn Rudstrom (2), Christer Martensson (1), Ragnar Kamp (skip).

Fig. 153   Air Canada Silver Broom, Bern, Switzerland, 1979. Winning rink, Norway. Left to right, Kristian Sørum (skip), Eigil Ramsfjell (2), Gunnar Meland (1), Morten Sørum (3).

Fig. 154   Air Canada Silver Broom, Moncton, Canada, 1980. Winning rink, Canada. Left to right, Jim Wilson (1), Rick Folk (skip), Tom Wilson (2), Ron Mills (3).

Fig. 155 Air Canada Silver Broom, Winnipeg, Canada, 1978. This picture gives a good impression of the pageantry which accompanies the opening of the World Championship. The great press interest can be judged from the press area in the foreground.

18
International Curling

Although the curling clubs of Ardrossan and Largs in Ayrshire had what might be termed international matches against Belfast in Ireland in the mid 1850s, the first truly international games were the one between Toronto and Buffalo in 1864, already alluded to; and the Canada-versus-U.S.A. series which followed it. Indeed for many years this series of matches provided the only international competition in the game.

When, at an annual meeting of the Royal Club in 1892, the suggestion was made, by some English curlers, of an international match between England and Scotland, the proposal was eagerly taken up by the Scots, who were no doubt keen to engage with the Auld Enemy on terms, and with weapons, which seemed clearly to favour them. Arrangements were enthusiastically entered into and on 29th January 1895 the first

Fig. 156   Scots v Rideau Hall Club, Ottawa, 1912, during the Canadian Tour of that year.

Fig. 157 Chamonix, France, 1924. The British curling team, led by their captain, Col. T.S.G.H. Robertson Aikman, at the opening of the Winter Olympic Games.

Scots-English match took place on Talkin Tarn at Brampton, near Carlisle, with 69 rinks on each side. The result was almost a foregone conclusion though the margin of the Scottish victory, 275 shots, was by no means the resounding triumph that the Scots had hoped for. Nonetheless it did enable one Scots participant to describe it as 'avenging Flodden'!

Only three further outdoor internationals have taken place, two at Lochmaben, and the last at Craigielands near Moffat in 1912. Since 1908 the International Match has been a douce indoor affair, more of a social event than a test of curling, played by small numbers of rinks at Glasgow, Manchester, Edinburgh and London.

Real international competition lay across the Atlantic Ocean. For half a century or more the Scots had been reading in their *Annuals* and elsewhere of the curling paradise that awaited them in the New World, but Canadian invitations to the Royal Club to send a curling team there and taste the pleasures at first hand met with no response. The distance, and the expense, were too great for a mere game. From the time, however, of Queen Victoria's Diamond Jubilee in 1898 other feelings began to motivate the Scots; patriotism overcame their

parsimony, and in the years following the turn of the century a patriotic fervour gripped the Royal Club. A curling tour of Canada was seen in terms of binding together the Empire, of strengthening the tie between the mother country and her North American colony. Had not the colonies rejoiced with us at the Diamond Jubilee, sorrowed with us on the death of the Queen; and stood by us and helped us in South Africa?

An invitation from the Canadian Branch was delivered personally by Dr Barclay from Montreal at a meeting of the Royal Club in 1901; pressure in the form of letters in the Scottish press was added; and the Royal Club, moved largely by the eloquence of the Rev. John Kerr, decided, at long last, to promote a Scottish tour to Canada and the U.S.

A team of 26 curlers, under the captaincy of John Kerr, set sail from Liverpool on 19 December 1902. The tour was a great success; the Scots were fêted wherever they went, and banquet after banquet followed bonspiel after bonspiel.

The tour, which lasted from 20th December 1902 until 28th February 1903, was remarkable for its length. Beginning at Halifax, it took the Scots about 5000 miles to St John, Quebec, Montreal, Ottawa, Peterborough, Toronto, Hamilton, Guelph, Stratford, London, Windsor, Winnipeg, Minneapolis, St Paul, Chicago, Utica and New York. The team played 99 set games, and won 47, lost 49 and peeled 3. There is no doubt that the Scots learned a lot, from the Canadians particularly, but it was from the point of view of the brotherhood of the rink that the tour was most successful.

A curling tour of Scotland by Canadians was obviously a much more precarious project from considerations of weather, but in 1907 Scotland's first indoor ice rink had been opened at Crossmyloof, Glasgow, guaranteeing ice; in 1909 the Canadians reciprocated with their first tour of Scotland. The invitation from the Royal Club specified two rinks from the Canadian Branch, two from the Ontario, two from the Manitoba and one from the Nova Scotia. 'When the message was flashed back that Canada cordially accepted the invitation, and that a team would be got ready to visit the mother country in the ensuing winter, the news was received with unmingled delight, and the curlers of Scotland were on the *qui vive*, the general expectation being that the visit of the Canadians to Scotland, like that of the Scots to Canada, would not only still further strengthen the bond of friendship between those who were kinsmen, but that the curlers of Scotland, once they had the Canadians over here, where they were figuratively on their native heath, would handsomely avenge any defeats sustained by the Scots on their visit to Canada, which by some strange system of perversion had been very much exaggerated.' (*Annual* for 1909-10, page cxxiii)

The plans prepared for the Canadian visitors provided for as much outdoor curling as possible but, taking account of the Scottish climate, realistically scheduled most of the games for the only ice rink in the country. Glasgow was thus the main centre for the tour, but the Canadians were transported to all quarters of the kingdom between 16th January and 23rd February 1909. At every stop, and at the end of each day's play, they were feasted and banqueted.

The planners had been wise to make the Crossmyloof arrangements, for only in the North did natural ice await them. All but three of their matches were played on Crossmyloof's artificial ice. The Canadians lost only 3 out of 26 matches: they won even on the natural ice at Moy against Inverness Province; at West Cults, Aberdeenshire, against the North East Province; and on the royal ponds at Balmoral. The Scots suffered crushing defeats in all the test matches for the Cup which had just been presented by Lord Strathcona. At the conclusion of the match at Balmoral, which was played in falling snow, C. W. Macpherson, an engineer of Dawson City, Manitoba,

remarked: 'We have played you indoors and out of doors in all conditions — what we want now to complete the tour is "to play you in mud".'

Since 1910 tours have alternated between Canada and Scotland, the present pattern being a tour of each country every alternate five years. Though the original idea behind such tours may have been international competition, the strenuous social demands made upon a tourist rendered this impossible. One Scottish curler after the 1902-3 tour suggested that the Scots might have done better had they sent out two teams — one for curling and one for banqueting.

The curling tour provides a chance for a keen curler to play abroad but the main purpose of a tour is to strengthen the ties of friendship between curling countries. The demands upon a tourist's constitution have always been immense; two games a day for weeks on end, constant travel, and little sleep can take their toll, not to mention the lavish hospitality which is such a feature of curling tours.

It appears to me that curling organisers try to do too much. What is the point of flying a Scottish team from Calgary to Vancouver at 7 a.m., having them play two games and flying them out again at 5.30 a.m. next day? What is the point of making a team of German tourists in Scotland play at every ice rink in the country, if the poor tourists can never spend more than one night in the same bed? No doubt they meet many curlers, but how many do they really get to know? Would it not be more sensible to station the visiting team in one place for several days and bring the local curlers to them? In that way the exigencies of curling travel and hospitality would be considerably reduced.

It was natural that the first international curling links to be forged should be between Scotland and Canada, but European ties were soon established also. In 1923 the Royal Club was host to a small official team from Sweden, which played a variety of opponents in Edinburgh Ice Rink. The Scots reciprocated in 1929, and since then tours have taken place from time to time. France, Germany and Switzerland have since the Second World War been added to the list. The U.S.A. has been hived off, as a separate New World tour.

Over the years the increasing part played in curling by the ladies has resulted in ladies' tours, for example, of Scotland by Canada, the U.S.A., Switzerland and Sweden; and tours of the New World are a well-established feature of the Scottish ladies' scene.

The most promising development in international curling tours has been made in recent years independently of the Royal Club. The Rotary movement

Fig. 158   The curling rink at the Winter Olympic Games, Chamonix, France, 1924.

is strong on both sides of the Atlantic, and in recent years Rotarians have made tours of limited duration and geographical compass.

In Scotland curling clubs are grouped under the Royal Club's constitution into Provinces, which are more, or less, active in promoting curling activities. The Twelfth Province, which comprises Renfrewshire and part of north Ayrshire, has for some years been one of the more active provinces. During an official tour of Scotland by a German team in 1974 the idea occurred to the Twelfth Province office bearers of organising a tour by the province in Germany. The plan was that a male team of twenty members should take themselves to Germany at their own expense, that they should be responsible for their own board and lodging, and that the German curlers should lay on curling and entertainment. In the event two wives went as playing members of the team. They curled at Garmisch-Partenkirchen, Oberstorf, München, and Iserlohn in the Düsseldorf area. In each place they stayed for at least two nights. So successful was the tour that arrangements were immediately put in hand for a tour to Denmark and Sweden which took place in 1977. In 1978 a mixed Danish team visited Scotland as guests of the Twelfth Province, and they curled at Crossmyloof, Hamilton, and Edinburgh. They were stationed in one hotel throughout the tour, and

were taken to the various ice rinks by bus. Since one of the oldest clubs in the province, Lochwinnoch, was holding its 150th anniversary celebrations, it was natural that the Danes should be invited to take part. By 1979 the Province were fully fledged foreign tourists, and they flew in that year to Canada with a mixed team of 22 to play at Perth, Ottawa, Toronto and Cambridge.

These tours have all been much less ambitious in scope than official Royal Club tours, and so long as the era of cheap air travel remains with us, it seems likely that such events will grow in popularity.

Apart from the earliest Scotch Cup series, there has not been an international match in the sense of the champion rink of one nation against the champions of another. There have, however, been opportunities for the champion rinks of Canada, Sweden, U.S.A. and Switzerland to be seen on Scottish ice apart from the Silver Broom, by virtue of invitations to compete in top quality competitions, and the rinks of Chuck Hay, Alec Torrance and Bill Muirhead from Scotland, and Ragnar Kamp and Kristian Sorum from Scandinavia have participated in the Curl Classic series sponsored by the Canadian Broadcasting Company; and in Scotland in recent years we have seen Otto Danieli and Peter Attinger from Switzerland; Kamp and Sørum; Bud Somerville and Scotty Baird from the U.S.A.; and Brier winners Jim Ursell, Orest Meleschuck, Harvey Mazinke and Doug Harrison, skipping Barry Fry's rink.

Such invitations would have been impossible in Scotland but for the growth of sponsored weekend invitation competitions such as the Perth Masters and the Edinburgh International. A considerable part of the sponsorship money has been wisely used to bring these foreign rinks to Scotland. Even those who abhor the very idea of sponsorship can scarcely deny that it is the presence of these foreign rinks that has at last encouraged both B.B.C. and Scottish Television to take some interest in curling, and to provide, albeit in tantalisingly brief programmes, coverage of the curler's favourite pastime.

That rinks of such calibre are prepared to travel such distance for a mere weekend's curling bespeaks not only their enjoyment of the game, but their realisation that the presence of champion rinks encourages spectator interest in the sport, and increases local enthusiasm. They are truly ambassadors for the game.

The Olympic Games have only once featured curling. In the Winter Olympics of 1924 at Chamonix in the French Alps, Great Britain sent a team, selected by the Royal Club, which emerged as world champions. The result is not surprising, since their only opponents were France and Sweden; Canada and the U.S.A. not being represented, and Switzerland having scratched at the last moment. The Scots, whose rink consisted of W.K. Jackson, Robin Welsh (father of the present Royal Club secretary), T.B. Murray and Lawrence Jackson, beat the Swedes by 38 shots to 7, and the French by 42 to 4 in games of 18 ends.

One reason for forming the International Curling Federation in 1966 was to create a body which could competently apply for the inclusion of curling in future Winter Olympics. One wonders whether the curling calendar is large enough to include not only the annual world championship, and the national championships which precede it, but also quadriennial Winter Olympics.

19

Trophies

In the earliest recorded matches the rinks battled more for honour, or perhaps for beef and greens and drink, than for prizes. Many a match was fought for charity, with the losers having to purchase a load of meal or coal for the poor of the winning parish. In fact the charitable tradition was observed in most parts where curling was played.

An interesting instance of this sort of challenge occurred in Ayrshire in 1830. The curlers of the various clubs in Kilmarnock, who had been curling 'almost every lawfull day' over a seven-week period, inserted the following advertisement in the *Ayr Advertiser*:

CHALLENGE

Sixty Curlers of the Town of Kilmarnock, offer to play, with two stones each, Sixty Curlers from any parish in the county of Air, for TWENTY SOVEREIGNS, to be expended for the benefit of the poor of the parish who gains the match. The ice to be chosen most central to the two parishes, and not more than fifteen miles distant from Kilmarnock, Address to the Curlers of Kilmarnock, care of Wm Rankine, Esq. Post-Office.

In order to give some idea of the value of the £20 involved in the challenge, regard may be had to the prices of various commodities printed in the newspaper on the same day. Eggs cost 8d. per dozen, cheese 6½d. per pound, butter 8d. per pound, and beef from 3d. to 6d. per pound. Each curler therefore stood to lose the price of 10 dozen eggs or from 13 to 27 pounds of beef.

The challenge was accepted by the curlers of Maybole, but the match never came off. It appears that the reason was a partial thaw followed by rain in Kilmarnock on the night before the match, 'and it now being very wet and apperiently going to be more rain', the Kilmarnockians thought it better to put off the match till another day. But the Maybole people did not agree, as the following humorous letter to the editor, published a week later, shows: 'SIR, — Were it not taking up too much room in your paper, I would tell the world through it, what a hoax I and almost the whole country-side have just suffered. The challenge of the Kilmarnock curlers, made through your last paper, was instantly accepted by the curlers of Maybole, and we were informed that yesterday at Lochsnipe the match was to be decided. So, away we

Fig. 159 Silver medal of Paisley United Curling Society, Renfrewshire, 1830. The large foot board used in this area is well depicted.

Fig. 160   Gold medal of Corstorphine Curling Club, Midlothian, 1830.

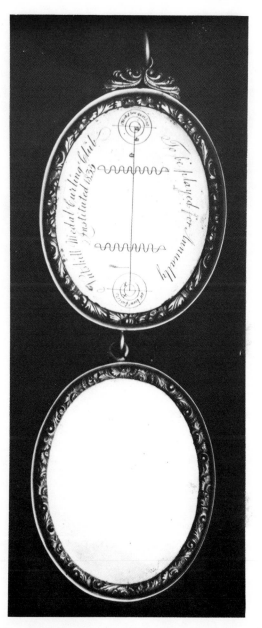

Fig. 161   Silver medal of Nitshill Curling Club, Renfrewshire, 1835. A most unusual medal, with a plan of the rink engraved upon it. Within the broughs are engraved 'All keen curlers' and 'two in and one guarding'.

set, in groups, to witness the grand bonspiel. Judges and lawyers, doctors and drapers, farmers and fiddlers, dandies and clowns, painters, pipers, and publicans, from every quarter were there, and the Maybole people were there too with their sovereigns in a bag, and their curling stones "Carrick for a man". But neither the Kilmarnock people — the public challengers — nor their money, were to be seen. Some inquiry should be made into the cause of this disappointment, and, should it be found that any of the Kilmarnock people have absconded with the money, the interest of the poor should be attended to. A reward should be offered for their detection, the advertisement beginning thus, "Whereas" etc. and running on in the usual strain of such notices. For myself, I intend to raise an action for reparation for my lost time, money and amusement — I am, etc.' Most

challenge matches, however, came off, and no doubt the poor of many a parish were grateful to the curlers for their public-spirited generosity.

The earliest form of trophy was the medal. Curiously, the two oldest extant medals appear to record victories rather than to be prizes. They both date from 1772 and are in the keeping of Coupar Angus and Kettins Curling Club. (See figs. 9 and 10.)

Fig. 162   Gold medal of Linlithgow Junior Curling Club, 1842. The curler on the reverse of the medal is a representation in low relief of the design that appeared until 1842 on the title page of *Annuals* of the Grand Club.

Fig. 163   Silver medal of Cambusnethan Curling Club, Lanarkshire, 1845.

Fig. 164   Silver medal of Corstorphine Curling Club, Midlothian, 1850.

The next oldest surviving medal is the Duddingston Society's gold medal for points. (See fig. 103.)

The next medal in point of date is one of considerable importance. Not only has it been played for continually since its manufacture, but it is the earliest prize medal to depict a curler at play, and on the reverse it contains a couplet which could not put the virtues of curling more succinctly:

> Simple, social, dextrous game,
> Source of pleasure, health and fame.

Moreover, it is recorded in the minutes of the Tarbolton club, whose property it is, that the purchase of the medal was one of the first acts of the newly founded club, and the price consumed more than half of the club's initial subscriptions in 1814. (See fig. 11.)

The next two surviving medals, Drum, 1820 (fig. 13), and Muirkirk, 1823 (fig. 12), provide a marked contrast in style. The Drum medal is an elegant gold oval with a fine engraving of a curler on the obverse, a prize suitable for sophisticated city people, for Drum was a country house, only five miles to the south of Edinburgh. The Muirkirk medal is a lively unsophisticated circular plate of silver, without even a rim, but the engraving is vigorous on front and back. Appropriately for an upland Ayrshire parish, there appears, below the engraving of a wee curler in the act of throwing his stone, a couplet adapted from a poem by the Ayrshire poet, Alexander Boswell:

Fig. 165   Silver medal of Airdrie Curling Society, Lanarkshire, 1850. The coat of arms of the burgh is engraved above a curling scene, which was also used in the medals in figs. 166 and 167. It was a Lanarkshire custom to attach to a trophy a small medallion or curling stone bearing the name of each year's winner.

Fig. 166   Silver medal of Straiton Curling Club, Ayrshire, 1855.

Fig. 167   Silver medal of Ardrossan Alma Curling Club, Ayrshire, 1855.

Fig. 168   Silver medal of Kirkintilloch Curling Club, 1854. The scene engraved on this medal takes its inspiration from Harvey's painting, *Curlers*, but the dress of the players and the shape of their stones show that it was meant to be a contemporary version.

> An ice stane and a guid broom cowe
> Will warm us like a bleezing lowe.

From the 1820s onwards medals survive in large numbers: some are simple discs with an inscription engraved on them, others have engravings of curlers at play, coats of arms, or curling objects on them. Sir George Harvey's painting of *Curlers* provided the design for numbers of medals, with each engraver adapting the basic design.

One particularly handsome group of medals deserves special mention, for mounted on the surface are miniature curling stones, variously made of silver or semi precious stone, placed between crossed besoms and a tee marker. The Coupar Angus and Kettins medal is the pride of this group. (See Plate 9.)

Such custom-made medals were no doubt costly; the Grand Club from its inception showed the way to a cheaper form, namely medals struck from dies, which

Fig. 169   Silver medal of Polmont and West Quarter Curling Club, Stirlingshire, 1862. The engraving shows in graphic form the much-vaunted boast of curlers that on the ice all men are equal. A brotherly handshake between tenant and laird. Obverse.

Fig. 170   Silver medal struck by Kirkwood of Edinburgh. This is an example of the 'off-the-peg' variety of medal which could be engraved for any purpose. This medal was given to the Stow curlers from their Musselburgh friends in 1891 to commemorate a memorable day on the ice.

they awarded as local and district medals. Very large numbers of these medals survive, but, in addition, medal makers, notably Kirkwoods of Edinburgh, provided a series of die-struck medals which could be bought 'off the peg' and engraved to suit the club's or the donor's requirements.

The curlers of Canada and the U.S.A. participated in the medal tradition at least from the beginning of the Grand/Royal Club, for district medals were awarded from their joining the Grand Club.

The medal tradition was fostered by the Grand National Curling Club of America. In 1869 Robert Gordon, the first patron of the club, presented a silver medal, now known as the Gordon Rink Medal, for which competition has been held annually. In 1870 Alexander Dalrymple presented two medals for competition between rinks in the eastern and western areas of the Grand Club: 'The Medal to be competed for annually by Members of the Club hailing from the North, against Members of the Club hailing from the South of Scotland.' And the border between north and south was fixed as the Forth and Clyde Canal.

Lord Dufferin, Governor General of Canada, who took up the game on his appointment, fostered the game by donating medals to every club in the Dominion for inter-club competition.

It was natural that curlers would use as trophies the reproduction of the object most characteristic of their game, namely the curling stone, just as the archers of old had competed for silver arrows, and the golfers for silver clubs.

Legend has it that King James IV of Scotland (1472-1513) gave a silver curling stone to be played for annually by the parishes in the Carse of Gowrie, as Sir Richard Broun (at page 62) reports. But John Kerr wittily puts Broun down by saying that without the silver stone there is no evidence to prove that James IV curled anywhere else than in Broun's imagination.

The earliest extant curling stone trophy bears the following inscription: 'This model of a Curling Stone, is presented by Mrs Howison Craufurd of Craufurdland, To the Curlers of Fenwick and Kilmarnock, as a trophy of Victory, to be won at a manly and innocent amusement.' (fig. 172). The stone, presented in 1828, was the object of keen competition until 1844 when, after a dispute, it became the property of the Fenwick curlers, and a new gold stone was given for competition among the clubs of Kilmarnock.

Leuchars in Fife also possessed an old silver snuff mull in the shape of a curling stone. Kettles, for the heating and holding of hot water for toddy, are also common.

Fig. 171A Silver medal of Dundonald Curling Club, Ayrshire, 1904. A fine contemporary scene in repoussé work. The medal was given by the son of Dr Alexander, who had been secretary of the club for 55 years. By 1904 the medal tradition was giving way to cups as trophies. Obverse.

Fig. 171B. Reverse of fig. 171A.

These are usually fashioned in the shape of curling stones, and are variously supported on wheeled carriages or a stand of crossed besoms.

The silver cup, or jug, or bowl, has become since the middle of the nineteenth century the commonest form of trophy in curling, as in most other sports. When the piece has been custom-made as a curling trophy, and enriched with engraved or repoussé work, the effect can be truly magnificent. One such jug was given to the curling clubs of the County of Ayr by the 13th Earl of Eglinton and Winton in 1851, and is still the most highly prized and most keenly fought trophy in Ayrshire.

Macdonald's Brier Trophy, surely the most hotly contested trophy in the world, is a good Canadian example of the cup form of trophy. A good Scottish example is the Scotch Cup, the forerunner of the Silver Broom. It is a simple silver quaich mounted on thistles, above a piece of Ailsa Craig Blue Hone, fashioned into the shape of the islet.

The other distinctive curling implement, the besom, has been utilised in some areas as a trophy. (Figs. 100, 101, and 102).

In the Atholl area the premier trophy was for many years the Duchess's Broom, given by the Duchess of Atholl in 1854 for annual competition. It is fitting that Air Canada should have chosen, as the trophy for the World Curling Championship that they have sponsored since 1968, a silver broom.

Fig. 172   Silver model of a curling stone, with jasper handle, Fenwick, Ayrshire, 1828. This appears to be the earliest surviving example of a trophy in the form of a curling stone. It bears the following quaint inscription: 'This Model of a Curling Stone, is presented by Mrs Howison Craufurd of Craufurdland To the Curlers of Fenwick and Kilmarnock, as a trophy of Victory, to be won at a manly & innocent amusement.'

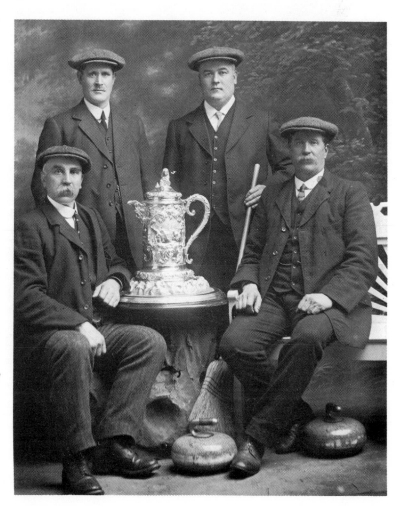

Fig. 173   The Eglinton Jug, given in 1851 by the 13th Earl of Eglinton to the curlers of Ayrshire for annual competition, and still the most highly prized trophy in the county. In Scotland the tradition is that the winning skip fills a trophy with whisky and passes it round the company in celebration. One winner informed the author that this trophy 'hauds fourteen bottle o' whisky!'

Fig. 174   Silver and crystal wine jug with engraved curling scene. Engraved: 'Glasgow Timber Trade Curling Club December 1881. To be won twice at the point game.'

Fig. 175 Detail of fig. 174.

Fig. 176 Further detail of fig. 174.

Fig. 177 The Scotch Cup, silver, 1959. This is the trophy given by the Scotch Whisky Association for competition between the champion rinks of Scotland and Canada. The cup, a traditional Scots quaich, is supported on thistles, and surmounts a piece of Blue Hone stone from Ailsa Craig, fashioned into the form of the island.

Fig. 178 Another modern silver trophy: The Haig Scottish Senior Curling Championship trophy.

Fig. 179 Directors' trophy, silver, Border Ice Rink, Kelso, Roxburghshire, 1967. A fine example of the silversmith's art in a modern idiom.

20

Après Curl

When a curling match was much more of an event than it is today, what more natural than that the curlers should repair to the nearest tavern and restore their energies with food and drink after the game? That this was the custom from early times can be inferred from Graeme's poem of 1771:

> The bonspeel o'er, hungry and cold, they hie
> To the next ale-house; where the game is play'd
> Again, and yet again, over the jug.

And from Fisher in 1810:

> and still the healthful sport goes on,
> till three huzzas declare the victor side;
> now off they go with appetite to dine, and drink,
> and spend in social glee the evening all . . .

Many a minute records a night spent in 'social glee' after the bonspiel. The Sanquhar Curling Society, whose minutes dating from 1774 are the second oldest in the world, generally played their games for dinner of beef and greens, and for drink; and this was a practice common throughout Scotland. Such a practice ensured a convivial evening after a day's sport.

The custom of dining after curling was carried across the Atlantic to Canada, for in the Rules and Regulations of the Montreal Club in 1807 we read:
'1st. The Club is to meet every Wednesday at 12 o'Clock to play till three . . .
2nd. The Club shall meet at Gillis' on every Wednesday fortnight, at 4 o'Clock, to dine on *Salt Beef & Greens*. The Clubs *Dinner & Wine* shall not exceed Seven Shillings and Sixpence a head . . .
6th. The Loosing Party of the day shall pay for a Bowl of *Whisky Toddy* to be placed in the middle of the Table, for those who may chuse it.'

Fig. 180   Wooden snuff mull, Mauchline, Ayrshire, 1835. The manufacture of wooden snuff and other boxes flourished in this small Ayrshire town in the early nineteenth century, as did curling: in 1845 there were, according to a correspondent in the *Ayr Advertiser*, no fewer than ten clubs.

Fig. 181 One of a pair of pottery toddy bowls, Delvine Curling Club, Perthshire, 1832. Inside and out the bowls are decorated with curling scenes in natural colours. The toddy bowl was an important piece of equipment for the revelry which followed bonspiels.

There we have it: a formal injunction upon all the members, not only to curl, but to socialise after the game; with an attempt to keep the socialising within bounds by providing an upper limit to the cost of food and drink.

The Montreal Club continued their socialising for at least 50 years. One of the club's most valued possessions is the handsome silver jug subscribed for in their jubilee year of 1857: 'the president shall take charge of the Jug during his term of office, and is at liberty to fill it as often as he pleases with anything except water, lemonade, tea, coffee, etc., etc. . . . .'

The Montreal limit of 7 shillings and 6 pence permitted pretty gluttonous affairs, if the menu of a dinner held by the Noddle Club at Largs on 10th December 1823 in the King's Arms Inn is any guide to Montreal prices. John

Cairnie of Curling Hall seems to have regarded this dinner as memorable, for not only has he printed an account of it in his *Essay on Curling* (at page 56), but he added the bill of fare in his own hand to the minute book: 'Bill 7/8½ each including supper. Bill of fare — Hare soup, Fryed whitings, a large Turbit, large Joint of corned beef, Roast Beef, Corned pork — 2 Tongues, 2 chickens, a large Goose, 4 grouse and vegetables — Dumpling pudding (custard), Jam Jellies etc — with 2 bottles of wine, drams, porter, Ale etc. The Dinner was excellent, and the party did not separate till ½ past 10 o'clock.'

Cairnie added a novelty to dining festivities at Largs. He encouraged 'what we call pic-nic dinners, where every Curler provides his own dish, and brings the drink he likes best. We, last season, had four of these pic-nic

Fig. 182   Tup's head snuff mull, Nitshill and Hurlet Curling Club, ca. 1876. A large communal snuff mull intended for use at a curling supper. The ivory mallet, the spike, rake and spoon are all part of the communal ritual of taking snuff. The lid of the snuff container is slightly open.

dinners, and the scene of festivity was on board of our cutter, lying high and dry upon her carriage, by the seaside.'

Most curling dinners, however, took place in the local inn or tavern, and at these dinners the corporate identity of the curling club was reinforced by the singing of songs in honour of the club, and often by the communal use of the few corporate possessions of the club, such as snuff mulls and toddy bowls.

Many clubs possessed snuff mulls that would be passed around the table while they dined. Three of the founder members of the Edinburgh club in 1841 gave to the club at its inception a handsome polished cowhorn snuff mull, mounted in silver and embellished with cut stones. Such mulls, made of cow and ram's horn, survive in appreciable numbers. One of the oldest and most unusual was given to the curlers of Broughton, Glenholm and Kilbucho in 1816 by the Rev. John Hamilton, the club's president from 1816 to 1854. It consists of a long curved goat's horn, 23 inches long, mounted in silver, with a polished agate in the lid and the following

inscription: 'The eager curlers manly play can make December's ice cold day, Seem genial, warm and mild as May.' Mr Hamilton was a fanatical curler who built his manse, in defiance of the heritors of the parish, on a site chosen by him because of its close proximity to the curling pond at Broughton: it is interesting that one of his earliest acts was to provide for the social aspects of the game by this gift.

Some snuff mulls are very ornate. The most elaborate and prestigious were fashioned out of a tup's head. Many such have fallen prey to moths and maggots, but one of the finest is still prized by the Royal Montreal Curling Club. Presented to the club in 1907 by the Scots curlers who had toured Canada in 1902-3, it is an eloquent tribute by the Scots to the oldest Canadian club.

Toddy, the mixture of whisky and hot water beloved by the early curlers, has given inspiration not only to curlers, but to curling poets and craftsmen. A curling poem was scarcely regarded as complete without a reference to the 'smoking toddy bowl'; and silver kettles, in the shape of curling stones, abound throughout

Scotland. Perhaps the finest toddy-inspired objects are a pair of bowls belonging to Delvine club. They are embellished inside and out with curling scenes painted in natural colours, along with some lines of poetry and a record of their donation to the club by John S.P. Muir Mackenzie in 1832.

Most club secretaries contented themselves with a bald record that the club had dined, on occasions adding that toasts had been drunk, and songs sung and the evening spent in convivial hilarity. On rarer occasions songs composed for the dinner were entered in the minute book.

It is rare that the real flavour of a nineteenth century curlers' dinner is captured on the written page and we are therefore fortunate that the minutes of Abdie club in Fife have been preserved. From the inception of the club in 1831 until 1849 the Secretary of the Abdie club was Mr George Dun, who records the doings of the curlers both on and off the ice in most elegant and humorous prose. A few examples will suffice to show the mischievous good humour that prevailed at Abdie dinners:

'Mr Pitcairn was with great applause fined in the sum of *twopence* for being on the Ice the previous day with an umbrella instead of a besom.'

'The next matter of business which came before the Meeting was the consideration of various delinquencies, faults, or foibles of the individual Members of the Club, which the Club as a body, hold themselves bound to take under their cognizance, and fine and punish as to them may seem meet. — The first case reported to the Meeting being a very serious one, occupied a good deal of time viz. That of Dr David Lyell on a recent occasion, in presence of witnesses now present, having shot at a Hare in her seat; This circumstance aggravated, by the fact of the Hare having been actually dead for some days previous, induced the Club to come to the resolution of fining Dr Lyell in the sum of One shilling, with the understanding that should ever a similar case come before the Club it should be treated with much less leniency.'

'The second ground of complaint laid before the meeting was the case of Charles Hill Esq. of Luthrie, *viz.* that of his Lady having presented him with a son and heir without consent of the Club — Mr Hill pled guilty, and was fined in the sum of 2/6.'

For several years a Dr Guthrie was fined 5/- for his non-attendance at meetings. In 1847 Dr Guthrie, 'having invariably been fined for a number of years for absence at the Annual Meetings was assessed in the sum of 5/- for deviating therefrom in so far as he had made his appearance on this occasion.' Poor Mr Pitcairn fell foul of the club again in 1848 'for being the first Member of the club who had submitted to take chloroform in extracting a tooth 1/-'.

In 1853 '. . . The dinner came off as usual with great conviviality, and when all were regretting the absence of J.O. Dalgleish, Esquire of Woodburne the Representative Member, they were disagreeably disappointed to find, that suddenly, and as if even by magic, he was represented at table in the shape of a *Basket* of *Champagne* and *Brandy* to which of course, the company did ample justice in drinking his health, and particularly that of the Donor, *David Martin Esq.,* Dundee, who in a polite letter to the President, pleaded guilty of having forcibly entered Woodburne House and surreptitiously carried off the Representative Member to Malvern, and being conscience struck and fearing the dread displeasure of "My Lord President", for his culpable conduct, sent the above as a peace offering, and as the only amends he could under the circumstances devise.'

At the meetings of many clubs new members were initiated into the mysteries of the curling brotherhood with greater or less ceremony. Such occasions could be boisterous, as the following minute of the Noddle Club, Largs, in 1822, in John Cairnie's own hand, shows: 'Mr Wm Scott of Greenock Mr Johnston factor at Kelburn and Dr Hector . . . who were initiated in the usual manner — in playing off his stone Mr Johnston took a wrong direction and played right upon a mahogany chair which stood on the one side of the room — report says the chair was a considerable sufferer from the accident being only half guarded by Mr Cairnie's legs which narrowly escaped an inwick.' Plus ca change!

When one contrasts some of the lively accounts of games and social evenings in some older minute books with the bald notes of motions made and seconded that pass for minutes nowadays, one cannot but feel regret. No doubt a minute is designed primarily as a record for the immediate utility of the club, but today's business records are tomorrow's history, and how much more valuable club minutes would be if they were enlivened by a bit of humorous description.

The tradition of after-curl activity continues. The social side of the Brier is as important as the sporting. Indeed, one recent writer, Jack Matheson, in *The First Fifty,* a nostalgic look at the Brier, by Doug Maxwell (1980), writes: 'At the Brier, the parties are interrupted twice a day by curling games, but nobody complains, because curling is what they came to see.'

At the Silver Broom, too, an opening and a closing banquet give spectators and players alike the chance to intermingle, and give spectators from all parts of the curling world a chance to form friendships.

21

Curlers' Courts

The representatives of the various curling societies who met in the Waterloo Hotel in July 1838 had gathered not merely to consider forming a Grand Club but, as the initial advertisement made clear, 'for the purpose of making the *mysteries* more uniform in future . . .' (My italics) At that historic meeting James Ogilvie Dalgleish, of the Abdie club, moved that a committee be appointed 'for the purpose of considering the mysteries and ceremonies, as also the rules and laws, of the Curling Clubs of Scotland, and to prepare a mode of initiation, and a set of rules and regulations'.

The constitution which the committee prepared was adopted in November 1838. Chapter 7 thereof was in the following terms:—

1*st*, That there shall be a fixed word of initiation, which no one, as an individual, is to commit to writing, without special permission from the Grand Caledonian Curling Club, or the Representative Committee, and which no Local Club is to communicate to any other which has not associated itself with the Grand Caledonian Curling Club. That every Club may insert in their respective minute-books certain cyphers, the connection between which and the word shall be divulged to the brethren only. That, in order to preserve the word to a letter, the Preses of each Club may, at their stated Annual General Meeting, (and then, however, for very special reasons only), direct it to be distinctly written down, but not more than one copy must be made, and this must be again carefully destroyed before the close of the said meeting.

2*d*, That there shall be a grip; and,

3*d*, That there shall be a pass- and counter-word.

No notice indicative of these two last to be written down; or communicated except to the initiated.

4*th*, That when once a Local Club has been initiated by the deputation empowered by the Representative Committee to do so, every new member afterwards admitted to their Club, shall be instructed in the secrets *in private*, in presence of at least three brethren appointed for that purpose by the Preses of the day.

It will be seen that the term 'Brotherhood of the Rink' had a deeper significance than the words impart at first glance.

The recently formed Dumbarton Club had sent their representatives to the November meeting, and the 'word' is faithfully preserved, in cyphers, in their minute book — the only surviving example of a club's following the Grand Club's injunction, although other clubs preserved the 'word' on wooden rods and in other ways.

The tradition of initiating curlers into the mysteries of the game had begun long before the Grand Club, and it has survived in most parts of Scotland to the present day. Indeed, the question: 'Are you a curler?' is not meant to establish whether the respondent plays the game but whether he is a member of the nationwide 'Brotherhood.' Nowadays the initiation is often referred to as 'making a curler,' and woe betide the 'made curler' who answers wrongly the question: 'Where were you made?' Some clubs, like Kinross, proudly maintain a tradition of an entirely 'made' membership. In others, the making ceremony occurs but seldom.

Initiation usually takes place as part of a curlers' court. Of this institution Sir Richard Broun says: 'The Curling Court is a sort of game of High Jinks, or mock heroic Tribunal, held under certain rules and regulations, before which it is competent to try, fine, and punish Curlers, for all trifling offences and misdemeanours committed upon the ice. No Curler can be a member of the court without a

196

previous private initiation — when after engaging to observe certain obligations, he receives the *Curler's grip and word*. After which, with all due formality, he is presented to "my Lord" in open Court, as a Brother of the Broom, and a keen, keen, keen Curler.'

'High Jinks' are the characteristic feature of most curlers' courts today. My Lord, the judge, is assisted by an Officer, or two, who incite the misdemeanours, report them to my Lord, and collect the fines in a pewter stoup, or mug; by an Initiator, who instructs the initiates, or 'nobodies', in the word and the grip; by a crowd of Henchmen, whose activities can be guessed at by the ubiquitous presence of a Surgeon! Goats and donkeys variously play their part, depending on the area in which the court takes place.

The court is usually preceded by a hearty dinner, at which traditional curlers' plain fare is helped down with draughts — sometimes copious — of the curlers' favourite drink. The meal over, the nobodies are banished, my Lord dons his robes, the court is formally 'fenced' by my Lord's Officer, and the fun begins. The success of the evening depends on the skill of my Lord, who must be adept at exciting enough misbehaviour to allow him to impose a constant stream of fines, yet exercise enough control, when the fun becomes fast and furious, to prevent the commission of real offences. To round off the evening the fines are rouped, or auctioned, to the highest bidder, and the proceeds of the sale, which may or may not exceed the contents of the stoup, are used towards defraying the expenses of the evening or given to a local charity.

In many areas of Scotland there are teams whose services in conducting courts are much sought after during the winter. At the time of writing Markinch Club have made their mark on curling by making many a curler throughout Scotland.

When the Silver Broom was last held in Scotland — in Perth in 1975 — with its emphasis on the history of the game in its homeland, the Earl of Elgin suggested that Perthshire clubs should hold courts for the instruction and initiation of the foreign visitors. It is to be hoped that, from the series of courts that were held as a result, this important part of the curling tradition will spread overseas.

22

Curlers' Jargon

Like most games, curling has its own specialised vocabulary, although unlike most games the source of much of curling jargon is the dialects of lowland Scotland. Just as the Scots dialect has retreated before the onslaught of standard English, so has the curling vocabulary become diminished, particularly in the face of Canadian terminology. Nonetheless a considerable number of picturesque curling terms still exists.

The first term I wish to get out of the road is *bonspiel*. Contrary to most widely accepted opinion, *bonspiel* in origin had no exclusive relationship with curling. Whatever its etymology — and there are doubts about it — *bonspiel* meant merely a game or contest. There are references to bonspiels at golf and archery — indeed, the seventeenth century records of the High Court of Justiciary record a prosecution for slaughter after 'ane bonspill at the golf' in Kelso kirkyard — but by the nineteenth century there is no doubt that curling had appropriated the word to describe a game in which large numbers played.

In that sense the word is still used in North America for what the Scots would call a competition, and the coinage *carspiel*, a bonspiel in which a motor car is the prize, shows that the word is still in full vigour west of the Atlantic. (If the time ever comes in Scotland, when cars are presented as prizes, one wonders what word will be invented for that).

Curiously, in Scotland, the word has narrowed in meaning, for a *bonspiel* now signifies a competition in which a number of clubs participate, each rink playing only one game, and the result is decided by the majority of shots for each club, divided by the number of rinks of that club participating. That explains why one can see on some trophies victories gained by margins such as $5\frac{2}{3}$ shots. The Grand Match is a bonspiel, in the modern Scottish sense, but it is never now called the Grand Bonspiel.

Rather than merely give a list of the terms along with their definitions, I propose to discuss them in relation to different aspects of the game.

Ice

The *sheet* of ice upon which a game is played is commonly known in Canada and Scotland as a *rink,* as is the team of four curlers. The building in which the *rinks* are situated is also the *rink*. In some parts of Scotland *rack* signified both the team and the sheet of ice; in others the ice on which the game took place was called the *lead*.

In relation to outdoor ice, there is a multiplicity of words to describe its quality. *Black ice* is ice which has frozen uninterruptedly. It is transparent, hard, and strong; and roars in response to the passage of stones over it. *White ice* occurs when melting snow is incorporated in the freezing process, the whiteness arising from entrapped air bubbles. The expression *white ice* was also used to describe the part of the rink in front of each hack, over which every stone passed in delivery.

Ice is now usually characterised as *keen,* or *dull,* or *heavy.* In Scotland heavy ice is still called *dour,* or *drug,* and sometimes *baugh.* If it is moist, it is *daughie.* The older curlers knew keen ice as *gleg,* or *slid.* Perfectly level ice is *true* or *honest.* Uneven ice can be *howe,* or hollow; or *biassed.* A *bias* is an unevenness which causes the stone to move from its expected course.

In these scientific days of artificial ice, the keenness is often described by the number of seconds taken by a drawing stone to travel from tee to tee; thus 26-second ice is very keen; 18 is very dull. Indoor ice is always *pebbled,* that is, given a spray of water which forms a large number of small bumps on the surface. The result is that at any moment there is very little of the stone actually in contact with ice. When the *pebble* wears down, stones are more responsive to the rotatory motion imparted to them in delivery, and the ice is said to be *swingy.*

The rink

On the rink are made the markings necessary for the game. Because these were originally scratched, or scored, into the ice they were known as *scores*. Even the Royal Club has now abandoned the term *score* in favour of *line* in its most recent revision of the rules.

At each end of the rink are drawn *circles*, or *rings*, 12 feet in diameter, with the *tee* as their centre. Both in Canada and in Scotland the area encompassed by the rings is the *house*. An older Scottish word for the rings was the *broughs* (pronounced bruchs, with the 'ch', as in 'loch'). The *tee* is a small hole drilled into the ice. In bygone days it was also known as the *toesee, gog, gogsee, cock, cockee, cogee, witter*. The current Canadian slang term is the *button*.

Within the outer rings are smaller rings of 8, and 4 feet diameter. The modern custom is to paint the ice between these rings in bright contrasting colours, so that the house can be readily seen from the hack. Such sophistication was unknown in the older days, and in many areas a wooden *bottle*, or *tee-marker*, was placed on the tee to give the curler a better idea of distance. When the Scots took curling to Switzerland, the Swiss called the bottle the *dolly*.

Canadians have developed a very useful battery of expressions to describe parts of the house. The front is generally known as the *front rings*; the back as the *back rings*. The area between the 12 foot and 8 foot circles is referrred to as the *12 foot*, the area between the 8 and 4 foot rings as the *8 foot*, and so on. The device for making the rings was called the *tee-ringer*, or *brough stick*. The distance scores are almost universally known as *hogscores*, or *lines*, but in central Ayrshire one can still hear an old curler or two refer to them as *colleys*, and in Kinross-shire they were called *collier scores*.

What the Scots call a *curling stone* is universally referred to by North Americans as a *rock*. In older times curling stones were known as *channel stanes* or *quoiting stanes*; and the ancestor of them all is the *loofie*.

In Scotland nowadays the stones are *soupit* to the *tee* with *brushes*: in North America the *rocks* are *swept* with *corn brooms*. The Scottish style of hair brush is given the name of *push broom* west of the Atlantic. The Scots word for *corn broom* was *besom*, and the ancestor of them all, the bunch of broom tied with string, was the *broom cowe*.

When a stone is to be thrown the curler stands on, or in, a *hack*; in North America, a foothold set into the ice; in Scotland, a small sloping platform set upon it. The name, however, derives from the notch, *hacked* into the ice, which was surely the earliest form of foothold. In parts of Scotland still, the hack is called the *trigger*, or *tricker*, which in its original form was a small pronged platform on which the curler supported one or both feet. In other areas these were known as *crisps, grips, grippers* or *prickles*. The *crampit*, in its original form of a piked device strapped onto the sole of the foot, is now no more, but Cairnie's *foot iron*, a long roughened platform of iron or wood, known, curiously, as the *crampit*, is still used by many Scots in outdoor play. It is also known as a *tramp*.

The game

Now that we have the ice prepared and the equipment ready, let us look at the teams. The captain of the *rink*, or *rack*, is almost universally known as *skip*. From his *directing*, or *controlling*, play, he used to be known as *director*, but there was a wealth of titles for him — *hin' han'* (hind hand: because he played behind all the others), *brandy, oversman, skipper*, and *douper* (the 'doup' in Scots is the backside, or 'behind': make of that title what you will). The *lead* leads off, or plays first; the *second* plays next; the *third*, or *vice-skip*, or, merely, *vice*, plays third.

The last end of a game might go as follows: With the lead crouched comfortably on the hack, the skip A, who is without last stone in the 10th and last end of the game and is trailing by 5 shots to 2, asks him to *draw* a stone to the *tee*. His *weight* is good, he has given it just enough momentum to allow it to be *swept*, or *soupit*, to the tee and it lies on top of the tee, a perfect *pot lid*. The opposing lead, who is asked to *take out*, or *strike*, the *shot*, borrows a bit of ice, and throws it outside the line of his skip's brush. The result is a *silent take-out*: he *fresh-airs* the *winner*, and misses. Skip A now asks his lead to lay on a *guard*, and by dint of powerful *souping* — to anxious cries of 'Hurry!, hurry!' from the skip — the *soupers* bring it just over the hog-score and leave it, a *long guard* directly in front of the *winner*. Skip B, feeling that his lead might be better with a cannier shot, asks him to draw round the guard and *crack an egg*, or *freeze*, on the winner, i.e. draw gently to it and lie against it. His stone is laid a bit *narrow*, or *tight*, of the skip's brush, and instead of *curling* behind the guard, it *wrecks* on it, sending both stones to different sides of the rink.

Skip A now asks his second to lay another guard. His stone bites the *twelve foot circle* directly in front of the winner.

Skip B asks his second to *take off*, or remove, the guard. His line is good, but his weight is excessive and his stone, instead of hitting the guard *on the nose* merely rubs it, and pushes it a foot or two to the front of the house, while his own stone careers through the house to end up out of play.

A's second lays a perfect guard within the 12 foot directly in front of the *winner*.

Skip B now decides to change tactics. He asks his second with his second stone to *raise the guard* directly on to the winner. He nearly succeeds, but because he fails to hit the guard directly on the nose the struck stone narrowly misses the winner. His stone, however, *rolls* to the left side of the house where it *hangs*, just *biting* the outer ring.

Skip A once again asks for a guard which lies in front of the winner biting the 12 foot.

There still appears to Skip B to be enough space between the guard and his own stone to allow a stone to be drawn through the *port* between them. His third's second stone is not heavy enough and blocks the port.

Skip A asks his *vice* to come hard at the two opposing stones lying at the front of the house within the *12 foot*. He makes a *double take out*, knocking out both stones, and lies in their place. A therefore *lie 4 shots*.

Matters are desperate for B. He tells his *vice* that he wishes him to attempt to *inwick* off the A's stone lying at the right of the house in front of the *tee*. (With luck his stone will come off it at the correct angle to hit the winner.) It succeeds. He *takes out* both stones and lies partly guarded behind A's guard.

Skip A with his first stone attempts a *straight raise* of his own guard onto the winner. He plays too heavy, the stone does not *bend*, or *curl*; it rubs the guard, pushing it a short way to his right and leaving it lying at about 45° to the winner, while careering over the *back score* and into the barrier at the back of the rink.

Skip B, who knows full well the advantage he has in playing last stone of the game, decides not to guard but to *freeze* his stone onto A's front angled stone. He is a couple of ounces too heavy, and the stones, instead of lying *frozen* together, are about a foot apart.

Skip A decides to *chap* B's front stone, so that it strikes B's other stone and clears them both out of the *house*. It succeeds and leaves A lying 3 shots. Unfortunately skip B has a clear road to the 4 foot with his last stone.

Skip B lays his stone well, a good draw weight, that will need swept all the road to the tee. In his excitement one of the sweepers touches the running stone with his brush: it is a *burnt* stone, and has to be removed from the ice.

Skip A, without the advantage of *the hammer*, as Canadians call the last stone, has *stolen* 3 shots, to make the score *peels*, and force an *extra end*.

23

The Curler's Library

The primary raw material for the history of curling is to be found in the minute books of clubs, but since these are scattered throughout the length and breadth of the curling world, the study of them is difficult, slow and laborious. It is the writer's hope that, as far as Scotland is concerned, there will be in the not too distant future a central repository for club records and minutes, as part of a Scottish curling museum, which is in the course of establishment. Not only would such an archive preserve and protect priceless records, but it would render them readily accessible to all serious curling historians.

Until that is accomplished, however, the researcher, wishing to consult a particular minute book, has to undertake the task of seeking out the custodier of the records, obtaining permission to consult them, and travelling to the place where they are kept. Some clubs guard their records jealously — to the extent of never letting them out of the Secretary's sight; others are more amenable, and allow them to be borrowed by the researcher; yet other clubs have been so careless of their minutes that they have been misplaced, lost or destroyed.

There is printed below, in chronological order, a list of the older surviving records up to the arbitrarily chosen date of 1820. The first is there by virtue of stretching the rules: the Muthill minutes were clearly written, from internal evidence, after 1820 but they do include a copy of the rules of the club at its inception in 1739 and a list of members from that date.

A comparison of the minutes listed below with those referred to in Kerr's *History* will show that some eighteenth century minutes, such as Hamilton, have been lost in the 90 years since he wrote, though others, notably Wanlockhead, Leadhills and Sorn, all unknown to Kerr, have come to light in only the last ten years. There has been a really tragic loss of a considerable **number of** early nineteenth century minute books,

written at a time when curling was rapidly expanding into the national game of Scotland.

The list includes the name of the club; the county in which it was situated; and the dates covered by the first volume. Where no location is given, the records are still in the possession of the club. The present writer has encouraged some clubs to deposit records for safe keeping on indefinite loan in the national archive, the Scottish Record Office, Register House, Edinburgh.

1. Muthill, Perthshire, 1739 — 15 July 1870.
2. Coupar Angus and Kettins, Perthshire, 1772 — Feb. 1881.
3. Sanquhar, Dumfriesshire, 21 Jan. 1774 — 31 Oct. 1873, S.R.O.
4. Wanlockhead, Dumfriesshire, 26 Dec. 1777 — Oct. 1854, Miners' Library, Wanlockhead.
5. Leadhills, Lanarkshire, 14 Feb. 1784 — Oct. 1854, Miners' Library, Leadhills.
6. Douglas, Lanarkshire, 25 Jan. 1792 — 7 Dec. 1847.
7. Duddingston, Midlothian, 17 Jan. 1795 — 18 Mar. 1853, S.R.O.
8. Sorn, Ayrshire, 21 Feb. 1795 — 21 Dec. 1815.
9. Blairgowrie, Perthshire, 20 Dec. 1796 — 7 Jan. 1811.
10. Kilmarnock Townend, Ayrshire, 6 Jan. 1814 — 17 Jan. 1838, S.R.O.
11. Meikleour, Perthshire, 8 Jan. 1814 — Jan. 1855.
12. Noddle (Largs), Ayrshire, spring 1814 — Feb. 1824, Largs History Society Museum.
13. Tarbolton, Ayrshire, 2 Nov. 1814 — 20 Oct. 1933, S.R.O.
14. Fenwick, Ayrshire, 15 Nov. 1814 — 25 Nov. 1834, S.R.O.
15. Penicuik, Midlothian, 20 Jan. 1815 — 9 Mar. 1832, Sir John Clerk, Penicuik House.

16. Sneddon (Paisley), Renfrewshire, 1815 — 14 Feb. 1880, Paisley Library.

17. Alyth, Perthshire, 18 Jan. 1815 — Jan. 1831.

18. Falkirk, Stirlingshire, 13 Mar. 1816 — 1869.

19. Kinross, Kinross-shire, 18 Feb. 1818 — 14 Jan. 1864.

20. Linlithgow Town and Parish, West Lothian, 22 Jan. 1820 — 9 Jan. 1839.

Another important primary source of material is reports of matches and other curling activities in newspapers. Some important evidence can be got from this source. For example, from the *Ayr Advertiser* of February 1803 comes the earliest reference to a gold curling medal; but newspaper research is very time-consuming, for few newspapers are indexed, and this sort of research involves scanning acre upon acre of small print: it is remarkable, though, how soon the eye can be trained to notice the words 'curl' or 'curling' wherever they appear on a newspaper page. Moreover, since newspapers printed news, one can reasonably restrict one's scrutiny to the curling months of the year.

A very important source of information is the various series of *Annuals* published by the Royal Caledonian Curling Club and other curling associations. Not only do these annuals include information as to the membership of clubs, office bearers and so on, but they also contain a wealth of articles of general and particular interest on curling.

The number of books and publications devoted exclusively to curling is small, but it can be supplemented by poems from anthologies and articles in periodicals and compendia.

The following list contains all the separately printed productions on curling, either published or privately printed, which my researches have thrown up. At the end of each entry is a note of the library or institution where the work may be consulted.

1. *Songs for the Curling-Club held at Canonmills. By a Member*. Edinburgh: Printed by J. Robertson, No. 39 South Bridge Street.　　　Pp. 16. 1792.
Canonmills Loch is shown in the earliest curling painting, by David Allan. See Plate 2. Very rare. National Library of Scotland.

2. [Ramsay, Rev. John], *An Account of the Game of Curling. By a Member of the Duddingston Curling Society*. Edinburgh: Printed at the *Correspondent* Office.　　　Pp. 46. 1811.
This is the earliest history of the game. Its influence was quite disproportionate to its length. It started the Scotland-versus-the Low Countries controversy about the origin of the game. By the inclusion of the rules of curling, recently adopted by the Duddingston Curling Society, it began the process of standardisation which was carried on by the Grand/Royal Caledonian Curling Club. Very rare. R.C.C.C.

3. *A Descriptive and Historical Sketch of Curling; also Rules, Practical Directions, Songs, Toasts, and a Glossary*. Published by H. Crawford, Kilmarnock.　　　Pp. 48. 1828.
The historical part was largely plagiarised from Ramsay. Very rare. R.C.C.C.

4. [Broun, Sir Richard], *Memorabilia Curliana Mabenensia*. Dumfries: Published by John Sinclair. Frontispiece, and plate at p. 99.　　Pp. 111. 1830.
A lively account of the game as played in Dumfriesshire. Sir Richard's motivation to write was a series of Bonspiels between his own parish of Lochmaben and their bitter rivals of Closeburn. The author planned a second edition, which was never published. I have recently discovered in the library of the Marquis of Bute an interleaved copy of the book, which belonged to the author, and contains copious manuscript notes for the second edition, including two attempted layouts of the title page. R.C.C.C.; Signet Library, Edinburgh; National Library of Scotland.

5. *Correspondence between the Kilmarnock and Maybole Curlers, regarding the challenge of the former which appeared in the* Ayr Advertiser, *of 4th February last [1830], to play Sixty Players of any parish in Ayrshire, within fifteen miles, for twenty sovereigns*. Ayr: Printed by W. Wilson.　　Pp. 28. 1830.
I have been unable to trace this publication. It appears to relate to the events described at p. 180.

6. Cairnie, John, *Essay on Curling, and Artificial Pond Making*. Frontispiece and three plates, pp. viii and 144. Glasgow, 1833.
The book was written largely to vindicate Cairnie's claim to be the inventor of artificial curling ponds. See p. 122. But his enthusiasm for the game led him to include lengthy notes from curling correspondents in various parts of Scotland. These are an invaluable source of material on local peculiarities. Both *Memorabilia* and Cairnie's *Essay* were reviewed widely in the newspaper and periodical press. It is perhaps not fanciful to suggest that their publication created the climate of opinion in which the establishment of the Grand Club in 1838 was possible. R.C.C.C.

7. Crawford, Dr. Andrew, of Johnshill, *The Crune of the Warlock of the Peil.* Pryce A Bawbee. Pp. 4. Prentit be W.C. Logan. 1838.
A quaint poem written in archaic Scots. Very rare. National Library of Scotland.

8. [Arnott, G.A.W.], *Laws in Curling; with Notes by Petrostes.* Printed for J. Whitehead, Kinross, and Maclachlan and Stewart, Edinburgh. Pp. 25. 1838.
I have been unable to trace any copy of this.

9. Bicket, John, *The Canadian Curler's Manual; or An Account of Curling, as practised in Canada, with remarks on the history of the game.* Published at the office of the *British Colonist,* for the Toronto Curling Club, 1840. Pp. 40.
The first non-Scottish publication on curling, by the Secretary of Toronto Curling Club. Very rare. National Library, Canada.

10. *The Douglas Bonspiel: A Poem.* Inscribed to Lieut. George Black, Fifty-second Regiment of Foot. 8th January 1806. Lanark: Printed by D. C. Budge. Pp. 23. 1842.
The work of Lieut. John Paterson, 1st Batt. 1st Regiment Bengal Native Infantry. The whole of the poem, with copious notes, is published in the Appendix to the *Annals of Lesmahagow,* by J. B. Greenshields.
Very rare. Douglas Curling Club.

11. *The Curler's Magazine; or, Curliana Memorabilia of the several Parishes and Clubs in Dumfriesshire, Galloway, Ayrshire, Lanarkshire, Renfrewshire, and generally throughout Scotland.* Printed and Published for the Proprietor and Editor at the Printing Office of the *Dumfries Times* Newspaper. Pp. 16. Dumfries, 1842.
Though referred to by Kerr, it is doubtful whether he saw a copy. There is a transcription of some pages of it among a collection of Kerr's MS. curling collection in Broughton House Library, Kirkcudbright. John Macnair, in the preface to *The Channel Stane,* says his copy was the only one he had ever seen.

12. *Report of Dinner and Presentation to Alexander Shedden, Esq. of Morrishill, 17th February 1846.* Beith: Printed by John Smith & Son. Pp. 24, two plates. 1846.
Very rare.

13. [Grierson, Rev. Thomas], *Four New Curling Songs: With a Dissertation on the Game of Curling. By an Old and Keen Curler, Author of 'Allan McGregor' and 'Autumnal Rambles.'* Pp. 16. Published by James Hogg. Edinburgh. N.D. *Circa* 1853.
Very rare. National Library of Scotland.

14. [Poet Tam], *Curliana. Dumfries v. Lochmaben and C., 17th February 1855.* Lockerbie: Printed by D. Halliday, Stationer. Pp. 8. 1855.
Very rare. Ewart Library, Dumfries.

15. *In Memoriam, Bathgate Curlers' Annual Dinner,* 1862. Edinburgh: R. & R. Clark. Pp. 63. 1863.
Very rare. R.C.C.C.

16. Brown, James, *History of the Sanquhar Curling Society. Published on the occasion of the Centenary of the Society, 21st January 1874.* Pp. 61. Printed at the Office of the *Dumfries and Galloway Courier,* 1874.
Rare.

17. *Gymnastics, Golf, Curling.* Chambers's Useful Handbooks, W. & R. Chambers, London and Edinburgh, pp. 49-66. 1877. Very rare.
Library of the University of Notre Dame, Indiana.

18. *The Curler's Guide.* Pp. 16. Toronto, 1880. By J. S. Russell.
I have been unable to trace this publication.

19. Smith, J. Guthrie, President of the Carbeth Curling Club, *His Havers.* 20th January 1881.
Verses spoken by Sheriff Guthrie Smith at the annual dinner of the C.C.C. at Strathblane. Privately printed at the request of the club. Pp. 8. 1881.
Very rare.

20. *Curling, Ye Glorious Pastime.* Reprint of Nos. 1 and 2 of this list, with Preface of Captain Macnair. Vignette. 250 copies privately printed. Pp. 80. 1882.
R.C.C.C.

21. Reprint of No. 3, under the title of *The Kilmarnock Treatise on Curling.* Preface by Captain Macnair. Vignette. Pp. 81. Edinburgh, 1883. Impression limited to 250 copies.
R.C.C.C.

22. Reprint of No. 3, to p. 48 of volume. From thence to p. 58 we have an account of 'The Scottish Game of Curling' by 'Maida' (T. Brown), and 'The Curler's Song,' by the late Francis Love of Stevenston. Pp. 60. J. McKie, Kilmarnock, 1883.
Rare. Dick Institute, Kilmarnock.

23. Macnair, Capt. John, *The Channel-Stane or Sweepings frae the Rinks,* 2 volumes, Richard Cameron, Edinburgh, 1883. A limited number were printed on parchment paper. Five copies had the title page printed in red.
A miscellany of curling articles from printed sources. Rare. Pp. 348.
R.C.C.C.

24. Taylor, James, *Curling, The Ancient Scottish Game.* William Paterson, Edinburgh, 1884, pp. 404.
    2nd Edition, 1887, pp. 404.
    A mixter-maxter of curling history, poems, jokes and anecdotes.   R.C.C.C.

25. Kerr, Rev. John, *Curling.* Vignette.   Pp. 16. 1884.   50 copies printed for private circulation. Broughton House Library, Kirkcudbright.

26. Crawford, Captain John, *Sixty-six Years of Curling: Being Records of North Woodside Curling Club, 1820-1886.* Edited by Captain Crawford. W. Weatherston & Son, Glasgow.   Pp. 144. 1886. Very rare.

27. *Curling Phrases and Tactics.* (Reprinted from the *Scotsman* of August 27, 1888). Alloa: Buchan Brothers. By the Rev. G. Murray, B.D., Sauchie. Printed for private circulation. Pp. 12.
    Very rare.

28. Kerr, Rev. John, *History of Curling, Scotland's Ain Game and Fifty Years of the Royal Caledonian Curling Club,* David Douglas, Edinburgh, 1890. Pp. 440.
    The curling historian's Bible, the result of a decision by the Royal Club to celebrate its jubilee in 1888 with a brief account of its first fifty years. The original plan was abandoned by Kerr, and all curlers have reason to be thankful to the indefatigable minister, whose thorough researches are incorporated in this lively, readable book.
    R.C.C.C.

29. Digby, James Drake, J.J.I., *Skating and Curling. The Glaciarium. A Brief History of the Invention and the Proposed Glaciarium Club.* Phipps and Connor, London, 1893. Pp. 35.
    A prospectus for a new ice rink in London on Professor Gamgee's principle.
    National Library of Scotland.

30. Campbell, Walter Douglas, *Auld Robin the Farmer, illustrated by Her Royal Highness, The Princess Louise, Marchioness of Lorne.* David Douglas, Edinburgh, 1894. Pp. 16.
    A brief sentimental curling poem, sentimentally illustrated.

31. Rossiter, Rev. S. B., D. D. *Curler's Sermons preached before the Grand National Curling Club at the North Presbyterian Church,* Bonnell, Silver & Co., New York.   Pp. 108. 1898.

32. Kerr, Rev. John, *Curling in Canada and the United States, a record of the Tour of the Scottish Team, 1902-3, and of the game in the dominion and the republic.* Edinburgh, Geo. A Morton, 42 George Street; Toronto, The Toronto News Co. Ltd., 1904. Pp. 787.
    A very full account of the historic first tour of Canada and the U.S.A. by the Scots. Written by the team captain, it contains, in addition to a wealth of material on the tour, a great deal on the history of curling in Canada and the U.S. up to the beginning of the twentieth century.
    R.C.C.C.

33. Bowie, Josh, *Curling, The Art of the Game,* John Anderson Weir, 74 pp. 1904.
    R.C.C.C.

34. Smith, Bertram, *The 'Shilling' Curler.* Richardson & Wroughton, London, n.d. (1912), pp. 39.
    A brief instruction manual.
    R.C.C.C.

35. Grant, J. Gordon, *The Complete Curler, being the history and practice of the game of curling.* Adam and Charles Black, London, 1914, pp. 220.
    R.C.C.C.

36. Marshall, Major M. H., *The Scottish Curlers in Canada and U.S.A. A Record of their Tour in 1922-23.* T. & A. Constable Ltd., Edinburgh, 1924, pp. 375.
    An encyclopaedic account of the tour by the tour secretary.
    R.C.C.C.

37. Noel Mobbs, A., and McDermott, F., *Curling in Switzerland, A Treatise on the Principles of the Game, and where and how to play it.* Arrowsmith, London, 1929, pp. 223.
    History, technique and strategy, plus descriptions of the Swiss Alpine resorts in which curling took place.
    R.C.C.C.

38. Steuart, J. Crurie, *An Old Curler's Letters to his Nephew.* Macniven & Wallace, Edinburgh, 1934, pp. 48.
    Quaint advice on the unwritten rules of the game.
    R.C.C.C.

39. Boase, Edward R., *How to Curl.* Edinburgh 1934, pp. 31.
    Basic instruction.
    R.C.C.C.

40. Beaumont, Major K. M., *Some Finer Points of Swiss Curling.* W. & J. Lloyd & Co.   pp. 12, 1935.
    R.C.C.C.

41. Talbot, Fritz B., *Mr Besom — starts Curling.* Privately printed by the Plimpton Press, Norwood, Massachusetts, 1936,   pp. 64.

42. Weyman, H.E., *An Analysis of the Art of Curling.* Lévis, Quebec, 1942-, 43, 44, 45, 46, 47, 48, 49, 51, 58, 60,   pp.108.

Fig. 183 A keen keen curler's last resting place, Tibbermore kirkyard, about four miles west of Perth. James Ritchie, late farmer of Cairney, who died in 1840, is commemorated by a representation of his ornate curling stones, his besom, and his pair of crampets.

A fascinating analysis of the mechanics of the curling stone delivery, and strategy. The later editions also contain full information about the making of ice and building of ice rinks.
R.C.C.C.

43. Creelman, William Albert, *Curling Past and Present, including 'An Analysis of the Art of Curling' by H. E. Weyman.* McClelland & Stewart, Ltd., Toronto, 1950,   pp. 256.
A reasonably comprehensive account of the history of the game in Scotland, Canada and the U.S.A.
R.C.C.C.

44. Watson, Ken, *Curling at a Glance.* Macdonald Tobacco Inc., Montreal, n.d., pp. 29.

45. Stevenson, John A., *Curling in Ontario, 1846-1946.* Ontario Curling Association, Toronto, 1950,   pp. 272.
A thorough and workmanlike history of curling and curling clubs in the province.
R.C.C.C.

46. Watson, Ken, *Ken Watson on Curling.* The Copp Clark Publishing Co., Toronto, 1950,   pp. 177.
The best book on curling techniques and strategy by the man who invented the sliding delivery. A curling classic.

47. Moir, Ken, *School Curling.* McMillan Press Ltd., St John, N.B., n.d. (ca. 1955),   pp. 22.

48. Curtis, Dar, *Curling . . . Fun for Everyone!* Winnetka, Illinois, 1959, pp. 30.
Basic instruction.

49. Richardson, Ernie, McKee, Joyce, and Maxwell, Doug., *Curling, an authoritative handbook of the techniques and strategy of the ancient game of curling.* Thomas Allen Limited, Toronto, 1962, pp. 180.
An interesting account of the techniques and strategy of the game.

50. Watson, James Kenneth, *Curling Today.* Harlequin Books, Winnipeg, 1962, pp. 224.

51. Hushagen, Earle, *Basic Curling.* Toronto, 1967, pp. 31.
Basic instruction.

52. Welsh, Robin W., *A Beginner's Guide to Curling.* Pelham Books, London, 1969, pp. 184.
A witty and readable account of all aspects of the game by the Secretary of the Royal Caledonian Curling Club since 1958.
R.C.C.C.

53. *Modernes Curling (Curling moderne).* Swiss Curling Federation, Geneva, n.d., pp. 35.
The first instruction booklets in the French and German languages.

54. Mulvoy, Mark, with Ernie Richardson, *Ernie Richardson's Curling: Techniques and Strategy.* McClelland and Stewart Ltd., Toronto, 1973, pp. 107.
A disappointingly uninformative book by arguably Canada's greatest skip.

55. Savage, Paul, *Canadian Curling 'Hack to House'.* Sportbook Ltd., Agincourt, Ontario, 1974, pp. 194.

56. Keith, Isabel, *Stones on the Ice. The Story of Curling.* Gordon Bennett Publications, Edinburgh, n.d., pp. 56.
The story of curling in verse.

57. Thiessen, Roy D., *Curling Handbook for Curlers, Teachers & Coaches.* Hancock House, Saanichton B.C.; Toronto; Seattle, 1977, pp. 88.
The best modern coaching manual.

58. Eggenberger, Henry, *Das grosse Buch vom Curling.* Verlag Gerhard Stalling AG, Oldenburg and Hamburg, 1977, pp. 144.
This, the first Swiss book on the game, is also the first not written in English. Lavishly and beautifully illustrated.

59. Eggenberger, Henry, *et al., Curling: Weltmeisterschaft 1979.* Weltrundschau-Verlag, Lugano, 1979, pp. 128.
A beautifully illustrated account of the 1979 Air Canada Silver Broom World Championship in Berne, 1979, with sections on the history of the game in Scotland, Switzerland, and Canada.

60. Maxwell, Doug. & Friends, *The First Fifty. A Nostalgic Look at the Brier.* Maxcurl Publications, Toronto, 1980, pp. 120.
A lively account of the history of Canada's national championship, with impressions of the event by participants and journalists.

An Account of the Game of Curling.

By a Member of the Duddingston Curling Society. Edinburgh: Printed at the Correspondent Office. 1811.

TO

THE PRESIDENT AND MEMBERS

OF

THE DUDDINGSTON CURLING SOCIETY,

THE FOLLOWING ACCOUNT OF THE

GAME OF CURLING

IS RESPECTFULLY INSCRIBED

BY

THE AUTHOR.

The following account is submitted to the Public, chiefly with the view of calling the attention of Curlers to one of our national amusements, that some additional information may thus be obtained respecting its origin and early history.

ON THE

GAME OF CURLING.

Every thing illustrative of national character is worthy of attention. But here the philosopher and the historian have often to regret the want of sufficient materials. From the earliest ages men have taken care to transmit to posterity the great revolutions which society has undergone: but the particular customs and amusements which prevail among a people, and which have no small influence in rendering them brave and virtuous, or effeminate and vicious, are too often overlooked by literary men, and allowed to sink into oblivion. How many of the amusements which contributed to brace the hardy limbs of our forefathers, and to generate that noble spirit of freedom which, after a struggle of many ages, reared at last that unrivalled constitution under which we have the happiness to live, are now unknown! Others, though still in existence, are fast hastening to decay. And, ere long, it is probable, even the names of some of them will be found only in the scattered fragments of our national poets. Every attempt, therefore, to preserve the memory of those which still remain, is certainly laudable.

The Game of Curling* may justly be regarded as one of our national amusements. It is practised in the winter during the time of frost, and consists in sliding stones along the ice to a particular mark. It has some resemblance to the games of bowls and billiards.

The stones employed in it are made from blocks of whinstone, or granite, of a close texture, free from cracks, and capable of taking a fine polish. Those whinstone nodules, of concentric texture, called *yolks*, on account of their toughness, and never breaking into large fragments, are reckoned the best. They are found in the beds of rivers, and on the sea-shore; sometimes not far removed from the shape which they are afterwards to assume. They are of a spherical form, flattened above and below, so that their breadth may be nearly equal to twice their thickness. The upper and under surfaces are

---

* *Curl,* from the German *kurzweil*; an amusement, a game; and *curling*, from *kurzweillen*, to play for amusement.

made parallel to one another, and the angles of both are rounded off. The under surface, or sole, as it is called, is polished as nicely as possible, that the stone may move easily along. Sometimes the sole is hollowed out in the middle, and sometimes it is made a little convex; but that which is perfectly level is unquestionably the best. In many parts of the country there are always a few misshapen blocks employed in the game. These, when well placed by the vigorous arms of those who take the lead, can with difficulty be removed. At Duddingston, however, none are admitted into the game, but such as are of a spherical form, and properly made. When thus prepared, a handle is inserted into the upper surface, generally of iron, sometimes of wood, and sometimes also of wood, screwed into an iron standard fixed in the stone. They are from 30 to 60 lbs. avoirdupois weight, according to the strength of the person who uses them.

The *rink** is that portion of the ice which is allotted for conducting the game. The chief thing to be attended to in chusing a rink, is, that the ice be level, smooth, and free from cracks, particularly such as are in a longitudinal or oblique direction. If it be not level, the stones naturally deviate from their proper course, and the game becomes in a great measure a game of chance. The place for the rink being chosen, a mark is made at each end, called a *tee,†* *toessee,* or *witter‡.* It is a small hole made in the ice, round which two circles of different diameters are drawn, that the relative distances of the stones from the tee may be calculated at sight, as actual measurement is not permitted till the playing at each end be finished. These circles, in the technical language of the game, are called the *broughs.* A score is then drawn across the rink, at each end, distant from the tee about a sixth part of the length of the rink. This is called the *hog-score.§* It is frequently made waving, to distinguish it from any accidental scratch. The length of the rink, from tee to tee, varies from thirty to fifty yards, according to the intensity of the frost, and the smoothness of the ice. The breadth is about ten or twelve feet. When the ice is covered with snow it must be cleared to that extent, and also ten or twelve feet beyond the tee, at each end, that those stones, which are impelled with too much force, may

have room to get far enough not to be of any use.

Formerly, that the players might be able to stand firm, when they threw the stones, they used to wear *crampits,* which are flat pieces of iron, with four sharp pikes below. They are bound to the sole of the shoe with a strap and buckle. But as the use of crampits is now very much laid aside, a longitudinal hollow is made to support the foot, close by the tee, and at right angles, with a line drawn from the one end of the rink to the other. This is called a *hack,** or *hatch.* Its situation is such, that, when discharging his stone, the player lifts it up, and makes it pass over the tee.

There are generally sixteen stones on a rink, each party having eight. At Duddingston, and in the neighbourhood of Edinburgh, each player uses two stones, so that there are eight players on each rink, four against four. But in most other parts of the country, where curling is practised, curlers have only one stone a-piece; in which case there are sixteen on a rink, eight against eight. There may be one or more rinks, according to the number of curlers. In some great matches, in which different parishes contend with one another, no less than six rinks have been engaged at once. The game may also be conducted by one person against another, by two against two, or three against three, each using one or more stones, as it may be agreed upon.

He who is reckoned the best curler, has generally the power of arranging the order of the game; and whoever is last in order gives directions to all the rest of his party. He is called the *driver,* and the first the *lead.* The origin of which appellations is sufficiently obvious.

It is necessary, too, that each curler be provided with a broom, the use of which will be sufficiently understood by reading the rules of the Duddingston Curling Society, annexed to this essay.

At first, the game is remarkably simple. The lead endeavours to lay his stone as near the tee as possible. If it be a little short of it, upon the middle of the rink, it is reckoned to be fully better laid than if it touched it. The object of the next in order is nearly the same as that of the lead. When he attempts to strike away the stone of his antagonist, if he miss his aim, his stone will pass by, and be completely useless. But if he place his stone near the tee, without minding that of his antagonist, it has a chance of remaining there, and gaining a shot to his party. The object of the next in order is to *guard†* the stone of his partner, if it be near the tee, or to strike off

---

* *Rink,* or *renk,* means a course, or race; probably from the ancient Saxon *hrink, hrineg* a strong man.
† *Tee,* probably from the Icelandic *tia,* demonstrare, q. as pointing out the place. Teut. *tijgh-en,* indicare.
‡ *witter,* to inform, to make known; Su. G. *wittra, notum facere, indicare.*
§ *Hog-score,* in some places called *coll,* or *coal-score,* means distance, line; because the stones which do not pass that line are, as it were, distanced, and thrown aside as useless.

---

* *Hack,* from the Icelandic *hiacka,* signifies a chop, a crack.
† To *guard* a stone, is to lay another in a direct line before it, so that the one who plays next, on the opposite side, may not be able to get it removed.

that of his antagonist, if it be nearer. The one who follows, if a stone belonging to his own party be nearest the *tee,* attempts to guard it; if one of the opposite party, to strike it off, or to *draw a shot,** if no stone be near the tee.

As the game advances it becomes always more intricate. Sometimes the stone nearest the *tee,* which is called the *winner,* is so guarded that there is no possibility of getting at it directly. It then becomes necessary, in order to get it removed, to strike another stone lying at the side, in an oblique direction. This is called *wicking,†* and is one of the nicest parts of the game. But when the winner cannot be reached, even in this way, the last in order but one or two must then endeavour to remove the opposing stones, by striking them with great force. If each curler use two stones, the driver may clear the ice with his first stone, in order to get at the winner with his last. Sometimes the stones are situated in such a critical manner, that the driver, to avoid the risk of losing any shots which his party may have gained, throws away his stone without attempting any thing.

It is astonishing what dexterity some curlers attain! Whether they have to draw, strike, wick, or *enter a port,‡* they will seldom deviate an inch from their aim. This, however, can only be effected when the ice is quite level, an advantage which, in our variable winters, is seldom to be met with. There is almost always some bias, which the curler must attend to, in order to gain his purpose. Much, too, depends upon the person who directs the game. However well individual curlers may acquit themselves, if they want a judicious and experienced director, all their art will not avail. — As the soldiers in an army, whatever may be their individual bravery, if not properly commanded, must yield to superior discipline; so also in a *bonspel,§* the skill of the curlers may be wasted by injudicious directions. When the stones on both sides have been all played, the one nearest the tee counts one;

---

* To *draw a shot,* is to make the stone rest as near the tee as possible.
† *Wick,* from Su. G. *wik,* angulus, a corner, because a corner or part of the stone only is hit.
‡ To *enter a port,* is to make a stone pass through an opening made by two others lying opposite to one another.
§ *Bonspel, bonspiel,* or *bonspeel,* a match at the diversion of curling on the ice, between two opposite parties. This has been derived from Fr. *bon,* Belg. *spel,* play q. a good game. But it will be found, that the same word is rarely formed from two different languages. It may, therefore, rather be traced to Belg. *bonne,* a village, a district, and *spel,* play; because the inhabitants of different villages or districts contend with each other in this sport, one parish, for example, challenging another. — *Jamieson's Dictionary.*

and if the second, third, fourth, &c. belong to the same side, all these count so many shots; thirty one of which, for each side, is the number usually played for.

The origin of this game is yet involved in darkness. Whilst most of our national amusements are to be found recorded in the writings of the antiquary and historian, we find no mention made of this before the beginning of the seventeenth century. About that time, the allusions to it are such as clearly prove that it was then pretty generally practised. It is probable, however, that its origin does not go much farther back; because, if it existed in the fifteenth, or about the beginning of the sixteenth century, it could hardly have been omitted in those lists which have been transmitted to us of the ancient amusements of our country. But in none of those lists do we find it ever mentioned, nor does any author make the least allusion to it, previous to that period. In the statutes of the fifteenth century, we find a list of amusements, amongst which are golf and foot-ball, particularly prohibited by authority, in order to promote the noble art of archery, as it is called. But nowhere do we find a single hint about the game of curling. It can be practised, it is true, only for a short time in winter; but when it is practised, it must, from its very nature, be public, and known to the whole neighbourhood. On which account, had it then existed, it could hardly have been overlooked by those who have particularly enumerated the Scottish amusements of the fifteenth and sixteenth centuries.

In later times, when it is known to have flourished in this country, we find it forming a favourite subject for poetic description. Not satisfied with allusions, the votaries of the muses have allotted to it whole poems, and expatiated, with the feelings of a curler, upon the various circumstances connected with this manly Scottish exercise. Now, since we do not find it even mentioned before that period, it is highly probable that it did not then exist, or that it was only in its infancy.

There is another circumstance, which would lead us to suppose, that the origin of curling, in this country at least, is not very remote. The stones, if we may judge from some specimens that still remain, seem once to have been unpolished blocks, used almost as they were found in the fields, and in the beds of rivers. In place of a handle, they appear to have had only a protuberance at top, with a niche for the finger and thumb. In which form they are still to be seen in several parts of the country. This gave place to the more convenient form of bent wooden, and iron handles. The improvement of the handle was connected with improvements in the stones themselves. They gradually laid aside their rude shape, and have now assumed an elegant and uniform appearance. This improvement is still going on, and has been so as far back as our information upon the subject extends. Now, had the game been of very ancient origin, we should expect many of these improvements to have been made long before the time when they actually were made. As society advances in improvement, arts and sciences advance at the same time. No human thing remains stationary. If, then, we find curling stones, at any period, in the rudest possible form, having received no improvements, we have reason to conclude, that the origin of the game cannot be far distant from that period. And since the earliest notices we have of it do not go farther back than the beginning of the seventeenth century, at which period curling stones were in the rudest form, the game was probably not known in this country sooner than the fifteenth or sixteenth century.

Connected with this is the inquiry respecting the country in which it originated. Upon this subject curlers are divided in their sentiments. Some seem to think that it was an amusement originally Scottish; others, that it was introduced into this country from the continent.

Upon examining its claims to a Scottish origin, we find those claims resting upon its existence here, and upon the want of sufficient evidence, that it existed, till lately, any where else. That it has now existed in this country more than two centuries, is beyond all doubt. This is fact, supported by direct historical evidence. It is also maintained that had the game been practised on the continent, in Germany, or the Low Countries, about or previous to the time when we have supposed it made its appearance in this country, it would most probably have been more or less practised still; or at least some traces of it would have remained sufficient to demonstrate its former existence. Now, persons who have resided long in those countries, and had the best opportunities of information, have all affirmed, that, at present, no such amusement exists, nor did they perceive any traces of its ever having existed. Such is the argument upon which those who favour the Scottish origin of curling rest their opinion.

With regard to the game of curling not being practised, at present, on the continent, this is a point which it is not very easy to ascertain. At this moment, perhaps, the half of the population of England, and a million of the inhabitants of Scotland, never heard of the game of curling. And of all the foreign travellers who have visited this country, and published their travels, not one has taken the smallest notice of it. The same thing may happen in Germany or the Low Countries. It may be practised in particular districts, and yet travellers, and even persons who have resided long in those parts of the country where it is not practised, may never have heard of such a game.

And even though it does not exist at present on the continent, and though no traces have been observed by many of our countrymen who resided there, of its ever having existed, still this circumstance is far from being sufficient to prove that it is not of continental origin. Within these two hundred years, the occupations, manners, and customs, of the different countries of Europe, have undergone the greatest revolutions. The vast improvements that have been made in agriculture and commerce, by giving employment to persons of all descriptions, have had a fatal influence upon our sports and amusements, particularly such as are practised in the open air. Hence, many of the amusements of former times are now forgotten, or fast going into disuse. The British youths, engaged from early life in the serious occupations of particular professions, have now little time for active amusements. Shut up in the sickening atmosphere of a public building, and doomed to the irksome task of watching a spindle, or forming a pin, they grow up like stunted trees in the midst of an overcrowded plantation. Curling, therefore, may have once flourished, where now, among an industrious and laborious people, it is completely forgotten.

Our want of written evidence is equally inadequate to prove that curling has not been known on the continent: for the game may have been practised, and yet no accounts of it published, or there may be accounts of it with which we are yet unacquainted. Even in our own country, where we know that it has prevailed for more than two centuries, it is not mentioned by one historian, and is only alluded to in one or two books of antiquities and of law. Now, it is not to be supposed that the Dutch or Flemings, had it prevailed among them two centuries ago, would be more careful to preserve the memory of it than we in this country have been. The game, therefore, may have existed in the Low Countries, and yet not be noticed in those books of history or antiquities which we have had an opportunity of consulting. Hence, the argument in favour of the Scottish origin of curling, drawn from the want of sufficient evidence that it existed till lately anywhere else, is by no means conclusive.

Let us next inquire, whether the opinion of those who suppose that it was introduced into this country from the continent be well founded. We have, indeed, no direct evidence that it ever existed on the continent, but we have all the evidence which etymology can give in favour of its continental origin. The terms being all Dutch or German, point to the Low Countries as the place in which it most probably originated, or, at least, from whence it was conveyed to us. For if it was not introduced from the continent, but was first invented in this country, it must have been at a time when the

German and Low Dutch were the prevailing languages. Now, though the Saxon was once pretty general in this country, and there are still many Dutch words in our language, yet those German dialects were never so general, as to make it credible, that our countrymen, in any particular invention, would employ them alone as the appropriate terms. In the history of inventions, such a phenomenon is not to be found. Had there been only one or two foreign terms, these would not have militated much against the domestic origin of the game, but the whole of the terms being continental, compel us to ascribe to it a continental origin.

But we have other evidence that curling, or something like it, was originally practised on the continent. Kilian, in his dictionary, renders the Teutonic *kluyten kalluyten,* (*ludere massis sive globis glaciatis, certare discis in equore glaciato.*) Whatever those round masses of ice were, they seem to have been employed in a game on the ice after the manner of quoits. Indeed, it appears highly probable, that the game, which we now call curling, was originally nothing else than the game of quoits practised upon the ice. Some of the very old stones which yet remain favour this conjecture. They are not only much smaller than those now employed, but instead of a handle, as was mentioned above, have a kind of niche for the finger and thumb, as if they had been intended to be thrown. Besides, the game to which we apply the name of curling, was, till lately, hardly known by that name among the common people. From one end of Scotland to the other, it was always named *kuting,** to curl, meaning nothing more than to slide upon the ice. In some parts of Ayrshire, we have heard, it is pronounced *coiting,* a circumstance which amounts almost to a proof that it was, at first, merely the game of quoits applied to the ice. Independently of the names, the games themselves have a considerable similarity. The one then might naturally arise out of the other, and assume that form in which it at present exists.

From all which there is a very strong probability, that the game of curling was introduced into this country by the Flemings, in the fifteenth, or about the beginning of the sixteenth century. It is well known, that in the reigns of Henry V. and VI. of England, and James I. of Scotland, many of them came over to this country, and settled as mechanics and manufacturers in our towns and villages, which had been much depopulated during the destructive wars betwixt the two kingdoms. Then,

however, it must have been in a very imperfect state, and probably had a nearer resemblance to the game of quoits.

Curling is said to have been carried into Ireland by the Scottish colonies who were planted there, so early as the reign of James I of England. In that country, however, it seems now to be completely unknown. It has made its appearance in some of the northern counties of England; and, within these few years, has even found its way to the capital of the British empire. There, the first essay was made upon the New River; but the crowd of spectators, attracted by such a novel spectacle, becoming very great, the ice threatened to give way, and the curlers were with reluctance compelled to desist. Whether it has again been attempted, and with what success, we have not been able to learn. It has not been confined within the boundaries of Europe; it has been carried over the Atlantic, and established in the frozen regions of North America. This information was communicated by a gentleman who was himself engaged in curling at Quebec. There, on account of the length and severity of the winter, it bids fair to attain a degree of celebrity unexampled in the milder climate of Scotland. Here, it can be practised only a few days in the season; so few, that for the last twenty years the average number is not more than eight; while, in that country, the amusement may be enjoyed the greater part of the winter.

The history of curling, in this country, is very little known. The earliest intimation of it, which we have been able to obtain, is in Cambden's Britannia, which was published by himself in 1607. 'To the east of the mainland,' (Orkney) he says, 'lies Copinsha, a little isle, but very conspicuous to seamen. In which, and in several other places of this country, are to be found in great plenty, excellent stones for the game called curling.* This intimation shews, that the game must have been pretty general, and in considerable repute, when stones were collected from a small island at such a distance from any place where the game could be practised.

Before the middle of the seventeenth century, curling had been generally practised on the Sunday. For Baillie, in his letters,† observes, 'Orkney's process came first before us. He was a curler on the Sabbath day.' It is hardly necessary to mention, that, before the reformation in this country, Sunday was the day particularly allotted for amusements of all kinds.

In 1684, we find the game noticed in Fountainhall's Decisions:‡ 'A party of the forces having been sent out to apprehend Sir William Scot of Harden, younger: one William Scot, in Langhope, getting notice of their

---

* Kuting, kuyten, probably from the Teutonic kluyten, kalluyten. If the word, however, be spelt *cootying,* with the Scotch sound of the double *o,* it is derived from the Dutch coete, a quoit.

* This extract is taken from Kippis' edition, vol. ii, p. 1473.
† Vol. i, p. 137.
‡ Vol, i, p. 328.

coming, went and acquainted Harden with it, as he was playing at the curling with Riddel of Haining, and others.'

Pennant, in his Tour in Scotland,* in 1792, thus describes the game. "Of all the sports of these parts, that of curling is a favourite, and one unknown in England. It is an amusement of the winter, and played on the ice, by sliding from one mark to another great stones of 40 to 70 lbs. weight, of an hemispherical form, with an iron or wooden handle at top. The object of the player is to lay his stone as near the mark as possible, to guard that of his partner which had been well laid before, or to strike off that of his antagonist."

Curling has never been universal in this country. But in some places where it once was, it is now no more; while in others it is flourishing as much as it ever did, at any former period. And, in many parishes, the number of players is double of what it was half a century ago. When our nobility resided upon their estates in the country, it was one of their favourite amusements. A challenge was sent from one baron to another, to engage in a bonspel with their respective tenants. The gentry in the country still partake of this interesting amusement. Matches are made up in a great variety of ways. One parish challenges another to contend with them upon some pond, or lake, or river, in the neighbourhood. And when the same parishes contend more than once, the conquerors in the last contest, have generally the privilege of choosing the place where they are to play next. Sometimes one part of a parish challenges another, or the married men those who are unmarried. Some districts too, have long been distinguished for their dexterity in the art, and at present, perhaps, none more so than the upper and middle wards of Lanarkshire, and certain parts of Dumfries-shire.

At Edinburgh, where curlers are collected from all the counties of Scotland, this amusement has been long enjoyed. And in so great repute was it towards the beginning of the last century, that the magistrates are said to have gone to it and returned in a body, with a band of music before them, playing tunes adapted to the occasion. Then it was practised chiefly on the North Loch, before it was drained, and at Canonmills. At which latter place a society was formed about fifty years ago, and continued to flourish a considerable time. Of late, however, it has dwindled away to nothing. Nearly about the same time, another society was formed at Duddingston; but this too was ready to die away, when it was reinstituted in 1795, under the title of the *Duddingston Curling Society*. Silver medals were struck off, to be worn as a badge of distinction by the members. The medals represent, on the one side, a party of curlers

* P. 93.

at play, and the church of Duddingston and Arthur's Seat on the background with this motto:

Sic Scoti, alii non aeque felices.

The other side has the following inscription:

Duddingston Curling Society, instituted 17th January 1795.

Since that time, the society has been rapidly increasing in respectability and numbers; new spirit has been infused into the game; and it seems to be fast rising to a degree of celebrity unexampled in the history of curling.

A gold medal, to be played for annually, was instituted by the society in 1809. This circumstance, by exciting a spirit of emulation among the members, must contribute not a little to promote their accuracy and dexterity in the art of curling. And as minutes of the proceedings of the society at Duddingston have now begun to be regularly kept, it will be easy, at any future period, to give an accurate history of these proceedings. Measures also will probably be taken to establish a correspondence betwixt the Duddingston society, and the different parts of Scotland where the game is practised. By which means an extensive and complete body of information may be collected, and produced when occasion requires.

There are few amusements which excite more interest than the game of curling. In the severest weather, a good curler, while engaged in his favourite amusement, feels no cold. In playing himself, and assisting his partners with his broom, he finds sufficient exercise to keep him warm. It must, therefore, be highly conducive to health; and being performed at a time when the labours of the field are at a stand, and when several mechanical employments cannot be carried on, it gives little interruption to business. It brings men together in social intercourse; it enlarges and strengthens the ties of friendship, and enlivens the dreary hours of winter with festivity and happiness. Games in which scenes of cruelty are exhibited, and amusements which go to enervate and debauch the soul, may well be allowed to sink into oblivion; but those which tend to strengthen the body and cheer the mind, without possessing any corrupting influence, ought surely to be encouraged and promoted. In the present state of society, care should be taken to counteract, by every possible method, that effeminate habit of thinking, and of acting, which the progress of luxury has a constant tendency to produce, and to call forth those exertions of the body and of the mind, which, when combined, constitute the perfection of the human character. That the game of curling is conducive to this object, is abundantly obvious to all who are acquainted with it. While the Scottish youths, then, shall continue to practise this manly exercise, they should know, for their encouragement, that they are engaged in one of the most innocent and healthy amusements which their fathers have transmitted to them.

This game has been noticed by some and minutely described by others of our national poets. Thus Pennycuick, who flourished in the seventeenth century, and whose poems were published in 1715,

> To curl on the ice doth greatly please,
> Being a manly Scottish exercise.
> It clears the brains, stirs up the native heat,
> And gives a gallant appetite for meat.

Allan Ramsay, who flourished about the beginning of the last century, alludes to it in the following words:

> ————the curling stane
> Slides murmuring o'er the icy plain.

So also Burns,

> He was the king o' a the core,
> To guard, or draw, or wick a bore,
> Or up the rink like Jehu roar,
>   In time o' need.

Graeme, a Scottish poet, who died at Lanark in 1785, describes the game with considerable minuteness and precision.

> The goals are marked out, the centre each
> Of a large random circle; distance scores
> Are drawn between, the dread of weakly arms.
> Firm on his cramp-bits stands the steady youth,
> Who leads the game. Low o'er the weighty stone
> He bends incumbent, and with nicest eye
> Surveys the farther goal, and in his mind
> Measures the distance, careful to bestow
> Just force enough; then balanced in his hand
> He flings it on direct; it glides along
> Hoarse murmuring, while playing hard before,
> Full many a besom sweeps away the snow,
> Or icicle, that might obstruct its course.

> But cease, my muse! what numbers can describe
> The various game. Say, can'st thou paint the blush
> Impurpled deep, that veils the strippling's cheek,
> When wand'ring wide the stone neglects the rank,
> And stops midway. His opponent is glad,

> Yet fears a similar fate, while every mouth
> Cries off the hog. — And Tinto joins the cry.
> Or could'st thou follow the experienc'd player
> Through all the mysteries of his art; or teach
> The undisciplined how to wick, to guard,
> Or ride full out the stone that blocks the pass.

Davidson, a poet of considerable genius, who wrote in the dialect of Kirkcudbrightshire, in his poem on Winter, thus describes the game:

> But manliest of all! the vig'rous youth
> In bold contention met, the channelstane,
> The bracing engine of a Scottish arm,
> To shoot wi' might and skill. Now to the lake
> At rising sun, with hopes of conquest flushed,
> The armed heroes meet. Frae dale to doon
> The salutation echoes — and amain,
> The baubee tossed, wha shall wi' ither fight,
> The cap'ring combatants the war commence,
> Hence loud throughout the vale, the noise is heard
> Of thumping rocks, and loud bravadoes' roar.

The author next gives an account of a bonspel, betwixt two rival chiefs, on Loch Ken, with considerable humour:

> God prosper long the hearty friends
>   Of honest pleasures all;
> A mighty curling match once did
>   At C***** W**k befal.

> To hurl the channelstane wi' skill,
>   Lanfloddan took his way;
> The child that's yet unborn will sing
>   The curling of that day.

> The champion of Ullisdale
>   A broad rash aith did make,
> His pleasure, near the Cam'ron isle,
>   Ae winter's day to take.

> Bold Ben o' Tudor sent him word
>   He'd match him at the sport;
> The chief o' Ken, on hearing this,
>   Did to the ice resort.

> Wi' channelstanes, baith glib an' strong,
>   His army did advance;
> Their crampets o' the trusty steel,
>   Like bucklers broad did glance.

A band wi' besoms high uprear'd,
    Weel made o' broom the best,
Before them like a moving wood,
    Unto the combat prest.

The gallant gamesters briskly mov'd,
    To meet the daring fae—
On Monday they had reach'd the loch,
    By breaking of the day.

The chieftains muster'd on the ice,
    Right eager to begin;
Their channelstanes, by special care,
    Were a' baith stout an' keen.

Their rocks they hurled up the rink,
    Ilk to bring in his hand;
An' hill an' valley, dale an' doon,
    Rang wi' the ardent band.

Glenbuck upo' the cockee stood,
    His merry men drew near;
Quoth he, Bentudor promised
    This morn to meet me here:

But if I thought he would not come,
    We'd join in social play.
With that the leader of the ice
    Unto Glenbuck did say:

Lo! yonder does Bentudor come,
    His men wi' crampets bright;
Twelve channelstanes, baith hard an' smooth,
    Come rolling in our sight:

All chosen rocks of Mulloch heugh,
    Fast by the tow'ring Screel.
Then tye your crampets, Glenbuck cries,
    Prepare ye for the speal.

And now with me, choice men of Ken,
    Your curling skill display;
For never was there curler yet,
    Of village or of brae,

That e'er wi' channelstane did come,
    But if he would submit
To hand to nieve I'd pledge this crag,
    I should his winner hit.

Bentudor, like a warrior bold,
    Came foremost o' them a';
A besom on his shouther slung,
    On's hans twa mittens bra.

An' with him forth came Tullochfern,
    An' Tom o' Broomyshaw;
Stout Robert o' Heston, Ratcliff, and
    Young John o' Fotheringhaw.

An wi' the laird o' Cairnyhowes,
    A curler guid an' true;
Good Ralph o' Titherbore, an' Slacks,
    Their marrows there are few.

Of Fernybank needs must I speak,
    As ane of aged skill;
Simon of Shots, the nephew bold
    Of Cairny on the hill.

With brave Glenbuck came curlers twelve,
    All dext'rous men of Dee;
Robin o' Mains, Clim o' the Cleugh,
    An' fam'd Montgomery.

Gamewell, the brisk, of Napplehowes,
    A valiant blade is he;
Harry o' Thorn, Gib o' the Glen,
    The stoutest o' the three.

An' the young heir of Birnyholm,
    Park, Craigs, Lamb o' the lin;
Allan of Airds, a sweeper good,
    An' Charley o' Lochfin.

Bentudor a Riscarrel crag,
    Twice up the ice hurled he,
Good sixty cloth yards and a span,
    Saying, so long let it be.

It pleased them a' — Ilk then wi' speed,
    Unto his weapon flew:
First Allan o' Airds his whinstane rock,
    Straight up the white ice drew.

A good beginning, cries Glenbuck;
    Slacks fidging at the sight,
Wi's bra blue-cap, lent Airds a smack,
    Then roared out, good night.

Next Robin o' Mains, a leader good,
    Close to the witter drew;
Ratcliff went by, an' 'cause he miss'd,
    Pronounc'd the ice untrue.

Gib o' the Glen, a noble herd,
    Behind the winner laid;
Then Fotheringhaw, a sidelin shot,
    Close to the circle play'd.

Montgomery, mettlefu' an' fain,
 A rackless stroke did draw;
But miss'd his aim, an' 'gainst the herd,
 Dang frae his clint a flaw.

With that stept forward Tullochfern,
 An' (saying, to hit, he'd try)
A leal shot ettled at the cock,
 Which shov'd the winner by.

Clim o' the Cleugh, on seeing that,
 Sten'd forth, an' frae his knee
A slow shot drew, wi' muckle care,
 Which settled on the tee.

Ralph, vexed at the fruitless play,
 The cockee butted fast;
His stane being glib, to the loch en',
 Close by the witter past.

Stout Robert o' Heston, wi' his broom,
 Came stepping up wi' might;
Quoth he, my abbey-burn-fit
 Shall win the speal this night.

With that brisk Gamewell, up the rink,
 His well mill'd rock did hurl,
Which rubbing Ratcliff on the cheek,
 Around the cock did twirl.

Now stept a noted gamester forth,
 Fernybank was his name,
Wha said he would not have it told,
 At C***** W**k for shame;

That e'er the chief o' Ken should bear
 The palm of victory.
Then heezing his Kilmarnock hood,
 Unto the cock drew he.

The stanes, wi' muckle martial din,
 Rebounding frae ilk shore;
Now thick, thick, thick, each other chas'd,
 An' up the rink did roar.

They closed fast on ev'ry side,
 A port could scarce be found;
An' many a broken channelstane
 Lay scattered up an' down.

Shew me the winner, cries Glenbuck,
 An' a' behind stan' aff;
Then rattled up the rocking crag,
 An' ran the port wi' life.

Bentudor flung his bonnet by,
 An' took his stane wi' speed;
Quoth he, my lads, the day is ours,
 Their chance is past remead.

Syne, hurlin through the crags o' Ken,
 Wi' inrings nice an' fair,
He struck the winner frae the cock,
 A lang claith yard an' mair.

The speal did last frae nine forenoon,
 Till setting o' the sun;
For when the hern scraich'd to her tree,
 The combat scarce was done.

Thus did Bentudor an' Glenbuck
 Their curling contest end;
They met baith merry i' the morn,
 At night they parted friends.

Grahame, a late poet, well known as the author of the Sabbath, a poem, in his British Georgics, has the following animated description:

Now rival parishes, and shrievedoms, keep,
On upland lochs, the long expected tryst
To play their yearly bonspiel. Agedmen,
Smit with the eagerness of youth, are there,
While love of conquest lights their beamless eyes,
New nerves their arms, and makes them young once more.

The sides when ranged, the distance meted out,
And duly traced the tees, some younger hand
Begins, with throbbing heart, and far o'ershoots,
Or sideward leaves, the mark. In vain he bends
His waist, and winds his hand, as if it still
Retained the power to guide the devious stone;
Which, onward hurling, makes the circling groupe
Quick start aside, to shun its reckless force.
But more and still more skilful arms succeed,
And near and nearer still around the tee,
This side, now that approaches, till at last,
Two seeming equidistant, straws or twigs
Decide as umpires 'tween contending coits.

Keen, keener still, as life itself were staked,
Kindles the friendly strife; one points the line
To him who, poising, aims and aims again;
Another runs and sweeps where nothing lies.

Success, alternately from side to side,
Changes, and quick the hours un-noted fly,
Till light begins to fail, and deep below,
The player, as he stoops to lift his coit,
Sees half incredulous, the rising moon.
But now the final, the decisive spell,
Begins; near and more near the sounding stones
Come winding in, some bearing straight along,
Crowd justling all around the mark, while one
Just slightly touching, victory depends
Upon the final aim: long swings the stone,
Then with full force, careering furious on,
Rattling it strikes aside both friend and foe,
Maintains its course, and takes the victor's place.
The social meal succeeds, and social glass;
In words the fight renewed is fought again,
While festive mirth forgets the winged hours.

A SONG,

COMPOSED AND SUNG BY ONE OF THE MEMBERS OF THE
DUDDINGSTON CURLING SOCIETY, AT THEIR ANNIVERSARY
DINNER.

CAULD, CAULD, FROSTY WEATHER.

Tune, — "Cauld Kail in Aberdeen."

Whan chittering birds, on flichtring wing,
    About the barn doors mingle,
And biting frost, and cranreuch cauld,
    Drive coofs around the ingle;
Then to the loch the curlers hie,
    Their hearts as light's a feather,
And mark the *tee* wi' mirth and glee,
    In cauld, cauld, frosty weather.

Our buirdly leaders down *white ice*
    Their whinstanes doure send snooving,
And birks and brooms ply hard before,
    Whan o'er the hog-score moving;
Till cheek by jowl within the brugh,
    They're laid 'side ane anither;
Then round the tee we flock wi' glee,
    In cauld, &c.

Wi' canny hand the neist play down
    Their stanes o' glibber metal;
Yet bunkers aften send aglee,
    Although they weel did ettle.

'Now strike — no — draw — come fill the port,'
    They roar, and cry, and blether;
As round the tee we flock wi' glee,
    In cauld, &c.

A stalwart chiel, to redd the ice,
    Drives roaring down like thunder;
Wi' awfu' crash the double guards
    At ance are burst asunder;
Rip-raping on frae random wicks
    The winner gets a yether;
Then round the tee we flock wi' glee,
    In cauld, &c.

Our chief, whase skill and steady arm
    Gain mony a bonspeel dinner,
Cries, 'open wide — stand off behind,
    'Fy John, fy show the winner;
'He goes — he moves — he rides him out
    'The length of ony tether,'
Huzzas wi' glee rise round the tee,
    In cauld, &c.

But now the moon glints thro' the mist,
    The wind blaws snell and freezing,
When straight we bicker aff in haste
    To where the ingle's bleezing;
In Curler Ha', sae beind and snug,
    About the board we gather,
Wi' mirth and glee, sirloin the tee,
    In cauld, &c.

In canty cracks, and sangs, and jokes,
    The night drives on wi' daffin,
And mony a kittle shot is ta'en,
    While we're the toddy quaffing.
Wi' heavy heart we're laith to part,
    But promise to forgather
Around the tee, neist morn wi' glee,
    If cauld, &c.

RULES IN CURLING

TO BE OBSERVED BY THE

DUDDINGSTON CURLING SOCIETY.

I.

The usual length of a rink is from thirty-six to forty-four yards, inclusive; but this will be regulated by circumstances, and the agreement of parties. When a game is begun, the rink is not to be changed or altered, unless by the consent of a majority of players: nor is it to be shortened, unless it clearly appears that the majority are unable to make up.

II.

The hog-score to be one-sixth part of the length of the rink distant from the tee; and every stone to be deemed a hog, the sole of which does not clear the score.

III.

Each player to foot in such a manner, that in delivering his stone, he brings it over the tee.

IV.

The order of playing adopted at the beginning, must be observed during the whole course of a game.

V.

All curling stones to be of a circular shape. No stone to be changed throughout a game, unless it happens to be broken; and the largest fragment of such stone to count, without any necessity of playing with it more. If a stone rolls or is upset, it must be placed upon its sole where it stops. Should the handle quit a stone in the delivery, the player must keep hold of it, otherwise he will not be entitled to re-play the shot.

VI.

A player may sweep his own stone the whole length of the rink; his party not to sweep until it has passed the hog-score at the farther end; and his adversaries not to sweep until it has passed the tee. The sweeping to be always to a side.

VII.

None of the players, upon any occasion, to cross or go upon the middle of the rink.

VIII.

If, in sweeping or otherwise, a running stone is marred by any of the party to which it belongs, it must be put off the ice: if by any of the adverse party, it must be placed agreeably to the direction which was given to the player; and if it is marred by any other means, the player may take his shot again. Should a stone at rest be accidentally displaced, it must be put as nearly as possible in its former situation.

IX.

Every player to be ready when his turn comes, and to take no more than a reasonable time to play his shot. Should he, by mistake, play with a wrong stone, it must be replaced where it stops, by the one with which he ought to have played.

X.

A doubtful shot is to be measured by some neutral person, whose determination shall be final.

XI.

Before beginning to play, each party must name one of their number, for directing the game. The players of his party may give their advice to the one so named, but they cannot control his direction; nor are they to address themselves to the person who is about to play. Each director, when it is his turn to play, to name one of his party to take the charge for him. Every player to follow the direction given to him.

XII.

Should any question arise, the determination of which may not be provided for by the words and spirit of the rules now established, each party to choose one of their number, in order to determine it. If the two so chosen differ in opinion, they are to name an umpire, whose decision shall be final.

The above rules received the probation and sanction of a general meeting of the society, held in the Curlers' Hall, Duddingston, upon the 6th January 1804.

Appendix B

The Canadian Curler's Manual;

or An Account of Curling, as practised in Canada: with remarks on the History of the Game.

'When winter muffles up his cloak,
And binds the mire like a rock,
THEN to the loch the Curlers flock
Wi' gleesome speed.'
BURNS.

By James Bicket, Secretary to The Toronto Curling Club. Toronto: Published at the Office of the British Colonist, for The Toronto Club: Sold Also by Henry Rowsell. Hugh Scobie, Printer. 1840.

CONTENTS.

PART I.

TO THE

PRESIDENT,

VICE-PRESIDENTS, MANAGERS,

AND

MEMBERS,

OF THE

TORONTO CURLING CLUB,

THIS MANUAL

IS MOST RESPECTFULLY INSCRIBED,

BY THEIR DEVOTED,

HUMBLE SERVANT,

THE AUTHOR.

218

PREFACE

This little pamphlet has been produced at the request of the TORONTO CURLING CLUB. The original object in its publication was simply to furnish the Members with a copy of the Constitution of the Club, and of the laws which they observe in playing. The design is now extended, so as to embrace a general description of Curling, with a brief history of the Game; and by thus making it to be understood, by those who have never seen it played, or who may have been only occasional spectators, to induce a more general participation in this most healthful and exhilirating amusement.

It is gratifying to observe the success of the efforts which have been made in this country, during the last few years, to promote and encourage the Game. It is now becoming, and must become, a favorite in Canada. It is admirably adapted to this climate, where the winter is generally cold enough to ensure good ice, and seldom so severe as to render the exercise unpleasant. Being played in the open air, during a season when few out-of-door recreations can be enjoyed, it is. well calculated to counteract the énfeebling influence of confinement to our close and heated winter houses. Many objections which may be brought against other sports, are not applicable to this. It calls up none of the low and degrading passions of our nature. Notwithstanding the intense interest which Curlers may feel in a well contested match, no betting ever takes place among them; the excitement arising from gambling, therefore, is altogether removed from the rink. Intoxication on the ice is also unknown among good players. The nice equilibrium of body and the firmness of nerve, essential to scientific Curling, would disappear on the first symptom of such a state. But the Game is sufficiently interesting without any extraneous stimulant. — While it imparts vigour to every limb, and every muscle, it engages the attention and awakens the judgment; and thus brings into healthful excitement those powers of the body and of the mind, the due exercise of which the Creator has allied with pleasure.

In the observations which will be found on the early history of Curling, a liberal use has been made of a small but valuable work on the subject, published anonymously, in Kilmarnock, in 1828. To the same authority the writer is indebted for the derivation of several of the words to be found in the Glossary; and it is only doing the Compilers of the work referred to, an act of justice, which they can have no wish should be omitted, to state, that they have availed of 'Doctor Jamieson's Dictionary,' 'Brewster's Encyclopedia,' and an 'Account of Curling, by a Member of the Duddingstone Society.' These, unfortunately, are not at present accessible to the writer. During the present year, he ordered from Edinburgh such publications on the Game, as could be found; but was disappointed on learning, that several excellent Treatises which he expected to receive, are now out of print — the only works which his Correspondent could procure, being the 'Annual of the Grand Caledonian Curling Club,' and the 'Rules of Curling, by Pretostes.'

The writer has affixed his name to this work — conceiving that from his official connection with the Toronto Curling Club, since its establishment, this may lend some weight to the opinions, and some authority to the statements therein contained.

Toronto, 30th November, 1840.

PART I.

Curling — Is a Game played upon the ice, by sliding stones, made for the purpose, from one point to another. In some respects it resembles Bowling, but with these differences, that the stones are slidden upon the ice, not rolled — neither are they made like Bowls, to curve on their passage; the points, also, to which the stones are played are stationary, whereas in Bowling the Jack is moveable: and in Curling, the ice in the path of the stone may be polished by sweeping — and thus the players may compensate for the want of force with which a stone may have been thrown.

Pennant, in his 'Tour through Scotland,' gives the following rough description of the Game:— 'Of all the sports in those parts, that of Curling is the favorite. It is an amusement of the winter, and played upon the ice, by sliding from one mark to another, great stones of 40 to 70 lbs. weight, of a hemispherical form, with a wooden or iron handle at top. The object of the player is to lay his stone as near the mark as possible, to guard that of his partner which has been well laid before, or to strike off that of his antagonist.' Such is a brief outline of that Game, a fuller description of which is attempted in the following pages.

Stones. — These are made of granite, or of any other stone which is hard, free from sand, and not liable to break. They are cut into a spherical form, flattened at top and bottom, and the angles rounded off and polished, particularly that at the sole. The handle is inserted in the top. Though they must all be made circular, the proportion of the diameter to the thickness varies in different districts; some being made more and some less than twice as wide as they are thick. The Grand Caledonian Curling Club has lately suggested the following scale — the first attempt that has been made to regulate the proportions of Curling Stones — and which for the sake of uniformity, it is hoped, will be adopted, viz:—

'When the weight is under

35 lbs. imp., the height not to be more than	$4\frac{1}{4}$	inches.
38 lbs.	$4\frac{1}{2}$	inches.
41 lbs.	$4\frac{3}{4}$	inches.
44 lbs.	5	inches.
47 lbs.	$5\frac{1}{4}$	inches.
50 lbs.	$5\frac{1}{2}$	inches.

'Whatever be the diameter or weight, the height ought never to exceed $6\frac{3}{8}$ inches, nor be less than $4\frac{1}{2}$ inches. — None ought to be allowed in a set game of greater diameter than 12 inches, nor of a greater weight than 50 lbs. imperial.'

Stones are sometimes so finished as to slide on either of the flattened surfaces, one of which in such cases, is made slightly concave, and on this side the stone is played when the ice is hard and keen; the other, a little convex, being used when the ice is soft and dull.

In some parts of Canada, where suitable stone cannot readily be procured, iron or wood has been substituted. At Quebec and Montreal, castings of iron, in the shape of Curling Stones, are played with — the intensity of the cold there, rendering the stones liable to break on striking against one another. Iron is used also by the Curlers at Dundas, in the Gore District; and at Guelph, where the Game has some ardent admirers, they play with blocks of hard wood. At Toronto, and the Curling localities in the neighborhood, stones only have been used; part having been imported from Scotland, and others having been made by the stone-cutter to the Club, from blocks of excellent quality picked up by him on the land in the vicinity. Several of the stones imported to Toronto have been made from Ailsa Crag, which, it appears, has long been known as an excellent material for the purpose; one of those now referred to having been played with by the father of the present owner, at least sixty years ago.

The Rink. — The ice on which the game is played is called the Rink. This should be a sheet of fifty yards in length and four yards in width; perfectly free from every inequality. At the distance of four yards from each end of the rink, and in the middle crosswise, a circular hole is made, about an inch in diameter and the same in depth, called the 'tee.' Round the tee two or more circular lines are drawn, the largest having a diameter of about five feet, the others smaller and at intermediate distances.

The space within the largest circle is called the 'brough.' The use of the circular lines is to shew, while the game is being played, the comparative nearness of the stones to the tee; actual measurement not being allowed until all the stones have been played to one end of the rink. A line is also drawn across the tee, at right angles with the rink lengthwise, and extending to the outermost circle, the use of which will be shewn in the remarks relating to sweeping. At the distance of seven yards from each of the tees a line is drawn across the rink, called the 'hog score,' and stones which on being played do not pass this score are called 'hogs,' and lose for that time the chance of counting, being distanced or thrown off the rink.

Playing. — When the player is about to throw his stones, he places himself at one end of the rink, rests his right foot in a notch, or 'hack' made in the ice* and in such a relation to the tee that when he delivers his stone it must pass over it. He is directed by one of the players of his own party, styled the 'skip,' who stands at or near the tee to which the stone is to be played, and who usually makes use of his broom to indicate the point to which, or the line along which, he wishes the stone to be played. Should the stone be delivered with the proper degree of strength, and in the direction pointed out to the player by the skip, it will either rest at the spot required, or receiving, as the skip intended, a new direction by coming in contact with some other stone, will effect the desired purpose. — The player on delivering his stone raises it off the ice, and swinging it once behind him to acquire a proper *impetus*, and to make surer of his aim, keeping his eye, at the same time, steadily fixed on the broom of the skip, or on any stone, or other object towards or against which he may be desired to play, throws it in that direction. The stone reaching the ice on its sole about two feet in front of the player — his body naturally following the same direction until the stone be fairly delivered.

Sweeping. — For the purpose of Sweeping, every player is furnished with a broom, by means of which the ice may sometimes be so polished that a stone may reach the tee, which, without sweeping, could not have passed the hog score. When a stone, therefore, in its progress up the rink

---

* Other contrivances than the hack are used in some places to prevent the foot of the player from slipping. Sometimes a thin board is laid on the ice, on which he places both his feet. At Toronto, the hack is considered the best, and although the Club has 'crampits' for the benefit of those accustomed to them, they are required only by strangers or novices, experience demonstrating their uselessness.

appears to the skip to have been thrown with insufficient force, he directs his party to sweep the ice in its path. The party opposed to that whose stone is coming up is not allowed to sweep in front of the line drawn across the brough, but may sweep behind it, so as to let the stone, if it should pass the tee, go far enough beyond it, to lose the chance of counting.

The brooms used in Scotland are usually made of 'broom,' sometimes of birch twigs, and occasionally of heather, as one or other may be found most convenient to the place of playing. In Canada, 'corn brooms' which have been used for domestic purposes a sufficient length of time to be stripped of the knotty parts which might break off and obstruct the progress of the stone, have been found to be the best. Some Curlers in Scarboro', near Toronto, who have immigrated from Lanarkshire, have imported stocks of the genuine Scotch broom, which, under their cultivation, thrives so well as to promise to supersede the use of every other material.

The Game. — The usual mode of playing the game is with 16 stones on a rink. This number is sufficient to impart interest to the playing, and more would towards the end of the head, crowd the ice. Sometimes these are played by four players on each side, playing two stones each, which mode may be preferable when a few only are exercising for practice; but in such case the sweeping, which — unless the ice be very keen — is essential to success, can never be properly attended to, as the skip and player being sufficiently occupied in their own departments, only two brooms can be effectively employed at the same time. The most interesting game, therefore, is where there are sixteen players on a rink, with one stone each, eight players on each side; and a game so played is now to be described.

The parties determine by lot which is to 'have the ice,' or in other words, which is to play the first stone. It is doubtful whether it be an advantage to win the ice, as the party who loses this plays the last stone — the most important in determining the result of the head. The side who wins the end plays the first stone on the end following.

The skip of the party who is to play first, stationing himself on that *tee* towards which the stones are to be thrown, directs the player who is to 'lead,' or play the first stone, on his side. When this stone is played the skip of the opposite party takes the same post, pointing out to his first player how he wishes his stone to be played. Each side plays one stone alternately, and the object of each successive player is to draw nearer the tee than any of his opponents, to strike out their winning shots, or to guard the winners of his own party. The earlier stages of the end

therefore appear simple enough; but after the first eight or ten stones have been played, especially when they have been played well, the game becomes more intricate and more interesting. One party may have a stone covering the tee, apparently guarded on every side, and impregnable to attack, the stones of their opponents having only strengthened its position; yet some stone which, either from a *ruse* on the part of the director, or from being badly played, has rested near the edge of the rink and seems to be lost for that end, may furnish a point to which another stone may be slidden, and receiving thence a new direction may reach the winner, and removing it from the tee, become itself the winning stone.

The director generally plays the last stone on his own side. The seventh player is usually appointed to that position in the order of the game on account of his being a correct and powerful player, so that he may, when necessary, open up a path for the stone of the 'hind hand.'

When the stones are all played to one end of the rink the game is counted, and every stone which either party has nearer the tee than any stone of their opponents, counts one shot or point; and such portion of the game is styled an 'end,' or 'head.'

The number of shots in a game is variable, depending on agreement. The Toronto Club usually play for 31, in a regular game; and in their matches among themselves, or with the Scarboro' Curlers, when more than one rink has been engaged, the practice has been, either to play to an hour specified, or to stop before that hour should the aggregate shots of either party on all the rinks collectively amount to thirty-one for each rink. In Scotland, where the continuance of the curling season is very precarious, all who have it in their power, play the whole of every day while the ice will permit, and, consequently, the number of shots played for is more uniform. At Toronto, where Curling may be practised almost daily, fully three months in the year, the rink is resorted to for one or two hours' recreation, and seven, thirteen, or twenty-one shots are frequently fixed on as the game, according to the time intended to be devoted to the exercise.

Laws of the Game. — In every district of Scotland, and in almost every club, some differences are to be found in the mode of conducting the game. Little difficulty, however, is there experienced from the want of written laws, the *lex non scripta* of every parish or county being perfectly understood where it is in force. Still in Edinburgh and a few other places where Curlers from distant Clubs are likely to meet, it has been found necessary to have their laws reduced to writing so that from whatever part of the country the player might come, he could not be ignorant of the rules by which his playing was to be governed. At Toronto, the want of a written code of laws, was for a number of years, felt to be inconvenient — few of the original Curlers having been accustomed to play exactly according to the same system. It was, therefore, one of the first objects of the Toronto Curling Club, after its formation, to draw up a set of Rules, founded on the prevailing practice in Scotland. The following, therefore, were agreed to — and although not applicable to every case that may be conceived, they have been found sufficient to decide, satisfactorily, every difficulty that has occurred during the experience of four years; and have been cheerfully agreed to by the Scarboro' Curlers, in their matches with those of Toronto:

1st. — The Rink to be forty-two yards from tee to tee* unless otherwise agreed upon by the parties. When a game is begun the rink cannot be changed or altered unless by the consent of a majority of players, and it can be shortened only when it is apparent that a majority cannot play the length.

2nd. — The hog score must be distant from the tee one-sixth part of the length of the rink. Every stone to be deemed a hog, the sole of which, when at rest, does not completely clear the score.

3rd. — Every player to foot so that in delivering his stone, it shall pass over the tee.

4th. — The order of playing adopted at the beginning must not be changed during a game.

5th. — Curling-stones must be of a circular shape. No stone to be changed during a game,† unless it happen to be broken; and the largest fragment of such stone to count, without any necessity of playing with it more. If a stone roll or be upset, it must be placed upon its sole where it stops. Should the handle quit a stone in the delivery, the player must keep hold of it, otherwise he will not be entitled to replay the shot.

6th. — The player may sweep his own stone the whole length of the rink; his party not to sweep until it has passed the first hog score, and his adversaries not to sweep until it has passed the tee — the sweeping to be always to a side.

7th. — None of the players, on any account, to cross or go upon the middle of the rink.

8th. — If, in sweeping or otherwise, a running stone is marred by any of the party to which it belongs, it must be put off the rink; if by any of the adverse party, it must be placed agreeably to the direction which was given to the player; and if it be marred by any other means, the player may take his shot again. Should a stone at rest be accidentally displaced, it must be put as near as possible in its former situation.

9th. — Every player must be ready when his turn comes,* and must take only a reasonable time to play his shot. — Should he, by mistake, play with a wrong stone, it must be replaced where it stops, by the one which he ought to have played.

10th. — A doubtful shot must be measured by a neutral person, whose determination shall be final.

11th. — The skips alone shall direct the game. The players of the respective skips may offer them their advice, but cannot control their directions; nor is any person, except the skip, to address him who is about to play. — Each skip may appoint one of his party to take the charge for him, when he is about to play. Every player to follow the direction given to him.

12th. — Should any question arise, the determination of which may not be provided for by the words and spirit of the preceding Rules, each party to choose one of their number, in order to determine it. If the two so chosen differ in opinion, they are to name an umpire, whose decision shall be final.

When a few players are curling for practice, or recreation, some of the above laws may not be rigidly enforced; but any relaxation should always be noticed, so that there may be no difficulty in strictly adhering to them when playing a Bonspiel, or set game.

The preceding account has been, as far as practicable, divested of technical terms, in order that it might be the more intelligible to the uninitiated. Many of the words

---

*The Grand Caledonian Curling Club recommend that rinks have double tees at each end, the one at least two yards behind the other: the whole four to be nearly as possible on the same line. The stones are to be delivered from the outer tee and played towards the inner; this saves the ice from being injured around the tee played up to.

†With regard to double-sided stones, the Grand Caledonian Curling Club has a law that the side commenced with shall not, under forfeiture of the match be changed during the progress of the game.

*An excellent method of obviating the confusion which is sometimes experienced in the early ends of a game, by players being doubtful of their places, is, that before commencing, the players on each side of a rink should 'fall in' in the order in which it is intended they shall play, and 'number off from right to left.' The player who makes a mistake after this has been done, is fit neither for a Curler nor a Soldier. This method has been practised at Toronto, since the winter of 1837-1838 — when military terms and ideas were infused into every department of life.

and phrases, however, used in Curling are peculiar to the game, — throwing light on its origin and history, — and it would now be as difficult for Curlers to abolish the language of the rink, as it would be for the gentlemen of certain learned professions, to substitute the Queen's English for their most unclassical Latin. An explanation of the following terms, which are in constant use, is therefore indispensable in a work of this nature:

Angled Guard — A stone which obliquely covers or guards one stone or more.

Bias — An inclination in the ice, tending to lead a stone off the direction given to it by the player.

Block the ice — See 'fill the ice.'

Boardhead — See 'brough.'

Bonspel, bonspiel, bonspeel — (French *bon*, good, and Belgic *spell*, a play — a good game: or Suio-Gothic, bonne, a husbandman; or Belgic, *bonne*, a village or district; because one district challenges another to play at this game.) — A match at Curling between two opposite parties.

Break an egg on — To strike one stone very gently with another.

Brough — (Alemanic, *bruchus*, a camp, often circular,) The space within the largest circle drawn round the tee.

Channel-stane — A Curling stone is so named in the southern counties of Scotland, probably from stones found in streams having been first used for curling.

Chuckle to — To make two or more inwicks up a *port* to a given stone.

Creep — (Come creeping up the rink,) the stones are said to creep when they are thrown with little force.

Curling — (German, *kurzweillin*, to play for amusement; or Teutonic, *krullen, krollen*, SINUARE, to bend, — as the great art of the game is to make the stones *bend, twist, (quod vide,)* CURL, towards the mark, when they cannot reach it in a straight line.) Sliding stones along the ice towards a mark.

Dead guard — A stone which completely covers another, concealing it from the view of the next player, is a dead guard upon that other.

Deliver — To throw the stone.

Director — The same as 'skip,' or 'skipper.'

Draw a shot — to play a spot pointed out by the director, having no other stone to strike or rest upon.

Dour, drug, dull — The state of the ice when the stone cannot easily be thrown the length of the rink.

End — That portion of the game in which the stones are all played to one end of the rink.

Guard — To lay a stone in a line before another; or the stone so laid.

Hack, or *hatch* — (Icelandic, *hiaka*, or Suio-Gothic *hacka*, a chop, cut, or crack,) a cut in the ice, in which the player places his foot to prevent it from slipping as he delivers his stone.

Head — See 'End.'

Hindhand — He who plays the last stone on his side.

Hog Score — The line drawn across the rink, about seven yards from the *tee*: stones which do not pass this are thrown aside.

How ice — The ice in the middle of the rink, *hollowed* by the friction of the stones; also called *white ice*.

Inring, inwick — See Wicking.

Keen — The opposite of dour.

Leader — He who plays first in order in his party.

Lie in the bosom of — To play a stone so as gently to touch and lie before another.

Outwick — See Wicking.

Pat lid — A Curling stone lying on the *tee*.

Port — An opening between two stones, wide enough to admit another to be played through.

Rack — A word used in some districts instead of rink.

Redd the ice — (Icelandic, *rada*, ORDINARE, to put in order; also, to warn, to advise,) to clear the ice, or to break the guards with a stone strongly played, so as to expose the tee or the winner; to 'ride' successfully.

Rest — To draw to any object or point so as not to pass it.

Ride — To throw a stone with great force towards one or more other stones, in order to remove them from their position.

Rink — The ice on which the game is played.

Shot — A stone played; in another sense, a stone which counts.

Skip, or *skipper* — (Probably from Suio-Gothic, *skeppare*, a master,) a director.

Tee — (Icelandic, *tia*, to point out the place: or, Teutonic, *tygh-en*, to point to,) the winning point to which the stones are played.

Twist — To give to a stone, on its being delivered, a rotary motion, so that it revolves on its sole as it slides along the rink, and bends from the straight line, when the force with which it has been thrown is nearly exhausted.

Wicking, wick, inwick — (Suio-Gothic *wick*, a corner: or Teutonic, *wyck*, a turning,) to make a stone take an oblique direction by striking another on the side.

PART II.

HISTORY OF CURLING.

The early history of Curling is involved in such obscurity, that the time even of the antiquarians might be better employed in eating Beef and Greens, or in playing the game, than in endeavoring to discover its origin. Some of these gentlemen have, from the definition given of a certain word in an old dictionary, come to the conclusion that Curling was originally the game of quoits played upon the ice. Kilian, in his Etymologica Teutonicae Linguae, renders the Teutonic words *'kluyten,'* *'kalluyten,'* *ludere massis, sive globis glaciatis; certare discis in aequore glaciato.* The term kluyte, or klyte, is still used in some parts of Scotland, where it always signifies to 'fall flat,' or to fall so that the broadest part of the falling body first comes in contact with the ground; but it never has any reference to moving on a plane surface. The words *ludere* and *certare* throw no light on the manner in which the *globus* or *discus* was used. But until it can be shown that they were moved upon the ice — not pitched through the air — it is difficult to perceive the relation between 'kluyten' and curling. As soon as the stones were played by being slidden — if the antiquarians could only determine the period of that event — a new game was introduced, affording opportunities equal to those of the quoit for muscular exercise, and a much wider field for the exercise of the judgment.

The earliest notice of Curling which has been discovered is in Cambden's Britannia, published in 1607. In it, Coppinsha, one of the Orkney islands, is mentioned as famous for 'excellent stones for the game called Curling.' This shews that it was then in considerable repute. In the 'Life of William Guthrie,' who in the year 1644 was ordained minister of Fenwick, in Ayrshire, it is stated that he was fond of the innocent recreations which then prevailed, 'among which was Curling.' In 1684, the game is taken notice of in Fountainhall's Decisions. Pennycuik, also in the seventeenth century, declares that

'To curl on the ice doth greatly please,
Being a manly Scottish exercise;'

And he celebrates the game as calculated

'To clear the brain, stir up the native heart,
And give a gallant appetite for meat.'

Ramsay has alluded to Curling. Burns, in 'Tam Samson's Elegy,' shows, in few words that he himself understood the game. Grahame, the author of the 'Sabbath,' has illumined the rink with the lustre of his own genius; and Curling forms the subject of a beautiful part of 'Fisher's Winter Season.'

Though the game has never been universal in Scotland, it has long been practised in almost every county south of the Forth and the Clyde. The shires of Ayr, Renfrew, Lanark and Dumfries are remarkable for their attachment to Curling. It is played in Perthshire, the Countess of Mansfield, being now patroness of the Scone

and Perth Club; but we are not aware of its having been, until lately, practised farther north. In Aberdeen — that city of northern lights — it is unknown. The Editor of the Aberdeen Herald, who is a native of a Curling district, laments in his paper of 13th January 1838 — that all was then bound up in the icy stillness of the season, and that in a place abounding with the material for making admirable curling stones, and with arms strong enough to wield them,

'No friendly combatants contested the field.'

The game was played near Inverness, in 1838, when Loch-na-Sanais (or the whispering-lake,) with the picturesque hills of Tomnahurich and Torvain, echoed, for the first time, to the booming of the stones over the ice.

Curling has long been held in high estimation in Edinburgh. About the beginning of last century 'the magistrates marched in a body to the North Loch, to spend the day in Curling. — In going and returning they were preceded by a band of music, playing appropriate airs.' It was the custom in Paisley, not many years ago, to send round the town drummer, after two or three nights' hard frost, to proclaim to the inhabitants where the Curlers should meet in the morning; and in the morning, should the frost continue, hundreds might be seen — manufacturers, bailies, weavers, and clergymen, — resorting promiscuously to the rendezvous; for on the ice all are on a *level* — all ordinary distinctions in society are, for the time, forgotten in the love of the game, and the noble and the learned are there willing to be directed by the most skilful player, though this should happen to be the humblest of their neighbors.

In some of the agricultural districts of Scotland, the extent of Curling Clubs is regulated by the legal divisions of the country, being again subdivided among themselves into rinks, who always play together under their respective skips; — the organization resembling in many respects that of the Militia of Canada — and on the occasion of a contest with another club, every man who, if in this country should be liable to serve as a soldier, turns out willingly for the honor of his *corps*. There, however, age procures no exemption from service. In the words of Grahame,

'When rival parishes and shrievedoms keep,
On upland loch, the long expected tryst,
To play this yearly bonspiel, AGED MEN,
Smit with the eagerness of youth, ARE THERE,
While love of conquest lights their beemless eyes,
Now nerves their arms and makes them young
once more.

On 20th January, 1838, the parish of Lesmahagow, in Lanarkshire, met the neighboring club of Avondale, on a sheet of ice, near Strathaven. Each club consisted of twenty-one rinks of eight players, making the number of players on each side one hundred and sixty-eight, so that three hundred and thirty-six Curlers were engaged in the match. Such a bonspiel as this may not take place every season, but this instance, which is referred to, as being of recent occurrence, is sufficient to shew the interest which in such districts is taken in the game, and, also, the excellence of the organization which could bring so many players together on a notice so short as that which can be given, where the continuance of hard frost cannot be depended on.

It is now about twenty years since Curling was introduced to Canada, and since that time the game has been regularly played at Quebec and Montreal. The Clubs of those Cities, in imitation of their friends on the other side of the Atlantic, have occasional contests with each other. The match which they last had, came off in March of the present year, and was played at both places on the same day — one-half of the players from each City having proceeded to the other — so that the result of the joint game could not be known at either place, until the parties had time to communicate. A few years ago, the Bonspiel took place at Three Rivers. The distance which, in those cases, the players had to travel, sufficiently shows how warmly they are devoted to the game.

During the last winter, the officers stationed at some of the posts to the south of Montreal, relieved the monotony of military duty, by engaging in Curling. The game has been practised at Perth, in the Bathurst District, although now fallen into disuse there. At Niagara, a rink was formed four years ago, one gentleman having imported a sufficient number of stones for their use, and great interest is now taken in the sport. At Newmarket, about 30 miles to the north of Toronto, there is a Curling Club, the minister, like many of his brethren at home, being an active promoter of the game, and an exact and skilful player. Curling is now also a favorite amusement at Dundas at the head of Lake Ontario; at Guelph in the new district of Wellington; and at Fergus, in the township of Nicholl. There are also, many first-rate players in Scarboro', who are always ready to measure their strength, in numbers and skill, with those of Toronto, and both enjoy the *certaminis gaudia* in their annual bonspiel. They played at Toronto, on 12th February last, with twenty-four players aside, when their Excellencies the Governor General and the Lieutenant Governor were spectators of the game.

The Fergus Club has been mentioned above, but is worthy of more particular notice, being perhaps, the first which was regularly organised in Upper Canada. The settlement of that neighborhood was begun in 1834, and the gloom of the first winter was dispelled by the introduction of the game. In the course of the winter following, the Honorable Adam Fergusson, who is the principal proprietor and the enlightened founder of the settlement, succeeded in forming the players into a club, of which he was the first President, and which now numbers upwards of thirty members. They play with blocks of hard wood, turned to the proper shape, which they have found to answer the purpose, except when the ice is dull. The experiment has been made of loading the blocks with lead, in order that the size and weight may bear about the same proportion to each other as in Curling stones, and this they consider a decided improvement.

The example of the Curlers of Fergus, in constituting a club, ought to be followed in every neighborhood where there are players sufficient for one rink. The permanency of the game and opportunities of playing, may thus be secured in places where, without such arrangement, the greatest difficulty might be experienced in bringing the players together. Although the game has been played at Toronto, every winter, since 1829, it was never enjoyed to the same extent as it has been since the formation of the Club in 1836. By the judicious arrangement of the managers, in appointing the hours of playing, and in having the ice ready before the Curlers meet, the time which was formerly wasted in preparations that may be performed by laborers, is now spent in the game; and thus the recreation can be shared by many, who should otherwise, by the nature of their occupations, be excluded from the rink. Wherever, on this continent, Curling has been introduced and not continued, its decline is attributable to the want of that system which the proper organization of a club would ensure. Wherever Curlers have been united, in the way now recommended, they have been enabled to attract constant accessions to their numbers and, by spreading throughout their respective neighborhoods a love of the game, to establish its permanency beyond the chance of decay.

Mr. John Graham, of New York, the best authority in the United States, in every matter connected with Scottish nationality, as existing there, — and who permits his name to be used on this occasion, — stated during his recent visit to Toronto, that the game was sometimes played at New York, but there being no club, a special arrangement was always necessary before any meeting on the ice could take place. If the New York curlers were to unite, there can be no doubt that the game would 'go a-head' there, and that in a few winters hence, we should hear of their having a bonspiel with their friends in Canada, either at Montreal or Toronto.

A few plain rules are sufficient for the government of a Curling Club. The following Constitution, which was agreed upon by the Toronto Curlers, has been found to answer every purpose for which it was intended. A few additional regulations have since been made, but these are only of a local or temporary nature:

CONSTITUTION

OF THE

TORONTO CURLING CLUB.

Article 1st. — The Office-bearers of the Club shall consist of a President, two Vice Presidents, four Managers, and a Secretary and Treasurer, who, after the first election, shall be elected at the Annual Meeting in December, to be called as provided in Article 5th.

Article 2nd. — Any person wishing to become a Member, may be proposed at any regular Meeting of the Club, and if the proposal be seconded, the election shall proceed, when the votes of a majority of three-fourths of the Members present, and the payment of the Entrance Fee and of one year's subscription, as provided in Article 3rd, shall be required for the admission of the applicant.

Article 3rd. — In order to provide a Fund to meet necessary expenses, Members shall pay on admission the sum of ____ as entrance fee, and also the sum of ____ as their first year's subscription; and shall afterwards pay such annual subscription as may be determined by the Club at the Annual Meeting.

Article 4th. — The Committee shall draw up the *Rules of the Game* according to the prevailing practice in Scotland; which Rules, when entered on the Books of the Club and read at a regular Meeting, shall regulate the playing, and shall be decisive in all disputes among the Members; and may also, in case of playing with other Clubs, regulate the match, unless objected to by such other Club.

Article 5th. — The Annual Meeting, when Office-bearers shall be elected, shall be held on the first Tuesday of December; and regular Meetings shall also be held on the first Tuesday in January, February and March in every year, at such a place as the President may appoint; to be properly intimated to the Members; and occasional Meetings of the Club may also be called by the President, whenever he may consider it expedient.

Article 6th. — Members shall pay their annual subscription to the Treasurer within one month after the amount of the same shall be determined; and on failing to do so, they shall be considered as having withdrawn from the Club.

Article 7th. — The Rules of the Club may be altered or new rules added, with the consent of three fourths of the Members present at any regular Meeting; such alterations or additions having been proposed at the regular Meeting preceding.

Index